Advanced Studies in Diginomics and Digitalization

Series Editors

Lars Hornuf, Faculty of Business Studies and Economics, University of Bremen, Bremen, Germany

Herbert Kotzab, Faculty of Business Studies and Economics, University of Bremen, Bremen, Germany

Markus Pelger, Management Science & Engineering, Stanford University, Stanford, CA, USA

The book series 'Advanced Studies in Diginomics and Digitalization' features the latest research in economic topics related to the digitization of labor, financial, and product markets. Books published in this series are primarily monographs and edited volumes that present new research results, both theoretical and empirical, on ethical, socio-political, psychological, economic and politically relevant questions about new digital markets. All books are published in print and digital formats and disseminated globally.

Lars Hornuf
Editor

Diginomics Research Perspectives

The Role of Digitalization in Business and Society

Springer

Editor
Lars Hornuf
Faculty of Business Studies and Economics
University of Bremen
Bremen, Germany

ISSN 2731-0477 ISSN 2731-0485 (electronic)
Advanced Studies in Diginomics and Digitalization
ISBN 978-3-031-04062-7 ISBN 978-3-031-04063-4 (eBook)
https://doi.org/10.1007/978-3-031-04063-4

This Springer imprint is published by the registered company Springer Nature Switzerland AG
The registered company address is: Gewerbestrasse 11, 6330 Cham, Switzerland

Foreword

This is a book full of creative ideas. Each of the ten chapters opens a new window of opportunities for researchers, educators, innovators, and entrepreneurs in the digital economy. I have been looking forward to reading this book ever since Prof. Dr. Lars Hornuf informed the idea of this project. I am truly honored to be among the first readers of the finished product. As a researcher, teacher, and editor in this space, *diginomics* is near and dear to my heart. To say that this book opened my eyes is an understatement. I am grateful to Lars and a cohort of creative scholars who have contributed to this body of state-of-the-art knowledge.

Allow me to share some of my initial takeaways from this well-designed book. The chapter "HumanRoboLab: Experiments with Chatbots in Management Education at Universities" by Denis Pijetlovic and Georg Müeller-Christ opens new opportunities in digitalizing higher education using artificial intelligence (AI) chatbots. The chapter "Marketing in a Digital World" by Kristina Klein, Maik Eisenbeiss, Maik Dulle, Nastaran Taherparvar, Mirko Wiemann, and Jan Wiezorrek brings us to the MarTech innovation space and showcases how firms can use AI creatively in purposeful marketing. The chapter "Human Resource Management in a Digital Environment" by Vera Hagemann and Katharina Klug advances our understanding on how human resource management is impacted by digitalization and people analytics. The chapter "Virtual Business Incubators: A Support for Entrepreneurship in Rural Areas?" by Jörg Freiling, Leon Marquardt, and Tatevik Reit explores an intriguing topic of how to start and scale rural area entrepreneurship via virtual business incubators. The chapter "Digital Dark Nudges" by Lars Hornuf and Sonja Mangold examines the dark side of the digital economy, particularly the consequences and remedies to address "digital dark nudges" (manipulative product and interface designs). The chapter "Machine Learning in Accounting Research" by Christian Fieberg, Matthies Hesse, Thomas Loy, and Daniel Metko brings accounting research to the frontier machine learning era, highlighting viable research opportunities offered by deep learning. The chapter "Asset Pricing in Digital Assets" by Steffen Günther, Tobias Glas, and Thorsten Poddig overviews the fascinating topic of digital assets, how they differ from traditional assets, their role in the global financial system, and investment strategies. The chapter

"Artificial Intelligence, Surveillance, and Big Data" by David Karpa, Torben Klarl, and Michael Rochlitz trade offs different political institutions on the impact of AI innovation and research quality. The chapter "Digital Transformation of Maritime Supply Chains Focusing on Ocean Shipping, Port Management, and Hinterland Connection" by Hans-Dietrich Haasis and Hapsatou reflects the opportunities and challenges for digital transformation in ocean shipping, port management, and hinterland connectivity, a timely topic due to the current supply chain crises. The chapter "Social Media Analytics in Operations and Supply Chain Management: Opportunities, Challenges, and Paradoxes" by Aseem Kinra, Fabian Siekmann, and Herbert Kotzab perfectly complements chapter "Digital Transformation of Maritime Supply Chains Focusing on Ocean Shipping, Port Management, and Hinterland Connection" by identifying social media analytics opportunities, challenges, and paradoxes in supply chain management.

An agenda-setting book. I hope readers will be inspired as much as I am, by the topics in this edited volume, whether you are a graduate student, professor, or practitioner. I promise you that reading this book opens a joyful discovery of your own creativity.

Ernest Scheller Jr. Chair in Innovation, D. J. Wu
Entrepreneurship and Commercialization,
Scheller College of Business, Georgia Institute of Technology,
Atlanta, GA, USA

Contents

HumanRoboLab: Experiments with Chatbots in Management Education at Universities

Denis Pijetlovic and Georg Mueller-Christ

1 AI-Based Chatbots in Higher Education Teaching: Why?

The development of algorithms in the field of artificial intelligence (AI) is a category of topics in computer science aiming to map and simulate human thinking, decision-making, and problem-solving behavior using computerized processes (Bendel, 2020). Chatbots fall into this category because they use elements of AI to simulate human communication behavior in such a way that people can talk to them using natural language. However, such a conception of AI-based chatbots is rather limiting in the context of application-oriented higher education teaching: It is too generally formulated and assumes expertise in cognitive sciences for its operational use to be possible. To circumvent this deficit, this chapter draws on Hammond's (2017) *Periodic Table of AI* (Fig. 1) in order to make the term "AI-based chatbots" suitable for practical use in higher education teaching. A German-language version of the periodic table of AI is provided by Bitkom (2018) in an online handbook. The authors make reference to Hammond's concept for systematizing AI functions: Hammond considers AI to be the combination of basic elements, similar to complementary LEGO bricks. Each AI element represents a sub-function that has historically established itself as an encapsulated functionality of a certain complexity and power. The author identifies a total of 28 AI elements that can be combined according to general criteria (Bitkom, 2018, p. 15).

Hammond's tabular arrangement of all AI elements is called a "periodic table," analogous to the physical sciences. Each AI element can be assigned to one of three groups: *Assess* is dark/light green, *Infer* is yellow/orange, and *Respond* is magenta.

D. Pijetlovic (✉) · G. Mueller-Christ
Faculty of Business Studies and Economics, University of Bremen, Bremen, Germany
e-mail: denis.pijetlovic@uni-bremen.de; gmc@uni-bremen.de

L. Hornuf (ed.), *Diginomics Research Perspectives*, Advanced Studies in Diginomics and Digitalization, https://doi.org/10.1007/978-3-031-04063-4_1

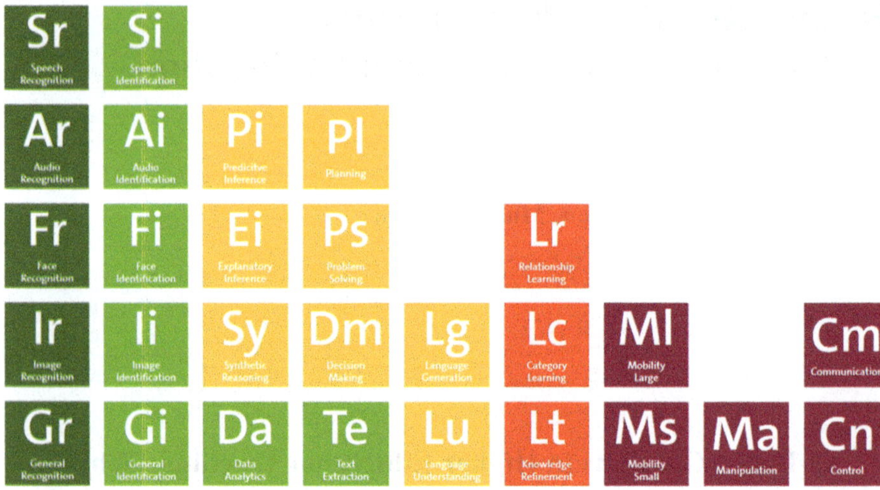

Fig. 1 Periodic table of artificial intelligence (Source: Bitkom, 2018, p. 7)

Through combinations of these different elements of AI, applications can in turn be derived and defined abstractly. In accordance with this, chatbots consist of the following AI elements:

Text extraction [Te] means that this AI element is proficient in analyzing texts. It does this by learning to differentiate between entities (e.g., people, organizations, cities, products) and terms (e.g., communication, innovation, production) in texts. This allows ambiguities in names and words to be resolved. A very everyday example of the ambiguity that AI aims to resolve would be the word *Müller*, which, depending on the context, could refer to the politician Gerd Müller, the footballer Thomas Müller, the drugstore chain Müller, or simply the German word for a person who operates a mill.

Language understanding [Lu] relates to the understanding of the information in the text, that is, the assignment to meaning. This AI element captures the relationships between entities and concepts meant in texts and thus solves two problems: first, it is clarified which entities and concepts in sentence structures are actually related to one another; second, the significance of this relationship is examined. The outcome of language understanding [Lu] in combination with text extraction [Te] is the translation of a possibly ambiguous text into an unambiguous machine representation (Bitkom, 2018).

Communication [Cm] as an AI element is used in turn to automatically answer large numbers of individual or recurring questions. In the course of this, models are trained based on specific case studies. These models are able to understand the meaning of incoming questions in order to suggest answers and conduct dialogs. In the case of chatbots, these datasets consist of language models that are trained by machine learning.

By fragmenting such a complex application as a chatbot, the AI periodic table helps to clarify the way in which the different elements of artificial intelligence are interrelated and work. Thus, reducing complexity by breaking it down into components with different functions helps make the broad field of artificial intelligence more workable.

1.1 Process Support as a Field of Application

The areas of application for chatbots are diverse. In basic terms, chatbots are used to support people in processes and to optimize processes. These areas of application can be divided into three overarching application scenarios: (a) decision-making, (b) communication, and (c) teaching and learning processes (see Fig. 2). These scenarios are considered in greater detail below.

(a) The use of chatbots in decision-making situations is still in its infancy. These specialized chatbots act as assistants for humans. For example, in an aerospace scenario, a decision-oriented chatbot can specify certain next (test) steps or calculate probabilities in dangerous situations. A chatbot developed by students in collaboration with OHB SE called Alan, the Astro Aid (see chapter "Virtual Business Incubators: A Support for Entrepreneurship in Rural Areas?"), for example, supports astronauts in resolving difficulties in handling the European Physiology Modules developed by OHB SE.
(b) Chatbots used for communication processes are primarily found in customer service. These chatbots can be used to book flights, order products, or process complaints (first-level support). By using these chatbots, companies can operate more efficiently and ensure better targeted customer service.
(c) Chatbots can also be used in teaching and learning processes as virtual training partners to help students consolidate the learning material (de Witt et al., 2020, p. 19). There are four different areas of application: (1) supporting learners, such as in an online community; (2) supporting learning activities; (3) testing knowledge and assessing performance; and (4) learning or career advice (Satow, 2018).

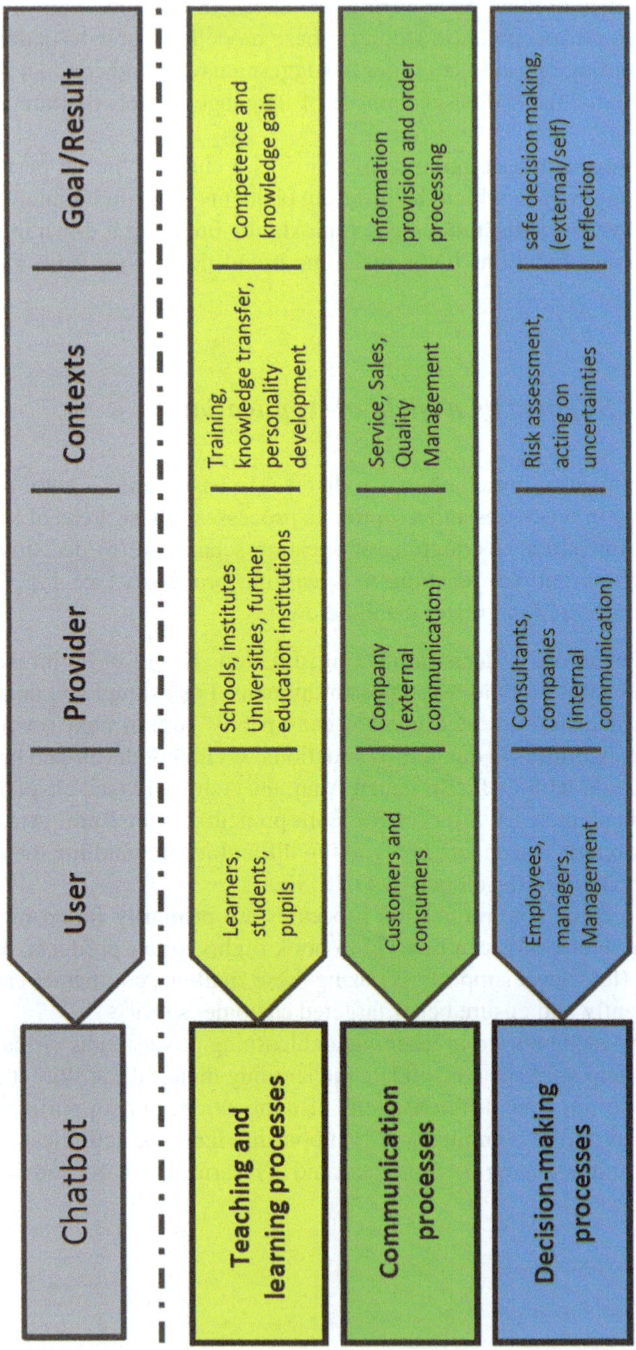

Fig. 2 Areas of application of chatbots in process support

1.2 Modeling and Training of Chatbots

Chatbot technology is not fundamentally new. The first prototypes were made back in the 1960s. ELIZA, developed by Joseph Weizenbaum, is considered to be the first fully functional chatbot and became known for its superficial simulation of a psychotherapist. In psychotherapy, targeted open questions are asked—a principle that Weizenbaum used by developing a program that applies the non-directive techniques of person-centered psychotherapy according to Carl Rogers (Höltgen & Baranovska, 2018). ELIZA used a structured dictionary for this, searching the sentences entered by users for terms from its dictionary. Given a matching word, the chatbot searches for generic terms or synonyms through which ELIZA can direct the conversation. Here is an example:

User: "I have a problem with my mother."
ELIZA: "Tell me more about your family!"

This form of database query is, however, no longer comparable with what is known today as artificial intelligence (in the sense of self-learning programs). Since ELIZA, chatbot technologies have steadily evolved, particularly with conversational AI, which enables human–machine interaction through natural language and which is becoming increasingly efficient (Lamprecht, 2016). Examples include AI-based applications such as OpenAI's GPT-3, Google Dialogflow, Microsoft Luis, Amazon Lex, and IBM's Watson Assistant. A special feature of these frameworks is that they enable even ordinary people to develop their own chatbot within a few hours without them having to be proficient in a programming language. The logic behind this technology is trivial: Chatbots are trained on specific content, known as *intents*, which are entered into the respective system. This allows the chatbots to respond to queries within seconds and enables interaction in real time. The extent to which the interaction *actually* succeeds depends on the interaction of the AI's algorithms with the language model. A key quality feature here is the structure of the chat design: the more comprehensively the user's possible intentions (in the form of questions, commands, and small talk) can be handled, the higher the probability that the interaction will be perceived as beneficial (McTear et al., 2016).

1.3 Chatbots as an Introduction to Machine Learning

In order to design an interactive chatbot, students must generate a language model for the respective case application, train it, and then optimize it based on initial test data. In this way, students can learn how machine learning (ML), a subfield of AI, works and how to control and monitor this learning process. The data for the language model is essential here. This data consists of three main parts—intents, entities, and dialog—that are input into a chatbot platform. ML uses the technology known as neural networks, which are algorithms with a similar structure to the human brain. They can recognize and match recurring patterns by using all the real-world information known to them (e.g., images, texts, time sequences) to translate familiar patterns into mathematical vectors. Using neural networks, the respective system can classify new information based on similarities and combine it into entities. These entities are designated with labels, such as "customers," "colleagues," and "order" (Roßbach, 2017, p. 13 f.; Schikora et al., 2020, p. 268).

There are three different types of ML: supervised learning, unsupervised learning, and reinforcement learning. In supervised learning, a program is given a sample dataset. This contains data that is already divided into certain categories (clusters) and labeled (labeled data). In this way, the program recognizes certain input parameters and can assign them to a result. With the data thus established, it becomes a model through training runs. Once the model has been created, unknown data can be supplied to the model and the program calculates a result (prediction). In unsupervised learning, the program generates a model for a given set of inputs. This model describes the inputs and enables predictions. The input data is divided through a cluster process into several categories which differ from one another by characteristic patterns. The program is able to independently create classifications according to which it categorizes the input patterns (Gomes et al., 2017, p. 23; Schikora et al., 2020, p. 270). Reinforcement learning allows a program to independently learn a strategy based on a reward function. The reward function (or utility function) describes the value of a particular state or action. Unlike supervised learning and unsupervised learning, reinforcement learning does not require any data in advance. Instead, the database is created by trial-and-error processes within a specially created simulation scenario. During the training runs, all required data is generated and highlighted. This learning method is most similar to the natural learning method of humans (Abdoos et al., 2015, p. 213).

Supervised learning is used in the chatbot projects as part of the HRL. This is so that students learn how useful functions for the chatbot program can be created and combined from pairs of inputs and outputs. In order for the machine learning process to work, students must provide the correct function values for an input. In this way, students learn to develop context-specific (language) models. This process is iterative and is usually constantly adapted and revised until a model works satisfactorily.

2 Chatbot Projects in the Real-World Laboratory

The chatbot projects carried out within the framework of the HRL (see chapter "Human Resource Management in a Digital Environment") are based on experimentation in real-world laboratories (Schneidewind, 2018); that is, they create a framework for "moving from knowledge to action." The ideal-typical process of the real-world laboratory according to this understanding takes place on a co-creative basis with practice partners who (1) develop the project together with the students, (2) implement the technical modeling or production of the chatbot, and (3) interpret and evaluate the outcome (Gibbons et al., 1994; Singer-Brodowski, 2016). This process reflects the concept on which the real-world laboratory approach is based: a transdisciplinary collaboration of scientists, students, and practice partners with the intention of facilitating research-based learning. The context dependence resulting from the application of knowledge enables continuous (self-) reflection and evaluation in order to repeatedly question the results and to adapt them to new conditions. Real-world laboratories are therefore learning settings for transdisciplinary exploratory research (Pijetlovic, 2020; Müller-Christ & Pijetlovic, 2018) that extend the usual focus of the development and application of AI technologies beyond the integration and synthesis of knowledge for potential application.

2.1 The HumanRoboLab Concept

The HRL seeks to integrate the testing of AI technologies in the real-world laboratory into economic and business psychology courses. It aims to integrate real-world learning environments into existing modules of teaching in these subjects, enabling the use of digital technologies while at the same time promoting the development of competencies for their meaningful design and reflection. The core of the HRL concept is the dovetailing of theoretical and methodological expertise, experience, and (self-) reflection.

Such a context imparts basic specialized knowledge in the topic groups of conversation-oriented artificial intelligence and communication theories, but also promotes the practical examination of the system, target, and transformation that the students apply in their respective chatbot projects. This concept is complemented by the methodological perspective of systemic exploratory research, which is composed of theories of "sciences of possibilities" ("*Möglichkeitswissenschaften*") (Pfriem, 2017) and futurology (Kreibich, 2017). This interplay of theory and practice is accompanied by exercises for (self-) reflection, which not only strengthens the learning experience, but also enables a critical look at one's own competencies and the influence of technology on human behavior. In this sense, the HRL concept attends to what is known as the "third mission" of higher education institution activities, meaning that, in addition to the other two missions of teaching and research, the higher education institution mutually interacts with the non-higher education world and uses socially relevant, reflective approaches and methods of transdisciplinary research for this purpose (Henke et al., 2016). The development of chatbot prototypes offers both students and their practice partners the opportunity not only to develop digital transformation spaces (Freiling et al., 2020) in an entrepreneurial way, but also to bring them into the socio-political context.

3 A Selection of the Chatbot Projects from the HRL

The HRL concept has been integrated into the bachelor's and master's degree courses in business administration and business psychology at the University of Bremen. A total of 84 students have participated in the HRL to date. The courses (six/nine credit points) are offered for one semester and conclude with a public project presentation of the developed chatbot prototypes. The students give these final presentations as part of the *Digital Assistant Conference*, which can also be attended by interested company representatives. This format has already helped some students to launch their careers through their project work. Practice partners who have been involved in HRL projects to date include Sparkasse Bremen AG, the aerospace technology group OHB SE, Techniker Krankenkasse, Beiersdorf AG, Universum GmbH, the University of Bremen, EWE AG, and Seghorn AG, which specializes in receivables management, as well as the tourism development of the city of Bremen. Students were free to decide which practice partners should support the work on their respective projects.

Below is a small selection of the projects from the HRL, providing a sampling of the practical contexts for which the students have already developed fully functional chatbots.

3.1 TIKAY BOT (Techniker Krankenkasse)

The TiKay bot optimizes the search for a space in a care home. By requesting specific information about the type of care, focus of care, level of care, and location of the care home desired, during the course of a chat, TiKay can compile a list of suitable care homes based on a database. This pre-selection gives searchers an informative overview of potentially suitable facilities and allows them to focus on contacting the selected providers. In addition, the TiKay bot is able to answer general questions on topics such as costs, services, and care support, or to establish direct contact with the source of the information.

3.2 Museum Bot XT-9U (Universum GmbH)

The XT-9U is a chatbot for the Digital Worlds area at the interactive museum Universum in Bremen, Germany. The XT-9U has knowledge about AI and robotics. Museum visitors learn from the chatbot itself what kind of AI it is based on, and what sensors are used by robots such as Pepper and NAO (developed by SoftBank Robotics) to be able to hold a conversation. The XT-9U is based on the model of an interested scientist who wants to discover new things and also likes to scrutinize visitors' answers. The digital assistant's name is inspired by the Star Wars robots

R2D2 and C3PO. The XT in XT-9U stands for eXtended Technology, the 9 for its development year 2019, and the U for Universum—the name of the interactive museum.

3.3 Design Thinking Bot (University of Bremen)

The task of the design thinking bot is to support participants in a design challenge based on the rules of design thinking throughout the development process of their products. This chatbot knows the individual process steps of design thinking and can guide the participants through the phases, answer questions about the process, and give useful tips for processing steps. The particular challenge of this project was to develop a chatbot that does not specify any requirements, but rather provides useful suggestions and encourages users to think creatively.

3.4 Alan (OHB SE)

Alan is a chatbot developed in collaboration with the OHB Group. Alan is designed to support astronauts in space in solving problems and addressing faults quickly and efficiently. Unlike experts on Earth, he can answer any questions without any delay in the transmission of the conversation, meaning that he enables real-time support. The focus of this bot project is the service element manufactured by OHB for the International Standard Payload Rack based on the European Physiology Module. This module is designed for experiments and represents an important research facility of the Columbus space laboratory on the International Space Station (ISS). In the first application scenario, Alan was used to help astronauts correct a power circuit fault that had already occurred on the ISS in 2010 and was made apparent by the fact that the power distribution unit no longer worked properly.

4 Competencies and Skills Learned

As part of the chatbot projects in the real-world laboratory, the students were able to acquire competencies (see Table 1) that, among other outcomes, enable them to better assess the relevance of dealing with chatbots in various areas of application, to clear up misunderstandings in the debate about AI and chatbots, and to better understand media reporting of AI developments and correctly classify them. In all chatbot projects, two key competence areas were prevalent. First is the generation of datasets in order to be able to set up and subsequently train an appropriate language model. These datasets can be compiled based on structured or unstructured data. The students in the real-world laboratory primarily generated

Table 1 Areas of competence of students in the HRL context

Area	Competency
Methodical	• *Machine learning (supervised learning)* • Data acquisition management • Dialog management
Technical	• *Knowledge of how digital dialog systems (chatbots) work* • Practical procedural knowledge regarding modeling strategies • Systemic perspective on AI
Personal	• *Development of an inquiring attitude toward AI applications* • Self-awareness from dealing with AI • Transfer of practice-oriented ideas to digital applications

unstructured data, which they then placed in if–then relationships to enable clear sequences of intents (input) and dialog (response). This process of data structuring is necessary because the chatbot program lacks simple background information that human users naturally bring to any communications. For example, users know that people greet each other when they first meet and only then interact in more depth, but a chatbot must first be taught this socio-culturally based convention through appropriate sequences of intents and dialog. The challenge for students is to become aware of self-evident things like these and to then prepare the data in such a way that enables successful meaningful interaction for a specific purpose. The second area of competency concerns the chatbot's satisfactory performance. For each case study that the chatbot is expected to master through appropriate interaction, the AI must also be able to identify the objective of the respective user and match it with a corresponding process of solution-oriented action. This is the only way that the interaction can ultimately lead to an outcome that is actually useful to the user.

The students therefore first develop an algorithm, that is, a rule that dictates how certain goals can be achieved step by step. In AI, an algorithm is a rule for solving a (mathematical) problem that has been translated into a programming language. The participants in the real-world laboratory conduct expert interviews in order to better understand the processes that the chatbot is expected to support, but also to generate suitable datasets for a language model exactly tailored to these processes. In this way, the student teams were able to gain initial experience in process analysis and modeling of language models—two key competencies for the confident use of AI.

By participating in the HRL, the students were able to find out whether a job in the field of chatbot development (or more generally in working with AI applications) would suit them personally, and whether after completing their chatbot project they would like to continue professionally developing in the direction of machine learning, user interaction design, or conversational user experience design. At the same time, the practice partners were able to record their own learning thanks to their work on the chatbot projects. The transdisciplinary approach of the real-world laboratory has contributed to (a) a culture of creativity and innovation, stimulating the exchange of knowledge between higher education teaching and business practices; (b) a better understanding among practice partners of chatbot technology and acquisition of transformational knowledge for their field; and (c) the opportunity for everyone involved to gather practical experience in collaborative agility.

5 What Is Next for the Chatbot Laboratory?

A look at the literature and visits to the corresponding platforms on the Internet show that chatbots are experiencing explosive growth in the higher education sector, although many examples give the impression that the technology is mostly used to deal with very simple dialogs and rule-based tasks. Chatbots commonly encountered in higher education are used to help students deal with tasks with predefined rules, such as in mathematics or learning a new language. For language acquisition, chatbots are used as dialog partners for practicing conversational scenarios or increasing vocabulary. The work of Bao (2019) provides insights into this area regarding the reducing of fear of foreign languages through chatbot interactions. There are also chatbots in higher education that provide support with administrative tasks. An example of this can be found in the study by Galko et al. (2018), where the enrollment process for students has been completely transitioned to a dialog with a chatbot.

These types of chatbots nevertheless involve predefined applications, and cannot be configured by users for their individual learning process. For higher education, therefore, these simple use cases are first steps, but they are far from maxing out the potential of AI. The presumably long road to successful (process/learning) support by chatbot systems should contribute to learners being able to reflect more on their own process of learning and deepen it in a self-directed manner. We believe that no one can solve this problem better than the students and learners themselves. What they need for this, however, is the knowledge and skills to develop such a chatbot as a learning companion in order to independently determine which learning goals are to be achieved and through which route. The assumption and hope is that, in this way, the AI potential of chatbots will be able to contribute to the development of greater learning and understanding among people and machines alike.

References

Abdoos, M., Mozayani, N., & Bazzan, A. (2015). Towards reinforcement learning for holonic multi-agent systems. *Intelligent Data Analysis, 19*(2), 211–232.

Bao, M. (2019). Can home use of speech-enabled artificial intelligence mitigate foreign language anxiety: Investigation of a concept. *AWEJ, 5*, 28–40. https://doi.org/10.24093/awej/call5.3

Bendel, O. (2020). Serviceroboter aus Sicht der Ethik. In M. Lindau & M. Meier Kressing (Eds.), *Schöne neue Welt? Zwischen technischen Möglichkeiten und ethischen Herausforderungen* (pp. 57–76). Transcript.

Bitkom. (2018). *Digitalisierung gestalten mit dem Periodensystem der Künstlichen Intelligenz – Ein Navigationssystem für Entscheider*. https://www.bitkom.org/sites/default/files/201812/181204_LF_Periodensystem_online_0.pdf Zugegriffen: 18. Dezember 2020.

de Witt, C., Rampelt, F., & Pinkwart, N. (Hrsg.) (2020). *Künstliche Intelligenz in der Hochschulbildung*. Whitepaper. KI-Campus.

Freiling, J., Holi, M., & Stührenberg, K. (2020). Exploration durch digitale Transformationsräume. Das Beispiel "future concepts Bremen." *Austrian Management Review*, 10(1), 47–59. Hrsg.: Wolfgang H. Güttel, Baden-Baden: Rainer Hampp Verlag.

Galko, L., Porubän, J., & Senko, J. (2018). Improving the user experience of electronic university enrolment. In F. Jakab (Ed.), *16th IEEE International Conference on Emerging eLearning Technologies and Applications, ICETA 2018*, Stary Smokovec, Slovakia, Nov 15–16, 2018 (pp. 179–184). IEEE. doi:https://doi.org/10.1109/ICETA.2018.8572054.

Gibbons, M., Limoges, C., Nowotny, H., Schwartzman, S., Peter, S., & Trow, M. (1994). *The new production of knowledge: The dynamics of science and research in contemporary societies*. Sage.

Gomes, H., Barddal, J., Enembreck, F., & Bifet, A. (2017). A survey on ensemble learning for data stream classification. *ACM Computing Surveys, 50*(2), 23:1–23:36. https://doi.org/10.1145/3054925

Hammond, K. (2017). *Here and now: Bringing AI into the enterprise*. https://conferences.oreilly.com/artificial-intelligence/ai-ny-2017/public/schedule/detail/59188 Zugegriffen: 18 Dezember 2020.

Henke, J., Pasternack, P., & Schmid, C. J. (2016). Third mission von Hochschulen. Eine Definition. *Das Hochschulwesen, 64*(1/2), 16–22.

Höltgen, S., & Baranovska, M. (Eds.). (2018). *Hello, I'm Eliza. 50 Jahre Gespräche mit Computern*. Projekt Verlag.

Kreibich, R. (2017). Wissenschaftsverständnis und Methodik der Zukunftsforschung. *Zukunftszeichen: Semiotik und Futurologie, Zeitschrift für Semiotik, 29*(2–3), 318.

Lamprecht, S. (2016). *Digitale Quasselstrippe – Interessante Chatbot-Gründungen*. eTailment vom 26. September 2016. https://etailment.de/news/stories/Digitale-Quasselstrippen%2D%2D-interessante-Chatbot-Gruendungen-4377 Zugegriffen: 20 Dezember 2020.

McTear, M., Callejas, Z., & Grigol, D. (2016). *The conversational interface: Talking to smart devices*. Springer International Publishing.

Müller-Christ, G., & Pijetlovic, D. (2018). *Komplexe Systeme lesen. Das Potential von Systemaufstellung für Wissenschaft und Praxis*. Springer Gabler.

Pfriem, R. (2017). Ökonomik als Möglichkeitswissenschaft. *Ökologisches Wirtschaften – Fachzeitschrift*, (2), 16–18.

Pijetlovic, D. (2020). *Das Potential der Pflege-Robotik. Eine systemische Erkundungsforschung*. Springer Gabler.

Roßbach, P. (2017). Machine learning, modern data analytics and artificial intelligence: What's new? *Banking and Information Technology, 18*(3), 13–19.

Satow, L. (2018). Lernen mit Chatbots und digitalen Assistenten. In K. Wilbers (Ed.), *Handbuch E-Learning* (pp. 1–14). Wolters Kluwer.

Schikora, C., Galster, S., & Högerl, D. (2020). Digitalisierung im recruiting: Chatbots. In M. Harwardt, P. J. Niermann, A. Schmutte, & A. Steuernagel (Eds.), *Führen und Managen in der digitalen Transformation* (pp. 266–281). Springer Gabler.

Schneidewind, U. (2018). *Die große Transformation: eine Einführung in die Kunst gesellschaftlichen Wandels*. Fischer Taschenbuch.

Singer-Brodowski, M. (2016). Transformative Bildung durch transformatives Lernen. Zur Notwendigkeit der erziehungswissenschaftlichen Fundierung einer neuen Idee. *ZEP: Zeitschrift für internationale Bildungsforschung und Entwicklungspädagogik, 39*(1), 13–17.

Marketing in a Digital World

Kristina Klein, Maik Eisenbeiss, Maik Dulle, Nastaran Taherparvar, Mirko Wiemann, and Jan Wiezorrek

1 Introduction

Marketing is not a static concept. Rather, the basic idea of marketing is based on the assumption that a firm's environment is constantly changing and that marketing must adapt to environmental changes in its strategic and operational design elements (Eisenbeiss, 2020). For more than two decades now, it is the technological environment that has been changing—and not slowly and moderately, but quickly and radically, with ongoing digitization regularly delivering innovative technology-based solutions that firms can then use to interact with consumers. According to an annual market study by Chiefmartec, the global count of marketing technologies has increased from about 150 solutions in 2011 to about 8000 solutions in 2020, corresponding to a growth of 5200% in under ten years (Chiefmartec, 2020). The solutions offered cover a wide range of marketing application areas, such as advertising and promotion, sales management, customer relationship management, social media management, content design, and data intelligence.

Technology providers and agencies promise that consumers can be addressed much more efficiently and effectively using these new marketing tools. This perspective, however, only attends to the technology side, which is all too frequently overemphasized. Marketing though is primarily about creating value for consumers. Thus, it is consumers rather than the technology itself that should be at the center of all corporate marketing decisions. Research has shown in many application areas that a technology, no matter how promising, often fails to achieve its goal as long as it is not aligned with the interests and needs of consumers (Malter &

K. Klein · M. Eisenbeiss (✉) · M. Dulle · N. Taherparvar · M. Wiemann · J. Wiezorrek
Faculty of Business Studies and Economics, markstones Institute of Marketing, Branding & Technology, University of Bremen, Bremen, Germany
e-mail: kklein@uni-bremen.de; eisenbeiss@uni-bremen.de; maik.dulle@uni-bremen.de; n.taherparvar@uni-bremen.de; mirko.wiemann@uni-bremen.de; jan.wiezorrek@uni-bremen.de

L. Hornuf (ed.), *Diginomics Research Perspectives*, Advanced Studies in Diginomics and Digitalization, https://doi.org/10.1007/978-3-031-04063-4_2

Rindfleisch, 2019). For example, in the context of retargeting, Bleier and Eisenbeiss (2015) illustrate that personalized online banners (which in theory should help consumers make purchasing decisions more easily) often elicit more negative than positive consumer responses. One of the reasons for this finding is the privacy concerns that consumers develop when they realize that their personal data is being processed. Another example is gamification (i.e., the use of game elements in non-game contexts, such as marketing; see Eppmann et al., 2018), which is intended to elicit joy and hence greater interest among consumers in performing certain (often monotonous) tasks, such as participating in a market research survey. However, Downes-Le Guin et al. (2012) and Warnock and Gantz (2017) have shown that while gamified surveys increase enjoyment among survey participants, at the same time, they also lead to higher dropout rates.

In this chapter, we suggest that marketing in a digital world is successful only when both perspectives (technology and the consumer) are taken into account. Modern marketing technologies only contribute to greater effectiveness and efficiency if consumers also recognize and value the benefits of these technological advancements. Analyzing previous research, this chapter shows how firms can combine innovative marketing technologies and consumer interests in a purposeful manner, using the examples of three application areas that will impact marketing in the future: (1) chatbots, (2) voice assistants, and (3) data privacy management.

2 Chatbots

The ways of interaction between individuals and machines have changed a lot over the last decades. Not only educational institutions use new technologies like chatbots more frequently, (see chapter "HumanRoboLab: Experiments with Chatbots in Management Education at Universities" by Pijetlovic & Mueller-Christ, 2022); firms are increasingly using them as an AI tool for interactions and communication with consumers (for a more advanced view on AI and machine learning in the context of accounting, see chapter "Machine Learning in Accounting Research" by Fieberg et al., 2022). It has been predicted that the world market for chatbots will grow about 24% annually to a value of 1.3 billion USD by 2024 (American Marketing Association, 2020), reflective of the fact that the technology has evolved and improved very rapidly over recent years. Basically, a chatbot is a text- or voice-based artificial intelligence that responds to text or voice inputs from a human being. This method of responding is made possible by *natural language processing* (NLP), which is based on an intelligent algorithm: inputs are analyzed in terms of the words that are produced by a human being. The algorithm is capable of understanding the content, extracting the important parts, and then answering properly (Adamopoulou & Moussiades, 2020a). The better the programming of the algorithm and the more (textual) information gained by prior conversations, the more accurately a chatbot can respond to specific topics. In a commercial setting, this capability is the basis for effective interaction between a software program representing the firm and consumers (Adamopoulou & Moussiades, 2020a).

From a technical perspective, two types of chatbots exist. What are known as *open-domain* chatbots can respond to any topic the user wants to talk about (e.g., the weather), even if the answer will not contain any relevant information (i.e., it is generic or makes no sense at all). In contrast, *closed-domain* chatbots operate only for specific topics or scenarios, such as customer services, and have only a limited repertoire of possible but well-fitting answers (Adamopoulou & Moussiades, 2020b). These are also called "rule-based" chatbots (Thorat & Jadhav, 2020). The interface design of chatbots is often very similar to the user interfaces of chat services such as WhatsApp or Facebook. In some cases, just speech bubbles appear within the chat, but more frequently, an avatar (i.e., a cartoon-style profile picture or the face of a real person) imbues the chatbot with some level of humanity.

Chatbots can offer several advantages for firms, including reduced costs through the automation of handling requests, increased time efficiency through their 24/7 availability, faster response time than human employees, and consequently a potentially better user experience and service quality. Of course, consumers also benefit from these aspects when using chatbots (Adam et al., 2021). This two-way interaction via chat has been shown to positively influence consumer outcomes such as satisfaction, intention to repurchase, trust, and word of mouth (Mero, 2018). Chatbots do not have only positive outcomes for consumers, however, and indeed may be a challenging proposition for firms. While consumers potentially can get solutions for their problems whenever needed, a large number of consumers also express concerns about or avoid interacting with a non-human "employee" (Gnewuch et al., 2017), as they sometimes perceive them as creepy or intrusive. Research has thus investigated parameters that might help reduce avoidance tendencies among consumers while interacting with chatbots. An important suggestion in this context is that consumers need to perceive a chatbot as a human-like being. This perception is called *anthropomorphism*, i.e., the attribution of human characteristics to a non-human being (Epley et al., 2007).

2.1 Humanness of Chatbots: A Two-Sided Coin

Interestingly, too much human-likeness can also backfire. In 1970, Masahiro Moto published his theory of the "uncanny valley," concerning the perception of industrial robots. The model explains the relationship between (positive and negative) familiarity with a non-human agent and the extent to which this agent is perceived as human-like. Overall, the theory states that the more human-like a non-human agent appears, the more familiar people perceive it to be (Gray & Wegner, 2012). However, if the agent seems to be "too" human-like, an overall positive familiarity becomes negative, traversing the so-called "uncanny valley." People then tend to exhibit a negative emotional response; agents are perceived as scary, creepy, strange or bizarre and people ultimately avoid any interaction (Blut et al., 2021). At the same time, the more human-like characteristics appear while seeing or interacting with a non-human agent, the more likely this agent will be perceived as a "real" entity (i.e., the non-human agent will be anthropomorphized), resulting in a positive emotional response towards the agent. The main purpose of this process of anthropomorphism from a consumer's perspective is to interact with one's environment effectively—reducing uncertainty, making sense of others' actions, and better predicting their behavior (Epley et al., 2007). Human-likeness is thus important in producing benefits for consumer experience.

In sum, the supposition that "the more human-like, the better it is" does not hold up in every case, which means that the extent to which a chatbot is designed to be human-like must be considered carefully.

2.2 Social Perceptions of Chatbots

Social cues (such as avatars, emojis, or language) should be the easiest and most efficient signals to increase the likelihood of anthropomorphism. These cues can also elicit social perceptions (Kim & Sundar, 2012), as they trigger what are called "human heuristics" (Sundar, 2008). These heuristics lead to an unconscious perception and evaluation of a chatbot, leading people to behave as they would in a social interaction with a human being. *Social response theory*, with its *computers-are-social-actors* (CASA) paradigm, provides a model to explain this phenomenon (Adam et al., 2021). This paradigm postulates that human–computer interactions are fundamentally social (i.e., applying social rules or norms) and driven by the evolutionary need for social orientation. This results in behavioral manners of consumers towards the chatbot (e.g., a specific way of responding, being polite, etc.) that can also be observed in social interactions between human beings. Perceiving a computer as a social actor happens both unconsciously and automatically (Nass et al., 1994; Nass & Moon, 2000) and can be triggered by social cues.

A primary goal of chatbot designers is thus to elicit a social perception of the agent while interacting with it (Go & Sundar, 2019) through the manipulation of parameters such as the overall design representing the corporate identity, how the chatbot is integrated into the website, and the use of various social cues. What consumers perceive while interacting with a chatbot are chiefly its appearance and the answers it gives. Feine et al. (2019) differentiate social cues into four categories: *verbal cues* (e.g., the content or style of responses), *visual cues* (e.g., the appearance of the chatbot, such as the avatar), *auditory cues* (e.g., the voice, which refers more to voice assistants) and *invisible cues* (e.g., response time). Figure 1 shows a typical structure of a chatbot.

At the bottom, consumers can type their messages. While an avatar (next to the messages of the chatbot) is the visual cue, the style in which the chatbot is writing (e.g., speech bubble, modern language with emojis) represents verbal cues. The typing indicator (three dots inside the second speech bubble) belongs to invisible cues, because it is strongly connected to response time.

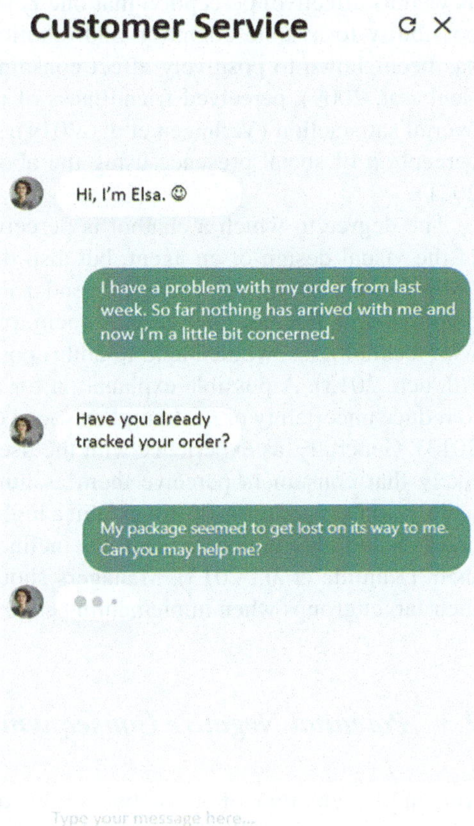

Fig. 1 Customer service chatbot Elsa (Bensemann, B. (2021). *Emotionen die Wahrnehmung von Chatbots? Eine empirische Untersuchung von Anthropomorphismus und Zufriedenheit im Kundenservice* [Unpublished master's thesis]. University of Bremen)

Most research so far has focused on visual cues. For example, giving chatbots a human name can elicit a social perception (Araujo, 2018; Koh & Sundar, 2010), which also occurs when using an avatar (Nowak & Rauh, 2005) or an animated typing indicator, but only for those consumers who have less experience with chatbots (Gnewuch et al., 2018). Recent research has shown that verbal cues such as language style (e.g., informal versus formal) can also increase the likelihood that consumers anthropomorphize a chatbot (Adam et al., 2021; Go & Sundar, 2019; Araujo, 2018). Through anthropomorphism then and an increased social perception, chatbots positively influence the intention to purchase in an e-commerce environment (Han, 2021), can increase conversion rates (Schanke et al., 2020), and lead to higher overall satisfaction (Chung et al., 2020; Yam et al., 2020).

Most of these effects do not occur directly, but are most likely mediated by other processes, a variety of which have been identified to gain a deeper understanding of how the perception of human-likeness of a chatbot and other agents is processed (Pelau et al., 2021). One of the underlying variables that can strengthen the perception of a social situation is *social presence*, that is, the subjective (cognitive as well as affective) perception that one is interacting with a human being and the possibility to assume cognition and emotion from the opposite. Social presence has been shown to positively affect consumers' trust (Toader et al., 2020; Qiu & Benbasat, 2009), perceived friendliness of the chatbot (Go & Sundar, 2019), and overall satisfaction (Verhagen et al., 2014). Managers should thus seek to create a perception of social presence using the above-mentioned social cues (Tsai et al., 2021).

The degree to which a chatbot is perceived as human-like is not only a result of the visual design of an agent, but also depends on consumers' predispositions (Waytz et al., 2014). For example, gender influences how chatbots will be anthropomorphized. Because men usually seem to be more interested in and experienced with technologies, women tend to anthropomorphize more often (De Graaf & Ben Allouch, 2013). A possible explanation for this finding can be their stronger need to reduce uncertainty or to strengthen social connections (De Graaf & Ben Allouch, 2013). Generally, as experience with the use of artificial agents increases, it is less likely that consumers perceive them as human beings (Blut et al., 2021). Thus, while middle-aged users do not exhibit a high tendency to anthropomorphize agents, children and elderly people are more inclined to attribute human characteristics to them (Kamide et al., 2013). Managers should thus consider the demographics of their target groups when implementing chatbot solutions.

2.3 Potential Negative Consequences of Chatbots

The implementation of a chatbot might also incur negative consequences. For example, Luo et al. (2019) found negative effects on the amount of purchases and contact time when consumers interact with a chatbot compared to a salesperson. While chatbots are comparably efficient, the study found that consumers perceived the chatbot to be less empathetic and knowledgeable, which ultimately led to a lower purchase rate. The reasons they identify are the awareness that one was interacting with a chatbot and limited prior experience with AI technologies. Ciechanowski et al. (2019) showed that a text-based chatbot with an animated avatar can lead to negative outcomes (e.g., affect or emotional arousal) and higher dissatisfaction. The former outcome likely occurred due to the "uncanny valley" effect, with the chatbot seeming to be "creepy and weird," while the latter decrease in satisfaction pertained to unmet expectations in chatbot performance. Crolic et al. (2021) investigated the effect on service satisfaction when angry (versus neutral) customers interacted with an anthropomorphized (versus non-anthropomorphized) chatbot. Overall, participants reported lower satisfaction with the service as well as lower purchase intention if they were angry and interacted with an anthropomorphized chatbot. These results overall show that specific context factors (such as the service situation) or the specific design (i.e., anthropomorphism) of a chatbot can lead to unwanted results.

2.3.1 In Sum: Chatbot Usage Must Be Carefully Considered

Anthropomorphized chatbots have generally been shown to be beneficial for consumer–firm interactions. They can increase purchase intentions, perceived service quality and overall satisfaction, and offer the possibility to communicate with consumers in a time- and cost-saving manner. However, managers need to consider many aspects when creating, testing, and implementing a chatbot for service purposes, taking into account not only the appearance of these AI-based agents, but also the context and target demographics with which they are likely to be used.

3 Voice Assistants

Chatbots are not the only emergent mode of interaction between firms and their consumers. Moving beyond interactions via keyboard, mouse, or touch interface, a new type of interaction via voice has become increasingly popular through the proliferation of voice assistants. These are voice-controlled devices that are able to perform a wide variety of tasks with or for humans (Mari, 2019). Voice interaction starts with a voice request from the user's side. Voice assistants recognize the voice request using automatic speech recognition (ASR) and natural language understanding (NLU) and return a voice response using text-to-speech (TTS) (Polyakov et al., 2018). Voice assistants also learn from previous conversations to continuously improve speech recognition using AI and machine learning (ML) (Hoy, 2018; for machine learning in accounting, see chapter "Machine Learning in Accounting Research" by Fieberg et al., 2022).

From a business perspective, voice assistants represent a new communication platform and new touchpoint with consumers. They collect users' data to recognize preferences and create personal profiles. These features enable voice assistants to provide immediate and personalized information and suggestions based on customers' queries and their profiles (Hoy, 2018), helping firms to acquire more insights into customers' preferences and purchase intentions, and opening up opportunities for targeted advertising and personalized product recommendations (Paluch & Wittkop, 2020). From a consumer perspective, the primary advantage of voice assistants is that they provide a quick and easy way to communicate their needs. Assistants offer a hands-free and eyes-free way of interaction that is faster and more natural than typing and does not require any additional equipment such as a keyboard (McLean & Osei-Frimpong, 2019).

Voice assistants come in a variety of forms. Apple introduced one of the first voice assistants, Siri, in 2011 and integrated it into its smartphones. Voice assistants are now also found on tablets, computers, and wearables, as well as in car navigation systems and voice-controlled smart home systems (Petrock, 2020). For instance, Amazon Echo, the world's first smart speaker [i.e., a digital speaker with an integrated assistant that is controlled by voice command (Bizzaco et al., 2021)], was introduced by Amazon in November 2014, followed by Apple with its Home Pod, Google with Google Home, Alibaba with Tmall Genie and Xiaomi with Mi.

The areas of application for voice assistants are also diverse. According to Paluch and Wittkop (2020), they can be divided into four main categories. The first category is *voice entertainment*, with applications such as music streaming services, podcasts, audiobooks, and radio and news programs, as well as games, quizzes, and fitness applications. The second category, *voice assistance*, encompasses applications to connect to and manage other smart devices in order to, say, control the lights, regulate the heating, or turn the coffee machine off and on. The third category is *voice search*, which includes information retrieval using spoken voice commands rather than typing, for example, when searching for products, news, weather, or recipes. The fourth category, *voice commerce*, includes all activities that involve shopping with voice assistants. Here, voice assistants act as intermediaries connecting firms and customers via voice apps. For Amazon voice assistants, these voice apps are called "skills," whereas, for Google voice assistants, they are called "actions." Firms need to create these apps, and consumers need to install them on their specific voice speakers. Then, for example, consumers can ask their Alexa to order a pizza or book an Uber. In January 2019, already 100,000 skills for Alexa and 4253 actions for Google Home existed (Kinsella, 2019).

Two key aspects of voice assistants might exert a strong influence on consumers' decision-making. First, voice assistants alter the way in which consumers search for and choose products (McLean & Osei-Frimpong, 2019). Based on the voice assistant's understanding of a consumer's request, it might offer a limited set of suggestions presented one after another, starting with the top search result in the underlying database. Voice assistants thus act as a filter and limit the amount of information given, generally reducing the number of suggested options based on context and existing user preferences. On the positive side, this filtering prevents information overload for the consumer and makes the purchase process more convenient and efficient. On the negative side, it can threaten one's sense of decision authority and self-determination by restricting a consumer's choices (Dellaert et al., 2020). The options suggested by voice assistants also might not guarantee the best option and can exclude more desirable options. Second, voice assistants limit consumers to the auditory sense and require consumers to choose from options without seeing them. Recalling all given information presented by a voice assistant could be difficult for consumers, especially in cases where they confront several options. This difficulty can enhance one's feeling of losing control over the received information, which reduces the customer's confidence in the product and results in an unpleasant experience (Pagani et al., 2019). Furthermore, many consumers prefer to see and/or touch a product before buying it, as this increases confidence in their decisions about the quality or value of a product (Peck & Childers, 2003). This lack of visual and tactile sensations might stop customers from using voice assistants to purchase products.

These two aspects portend new challenges for firms. First, they need to ensure that they maintain their customers in the transition to voice commerce. The algorithm behind voice assistants that ranks and suggests products/brands is not openly accessible; sometimes voice assistants might, for instance, recommend a private label over a national brand, which might result in the loss of brand visibility for the national brand. Moreover, specific data (e.g., how the algorithm works and what it includes) are only available to the manufacturer of the smart speakers, such as Amazon with Alexa. Consequently, the hardware and software provider becomes a gatekeeper, with some brands not being chosen by a particular voice assistant (Mari, 2019). Firms need to be aware of this potential negative effect on their "presentation" to consumers.

Second, firms need to fundamentally rethink the design of content provided to consumers. Instead of classic visual representations, only audio-based content is needed. The design of audio-based advertising messages can increase costs without guaranteeing acceptance of the message (Lenz-Kesekamp & Weber, 2018). Due to the limited capacity of memory in the auditory sense, consumers might simply forget the content they have heard, particularly if several options are presented to them. These restrictions make advertising more difficult, potentially increasing advertising costs (Mari, 2019).

Another more general challenge for firms is to find new solutions that enhance data protection. As voice assistants can constantly listen to conversations and collect information, many users are concerned about data privacy and security. Because such data are vulnerable to theft by hackers or being published in the event of data leaks (Hoy, 2018), developing a strategy for such situations is crucial for firms.

Despite the increasing popularity of voice assistants, firms are still reluctant to heavily invest in this point of contact with consumers. However, if firms want to rely on voice assistants in the future, they should make them customer-centric first and foremost. The (relatively sparse) literature to date already provides several starting points for this in two key decision areas:

I. Factors influencing the usage of voice assistants
II. Design factors for the interaction between voice assistants and consumers

3.1 Factors Influencing the Usage of Voice Assistants

The *technology acceptance model* provides a valuable lens for understanding users' adoption and use of new technology (Davis, 1989). Based on this model, hedonic elements such as perceived enjoyment (Pitardi & Marriott, 2021) as well as functional elements such as perceived usefulness and perceived ease of use are main antecedents influencing users' attitude towards using voice assistants for both transactional activities (e.g., purchasing) and non-transactional activities (e.g., searching information) (Moriuchi, 2019). A favorable attitude towards using voice assistants positively influences consumers' loyalty (i.e., behavioral intention) towards firms integrating voice assistants into their marketing strategies (Moriuchi, 2019).

There are three primary motives driving consumers to use voice assistants. The first motive is related to *utilitarian benefits* that emerge when consumers see voice assistants as a useful and convenient way to accomplish tasks (McLean et al., 2021). The second motive relates to *symbolic benefits* that reflect an individual's sense of self or social identity. The use of a voice assistant gives consumers the feeling that they can improve their social status. Third, consumers derive *social benefits* through treating voice assistants as a social entity and feel a human-like relationship when interacting with them (McLean & Osei-Frimpong, 2019; McLean et al., 2021).

In addition to these general usage motives, the underlying perception of a voice assistant also influences consumers' usage intention/behavior (Schweitzer et al., 2019). Voice assistants can be perceived by consumers in one of three forms: servant, partner, or master. The role of a servant is characterized by such traits as kindness, loyalty, friendliness, helpfulness, and reliability, and is seen as one that can help consumers to conduct daily tasks. A partner is perky, humorous, intelligent, factual, and serious, and one who deftly organizes situations. A master is perceived as ignorant, inflexible, annoying, obstinate, and erratic. Increased future usage of a voice assistant is most likely when consumers perceive the assistant as a servant, imparting a feeling of control, mastery, and superiority that inspires continued usage. In contrast, consumers who perceive voice assistants as masters see themselves as servants who must follow the voice assistant's rules, resulting in reduced usage intentions (Schweitzer et al., 2019).

3.2 Design Factors for the Interaction Between Voice Assistants and Consumers

Compared to other digital channels such as websites, interaction with voice assistants can become relatively complex for consumers, which can lead to different patterns of usage. When shopping, for example, consumers perceive recommended products on websites more positively than with voice assistants. This is because they regard voice assistants as pseudo-human agents detached from the firm, while they view websites as a tool or interface used by the firm (Whang & Im, 2020). Recommendations in auditory form (as opposed to visually) also increase difficulty in information processing, resulting in consumers being less able to differentiate among options. Consequently, an auditory form leads to a higher likelihood of accepting recommended options, but also a higher probability of deferring choice altogether compared to options presented visually (Munz & Morwitz, 2019). Finally, voice presentation changes the level of cognitive effort exerted by individuals, resulting in reduced personal engagement and brand trust (Pagani et al., 2019).

Because of this potential increased complexity in the interaction between voice assistants and consumers, it is recommended that marketers build a voice assistant system that (1) understands the user's mental model in a voice interaction context, (2) recognizes and expresses emotions, (3) determines users' short-term and long-term goals for voice interaction, (4) provides advice that matches consumers' goals,

(5) leads the dialog in the desired direction by requesting information that is missing ("pull" dialog) or providing information that the user needs ("push" dialog), and (6) predicts the user's future goals (Dellaert et al., 2020).

The type of marketing messages conveyed via voice assistant is another important design factor to consider. Consumers are more likely to accept marketing messages on voice assistants if (1) they include information about the availability and location of a product/service, (2) they provide information about sales or discounts, (3) they offer products/services that the consumer has specifically inquired about, (4) they explain how beneficial the product is for the consumer, (5) they can be skipped and repeated if desired, (6) they can provide detailed information if asked (Smith, 2018), and (7) they include personalized and relevant content that matches consumers' preferences (Rhee & Choi, 2020; Jones, 2018).

3.2.1 Voice Assistants: A Field with Vast Research Potential

Due to the novelty of these technical devices, research into voice assistants and their effects is still in its infancy. While much is known about how consumers make decisions in traditional web environments, far less is known about whether and how search behavior and product choices change in voice environments. In addition, no study has compared consumers' choice behavior regarding products with different involvement levels or different categories to investigate which circumstances favor or inhibit the use of voice assistants. Nor has a study examined how the interaction between consumers and voice assistants changes over time. A longitudinal study could bring interesting insights into how interactions change and affect customer behavior. Furthermore, no study has examined the effectiveness of voice assistants when integrated with other platforms such as PCs or mobile devices. Voice assistants cannot be seen as a single channel in isolation; they might have a stronger effect on consumer behavior when they are combined with other online or offline channels.

4 Data Privacy Management

Both chatbots and voice assistants are examples of marketing technologies that only work if they draw on (personal) consumer data. In general, collecting consumer data and creating consumer insights is at the heart of many contemporary marketing activities (Bleier et al., 2020). Through processing consumers' data, marketers can increase the effectiveness of digital marketing while at the same time creating value at the individual consumer level regarding price (e.g., individual discounts), product (e.g., personalized recommendations), and promotion (e.g., geotargeting) (Erevelles et al., 2016). Given the importance of consumer data for marketing, Martin and Murphy (2017) have identified a shift in privacy research. While early scholarship concentrated more on whether consumers are willing to reveal personal data (e.g., Acquisti & Grossklags, 2005), recent studies have focused more on how consumers react to unavoidable data disclosure (e.g., "cookie walls" as a necessity to enter or use a website; Nouwens et al., 2020) and tailored marketing activities. The increasing focus on consumers' reactions towards data collection practices is directly connected to the construct of data privacy (Martin & Murphy, 2017). When examining how consumers react to certain disclosure situations, it is indispensable also to study consumers' perception of data privacy and the consequences of this perception (e.g., privacy concerns; see Goldfarb & Tucker, 2012).

Martin et al. (2020) point out that other parties besides consumers are important in the context of data privacy. That is why they present consumers, regulators, and firms as "germane key players" in data privacy and highlight the triangulated, dependent relationship among them. Regulations (through such laws as the General Data Protection Regulation or the California Consumer Privacy Act) are implemented and monitored by governments; they set the context of data handling and regulate what data collection practices are allowed and what requirements firms have to meet when they want to collect consumer data (Martin et al., 2020). From a consumer perspective, data privacy and the privacy trade-off cuts both ways. While consumers can perceive services built on personal data (e.g., personalized recommendations) as beneficial and useful (Bleier & Eisenbeiss, 2015; Kokolakis, 2017), data collection practices can also lead to consumer discomfort (Aguirre et al., 2015), increased perceived data vulnerability (Martin et al., 2017), increased privacy concerns (Goldfarb & Tucker, 2012; Bleier & Eisenbeiss 2015; Xu et al., 2012), and cause protective behavior (e.g., falsified identification.; Malhotra et al., 2004). The third key players involved are firms. Several studies suggest that firms can use data privacy/privacy protection as a proactive strategy to gain a competitive edge over their competitors (Casadesus-Masanell & Hervas-Drane, 2015; Gerlach et al., 2019; Martin & Murphy, 2017). In practice, more and more corporations are emphasizing the protection of consumer privacy. Apple, for example, describes privacy as a" fundamental human right "and one of its "core values" (Apple, 2021). This theme is woven into several of the company's advertising campaigns titled "Privacy. That's iPhone," demonstrating that corporations increasingly view privacy protection as a core component of their strategic positioning. And by including data privacy in their corporate strategy, firms can reduce the negative effects of data collection practices (e.g., privacy concerns; Wirtz et al., 2007) opening up more personal data to be collected for management decision-making (e.g., customer relationship management; Malthouse et al., 2013).

The dependency of the three perspectives—regulation, consumer, firm—underlines that managing consumers' data/privacy is a complex topic for firms. If firms want to take advantage of innovative marketing technologies that build on personal data and avoid negative outcomes, they must increasingly address the issue of data privacy management in the future. In the following, we highlight several starting points and findings from scientific literature that have been shown to be helpful for effective privacy management:

I. Transparency
II. Privacy control and data sovereignty
III. Privacy customization
IV. Data handling

4.1 Transparency

Legislation such as those described above aims to protect consumers' informational self-determination by requiring firms to be transparent about their data collection practices. Transparency entails that firms act comprehensibly and fairly to obtain consent for information collection and further information processing from consumers (Ghosh, 2018; Martin et al., 2020). But transparency should go beyond meeting legal requirements, as various advantages are associated with it. Firms can reduce privacy concerns through transparent data management (Malhotra et al., 2004; Oulasvirta et al., 2014). Consumers reward transparency, for example, by sharing more personal information when websites use privacy policies (Hui et al., 2007), and report a higher likelihood to purchase if privacy policies are easily accessible and likewise comprehensible (Tsai et al., 2011).

Likewise, non-transparent procedures by firms can result in disadvantages. For instance, the perceived vulnerability of consumers can increase when data for personalized advertising is collected in a non-transparent manner (Aguirre et al., 2015). However, understandability and fairness of transparency features are a necessity for their success (Martin & Murphy, 2017). Fairness refers to the perceived benefits consumers receive for sharing their data and must outweigh the perceived disadvantages. This trade-off should be in balance so that it is perceived as fair by consumers (Li et al., 2010). Finally, transparency measures must be understandable for consumers. Privacy policies that are incomprehensible for consumers, for example, are judged as unfair and reduce trust in the firm (Vail et al., 2008). Together, these measures should enable consumers to better understand the consequences of their data disclosure and build trust (Martin & Murphy, 2017). Transparency should therefore only be one part of an overarching privacy strategy that takes other elements into account.

4.2 Privacy Control and Data Sovereignty

Transparency is interlinked with privacy control. It enables consumers to have the necessary information about the use of their personal information and is deemed a prerequisite for consumers to gain control over their privacy (Morey et al., 2015). Privacy control involves consumers believing that they can exercise choice over their data and give explicit consent to share it (Iyengar, 2010; Tucker, 2014). Privacy control thus has a profound impact on all consumer decisions related to personal data (Mothersbaugh et al., 2012; Tucker, 2014). When consumers perceive that they have control over their privacy, privacy concerns are reduced (Xu et al., 2012), and consumers have stronger feelings of empowerment (Martin et al., 2017). Moreover, privacy control can reduce consumer reactance towards marketing efforts (Taylor, 1979), increase consumers' willingness to share personal data via control mechanisms such as opting into or opting out of data sharing agreements (Martin et al., 2017), and increase the effectiveness of personalized advertising (Tucker, 2014). Consumers can decide for themselves when, how, and for what purposes they want to disclose their personal data. Ultimately, it may result in consumers exercising data sovereignty.

4.3 Privacy Customization

Privacy customization is linked to the construct of control as it concerns the idea of giving consumers complete control over their data by letting them choose what to disclose. Following the privacy customization approach (Eisenbeiss & Wiegand, 2019), consumers can configure which data they share for certain marketing purposes and which they do not. Although privacy customization may result in fewer data points being released by consumers, several positive effects also result from this approach (Eisenbeiss & Wiegand, 2019). In particular, consumers who are willing to share their data have a higher degree of self-disclosure (e.g., Facebook users customizing their privacy settings are more likely to have a high self-disclosure; Lankton et al., 2017), mostly because of various psychological benefits that are elicited through customization, such as an increased feeling of exercised control and empowerment (Van Dyke et al., 2007). Letting consumers customize their privacy settings may also lead to a higher feeling of psychological ownership (Franke et al., 2010), an increased sense of control (Eisenbeiss & Wiegand, 2019), and decreased privacy concerns (Zhang & Sundar, 2019). Overall, the positive effects of customization can outweigh the negative effects, as shown in the context of display banner advertising by Eisenbeiss and Wiegand (2019). Likewise, Bornschein et al. (2020) showed that privacy customization options (in a cookie notification context) can increase consumers' purchase intention. Lastly, Zhou and Piramuthu (2015, p. 29) concluded that privacy customization can increase firms' profits, and therefore it is a "win-win situation for both business and consumers."

4.4 Data Handling

Fueled by the rapid development of technology, consumers' general privacy concerns are rising (Statista, 2019). More precisely, studies have shown that data collection by firms can be a driver of consumers' privacy concerns (e.g., Lwin et al., 2007; Bleier et al., 2020; Martin et al., 2020). In order to mitigate those concerns, firms can offer additional services. Wiezorrek and Dulle (2021) however showed that there is no suitable "trading good" for highly sensitive data. In light of these findings, it becomes even more important for firms to reflect on exactly what data improves their ability to offer their services. Hence, firms should answer the following questions (based on the suggestion by Stewart, 2017) before collecting consumer data:

1. What consumer data is actually required to enable us to offer our services?
2. How sensitive is the data we asked for in our consumers'perception?
3. How can we ensure safety for the data we collect?
4. Who has access to the data?

The first studies in this still-young field of research have argued that focusing on data handling should be part of the strategic focus of firms (Martin et al., 2020). Possible starting points to strategically approaching data handling can be data minimization (Ogonji et al., 2020), privacy as a default setting (Noain-Sánchez, 2016), privacy-by-design (e.g., through privacy-friendly interface design; Emanuel & Koohborfardhaghighi, 2020) and giving consumers more configurative power through privacy customization (Eisenbeiss & Wiegand, 2019).

5 Conclusion

This chapter has introduced two new ways of interaction with consumers that technology and digitization have enabled and has shed light on the very important issue of privacy management that accompanies new technologies based on data. The chapter has highlighted that consumers and their needs must always be at the forefront of firms' considerations, as it is consumer perceptions that will "make or break" a new technology and be decisive in its success.

References

Acquisti, A., & Grossklags, J. (2005). Privacy and rationality in individual decision making. *IEEE Security and Privacy, 3*(1), 26–33. https://doi.org/10.1109/MSP.2005.22

Adam, M., Wessel, M., & Benlian, A. (2021). AI-based chatbots in customer service and their effects on user compliance. *Electronic Markets, 31*(2), 427–445. https://doi.org/10.1007/s12525-020-00414-7

Adamopoulou, E., & Moussiades, L. (2020a). An overview of chatbot technology. In I. Maglogiannis, L. Iliadis, & E. Pimenidis (Eds.), *IFIP Advances in information and communication technology. Artificial intelligence applications and innovations* (pp. 373–383). Springer.

Adamopoulou, E., & Moussiades, L. (2020b). Chatbots: History, technology, and applications. *Machine Learning with Applications, 2*(100), 006. https://doi.org/10.1016/j.mlwa.2020.100006

Aguirre, E., Mahr, D., Grewal, D., De Ruyter, K., & Wetzels, M. (2015). Unraveling the personalization paradox: The effect of information collection and trust-building strategies on online advertisement effectiveness. *Journal of Retailing, 91*(1), 34–49. https://doi.org/10.1016/j.jretai.2014.09.005

American Marketing Association. (2020). *Chatbots and customer experience in 2020*. Retrieved August 11, 2021, from https://www.ama.org/marketing-news/chatbots-and-customer-experience-in-2020/

Apple. (2021). *Privacy*. Retrieved July 7, 2021, from https://www.apple.com/privacy

Araujo, T. (2018). Living up to the chatbot hype: The influence of anthropomorphic design cues and communicative agency framing on conversational agent and firm perceptions. *Computers in Human Behavior, 85*, 183–189. https://doi.org/10.1016/j.chb.2018.03.051

Bizzaco, M., Rawes, E., & Wetzel, K. (2021, March 30). What is Alexa? It's Amazon's new virtual assistant. *digitaltrends*. Retrieved September 28, 2021, from https://www. digitaltrends.com/home/what-is-amazons-alexa-and-what-can-it-do/

Bleier, A., & Eisenbeiss, M. (2015). The importance of trust for personalized online advertising. *Journal of Retailing, 91*(3), 390–409. https://doi.org/10.1016/j.jretai.2015.04.001

Bleier, A., Goldfarb, A., & Tucker, C. (2020). Consumer privacy and the future of data-based innovation and marketing. *International Journal of Research in Marketing, 37*(3), 466–480. https://doi.org/10.1016/j.ijresmar.2020.03.006

Blut, M., Wang, C., Wünderlich, N. V., & Brock, C. (2021). Understanding anthropomorphism in service provision: A meta-analysis of physical robots, chatbots, and other AI. *Journal of the Academy of Marketing Science*. https://doi.org/10.1007/s11747-020-00762-y

Bornschein, R., Schmidt, L., & Maier, E. (2020). The effect of consumers' perceived power and risk in digital information privacy: The example of cookie notices. *Journal of Public Policy and Marketing, 39*(2), 135–154. https://doi.org/10.1177/0743915620902143

Casadesus-Masanell, R., & Hervas-Drane, A. (2015). Competing with privacy. *Management Science, 61*(1), 229–246. https://doi.org/10.1287/mnsc.2014.2023

Chiefmartec. (2020). *Marketing technology landscape supergraphic (2020): Martech 5000 – really 8,000, but who's counting?* Retrieved October 8, 2021 from: https://chiefmartec.com/2020/04/marketing-technology-landscape-2020-martech-5000/

Chung, M., Ko, E., Joung, H., & Kim, S. J. (2020). Chatbot e-service and customer satisfaction regarding luxury brands. *Journal of Business Research, 117*, 587–595. https://doi.org/10.1016/j.jbusres.2018.10.004

Ciechanowski, L., Przegalinska, A., Magnuski, M., & Gloor, P. (2019). In the shades of the uncanny valley: An experimental study of human–chatbot interaction. *Future Generation Computer Systems, 92*, 539–548. https://doi.org/10.1016/j.future.2018.01.055

Crolic, C., Thomaz, F., Hadi, R., & Stephen, A. T. (2021). Blame the bot: Anthropomorphism and anger in customer–chatbot interactions. *Journal of Marketing, 86*(1), 132–148. https://doi.org/10.1177/00222429211045687

Davis, F. D. (1989). Perceived usefulness, perceived wase of use, and user acceptance of information technology. *MIS Quarterly, 13*(3), 319–340. https://doi.org/10.2307/249008

De Graaf, M. M., & Ben Allouch, S. (2013). Exploring influencing variables for the acceptance of social robots. *Robotics and Autonomous Systems, 61*(12), 1476–1486. https://doi.org/10.1016/j.robot.2013.07.007

Dellaert, B. G. C., Shu, S. B., Arentze, T. A., Baker, T., Diehl, K., Donkers, B., Fast, N. J., Häubl, G., Johnson, H., Karmarkar, U. R., Oppewal, H., Schmitt, B. H., Schroeder, J., Spiller, S. A., & Steffel, M. (2020). Consumer decisions with artificially intelligent voice assistants. *Marketing Letters, 31*(4), 335–347. https://doi.org/10.1007/s11002-020-09537-5

Downes-Le Guin, T., Baker, R., Mechling, J., & Ruyle, E. (2012). Myths and realities of respondent engagement in online surveys. *International Journal of Market Research, 54*(5), 613–633. https://doi.org/10.2501/IJMR-54-5-613-633

Eisenbeiss, M. (2020). Privatsphäre-Management im digitalen Zeitalter. In M. Bruhn, C. Burmann, & M. Kirchgeorg (Eds.), *Marketing Weiterdenken* (pp. 631–645). Springer Gabler.

Eisenbeiss, M., & Wiegand, N. (2019). *Privacy customization. Working paper*. University of Bremen.

Emanuel, E., & Koohborfardhaghighi, S. (2020). Delivering privacy-friendly location-based advertising over smartwatches: Effect of virtual user interface. In K. Djemame, J. Altmann, J. Á. Bañares, O. Agmon Ben-Yehuda, V. Stankovski, & B. Tuffin (Eds.), *International conference on the economics of grids, clouds, systems, and services* (pp. 41–53). Springer.

Epley, N., Waytz, A., & Cacioppo, J. T. (2007). On seeing human: A three-factor theory of anthropomorphism. *Psychological Review, 114*(4), 864–886. https://doi.org/10.1037/0033-295X.114.4.864

Eppmann, R., Bekk, M., & Klein, K. (2018). Gameful experience in gamification: Construction and validation of a gameful experience scale [GAMEX]. *Journal of Interactive Marketing, 43*, 98–115. https://doi.org/10.1016/j.intmar.2018.03.002

Erevelles, S., Fukawa, N., & Swayne, L. (2016). Big data consumer analytics and the transformation of marketing. *Journal of Business Research, 69*(2), 897–904. https://doi.org/10.1016/j.jbusres.2015.07.001

Feine, J., Gnewuch, U., Morana, S., & Maedche, A. (2019). A taxonomy of social cues for conversational agents. *International Journal of Human–Computer Studies, 132*, 138–161. https://doi.org/10.1016/j.ijhcs.2019.07.009

Fieberg, C., Hesse, M., Loy, T., & Metko, D. (2022). Machine learning in accounting research. In L. Hornuf (Ed.), *Diginomics research perspectives: The role of digitalization in business and society*. Springer International Publishing.

Franke, N., Schreier, M., & Kaiser, U. (2010). The "I designed it myself" effect in mass customization. *Management Science, 56*(1), 125–140. https://doi.org/10.1287/mnsc.1090.1077

Gerlach, J. P., Eling, N., Wessels, N., & Buxmann, P. (2019). Flamingos on a slackline: Firms' challenges of balancing the competing demands of handling customer information and privacy. *Information Systems Journal, 29*(2), 548–575. https://doi.org/10.1111/isj.12222

Ghosh, D. (2018). What you need to know about California's new data privacy law. *Harvard Business Review Digital Articles*. Retrieved June 27, 2021, from https://hbr.org/2018/07/what-you-need-to-know-about-californias-new-data-privacy-law

Gnewuch, U., Morana, S., & Maedche, A. (2017). Towards designing cooperative and social conversational agents for customer service. In *Proceedings of the 38th International Conference on Information Systems (ICIS)*, pp. 1–13.

Gnewuch, U., Adam, M. T. P., Morana, S., and Maedche, A. (2018). 'The chatbot Is typing ...' – The role of typing indicators in human–chatbot interaction. In *Proceedings of the 17th Annual Pre-ICIS Workshop on HCI Research in MIS*, 0–5.

Go, E., & Sundar, S. S. (2019). Humanizing chatbots: The effects of visual, identity and conversational cues on humanness perceptions. *Computers in Human Behavior, 97*, 304–316. https://doi.org/10.1016/j.chb.2019.01.020

Goldfarb, A., & Tucker, C. (2012). Shifts in privacy concerns. *American Economic Review, 102*(3), 349–353. https://doi.org/10.1257/aer.102.3.349

Gray, K., & Wegner, D. M. (2012). Feeling robots and human zombies: Mind perception and the uncanny valley. *Cognition, 125*(1), 125–130. https://doi.org/10.1016/j.cognition.2012.06.007

Han, M. C. (2021). The impact of anthropomorphism on consumers' purchase decision in chatbot commerce. *Journal of Internet Commerce, 20*(1), 46–65. https://doi.org/10.1080/15332861.2020.1863022

Hoy, M. B. (2018). Alexa, Siri, Cortana, and more: An introduction to voice assistants. *Medical Reference Services Quarterly, 37*(1), 81–88. https://doi.org/10.1080/02763869.2018.1404391

Hui, K. L., Teo, H. H., & Lee, S. Y. T. (2007). The value of privacy assurance: An exploratory field experiment. *MIS Quarterly: Management Information Systems, 31*(1), 19. https://doi.org/10.2307/25148779

Iyengar, S. (2010). *The art of choosing*. Twelve.

Jones, V. K. (2018). Voice-activated change: Marketing in the age of artificial intelligence and virtual assistants. *Journal of Brand Strategy, 7*(3), 239–251.

Kamide, H., Kawabe, K., Shigemi, S., & Arai, T. (2013). Development of a psychological scale for general impressions of humanoid. *Advanced Robotics, 27*(1), 3–17. https://doi.org/10.1080/01691864.2013.751159

Kim, Y., & Sundar, S. S. (2012). Anthropomorphism of computers: Is it mindful or mindless? *Computers in Human Behavior, 28*(1), 241–250. https://doi.org/10.1016/j.chb.2011.09.006

Kinsella, B. (2019, February 15). *Google assistant actions total 4,253 in January 2019, Up 2.5x in past year but 7.5% the total number Alexa skills in U.S. Voicebot.ai*. Retrieved April 28, 2021, from https://voicebot.ai/2019/02/15/google-assistant-actions-total-4253-in-january-2019-up-2-5x-in-past-year-but-7-5-the-total-number-alexa-skills-in-u-s/

Koh, Y. J., & Sundar, S. S. (2010). Heuristic versus systematic processing of specialist versus generalist sources in online media. *Human Communication Research, 36*(2), 103–124. https://doi.org/10.1111/j.1468-2958.2010.01370.x
Kokolakis, S. (2017). Privacy attitudes and privacy behaviour: A review of current research on the privacy paradox phenomenon. *Computers and Security, 64*, 122–134. https://doi.org/10.1016/j.cose.2015.07.002
Lankton, N. K., McKnight, D. H., & Tripp, J. F. (2017). Facebook privacy management strategies: A cluster analysis of user privacy behaviors. *Computers in Human Behavior, 76*, 149–163. https://doi.org/10.1016/j.chb.2017.07.015
Lenz-Kesekamp, V., & Weber, T. (2018). Alexa Skills: Welche Chancen und Risiken sind damit verbunden? *Wirtschaftsinformatik and Management, 10*(12), 18–25. https://doi.org/10.1007/s35764-018-0115-9
Li, H., Sarathy, R., & Xu, H. (2010). Understanding situational online information disclosure as a privacy calculus. *Journal of Computer Information Systems, 51*(1), 62–71. https://doi.org/10.1080/08874417.2010.11645450
Luo, X., Tong, S., Fang, Z., & Qu, Z. (2019). Frontiers: Machines vs. humans: The impact of artificial intelligence chatbot disclosure on customer purchases. *Marketing Science, 38*(6), 937–947. https://doi.org/10.1287/mksc.2019.1192
Lwin, M., Wirtz, J., & Williams, J. D. (2007). Consumer online privacy concerns and responses: A power–responsibility equilibrium perspective. *Journal of the Academy of Marketing Science, 35*(4), 572–585. https://doi.org/10.1007/s11747-006-0003-3
Malhotra, N. K., Kim, S. S., & Agarwal, J. (2004). Internet users' information privacy concerns (IUIPC): The construct, the scale, and a causal model. *Information Systems Research, 15*(4), 336–355. https://doi.org/10.1287/isre.1040.0032
Malter, A. J., & Rindfleisch, A. (2019). *Marketing in a digital world.* Emerald Publishing Limited.
Malthouse, E. C., Haenlein, M., Skiera, B., Wege, E., & Zhang, M. (2013). Managing customer relationships in the social media era: Introducing the social CRM house. *Journal of Interactive Marketing, 27*(4), 270–280. https://doi.org/10.1016/j.intmar.2013.09.008
Mari, A. (2019). Voice commerce: Understanding shopping-related voice assistants and their effect on brands. *IMMAA Annual Conference.*
Martin, K. D., & Murphy, P. E. (2017). The role of data privacy in marketing. *Journal of the Academy of Marketing Science, 45*(2), 135–155. https://doi.org/10.1007/s11747-016-0495-4
Martin, K. D., Borah, A., & Palmatier, R. W. (2017). Data privacy: Effects on customer and firm performance. *Journal of Marketing, 81*(1), 36–58. 10.1509%2Fjm.15.0497
Martin, K. D., Kim, J. J., Palmatier, R. W., Steinhoff, L., Stewart, D. W., Walker, B. A., Wang, Y., & Weaven, S. K. (2020). Data privacy in retail. *Journal of Retailing, 96*(4), 474–489. https://doi.org/10.1016/j.jretai.2020.08.003
McLean, G., & Osei-Frimpong, K. (2019). Hey Alexa … Examine the variables influencing the use of artificial intelligent in-home voice assistants. *Computers in Human Behavior, 99*(10), 28–37. https://doi.org/10.1016/j.chb.2019.05.009
McLean, G., Osei-Frimpong, K., & Barhorst, J. (2021). Alexa, do voice assistants influence consumer brand engagement? Examining the role of AI powered voice assistants in influencing consumer brand engagement. *Journal of Business Research, 124*(1), 312–328. https://doi.org/10.1016/j.jbusres.2020.11.045
Mero, J. (2018). The effects of two-way communication and chat service usage on consumer attitudes in the e-commerce retailing sector. *Electronic Markets, 28*(2), 205–217. https://doi.org/10.1007/s12525-017-0281-2
Morey, T., Forbath, T., & Schoop, A. (2015). Customer data: Designing for transparency and trust. *Harvard Business Review, 93*(5), 96–105.
Moriuchi, E. (2019). Okay, Google!: An empirical study on voice assistants on consumer engagement and loyalty. *Psychology and Marketing, 36*(5), 489–501. https://doi.org/10.1002/mar.21192

Mothersbaugh, D. L., Foxx, W. K., Beatty, S. E., & Wang, S. (2012). Disclosure antecedents in an online service context: The role of sensitivity of information. *Journal of Service Research, 15*(1), 76–98. https://doi.org/10.1177/1094670511424924

Munz, K., & Morwitz, V. (2019). *Not-so-easy listening: Roots and repercussions of auditory choice difficulty in voice commerce*. NYU Stern School of Business. https://doi.org/10.2139/ssrn.3462714.

Nass, C., & Moon, Y. (2000). Machines and mindlessness: Social responses to computers. *Journal of Social Issues, 56*(1), 81–103. https://doi.org/10.1111/0022-4537.00153

Nass, C., Steuer, J., & Tauber, E. R. (1994). Computers are social actors. In *Proceedings of the SiGCHI Conference on Human Factors in Computing Systems.*https://doi.org/10.1145/259963.260288.

Noain-Sánchez, A. (2016). "Privacy by default" and active "informed consent" by layers: Essential measures to protect ICT users' privacy. *Journal of Information, Communication and Ethics in Society, 14*(2), 124–136. https://doi.org/10.1108/JICES-10-2014-0040

Nouwens, M., Liccardi, I., Veale, M., Karger, D., & Kagal, L. (2020). Dark patterns after the GDPR: Scraping consent pop-ups and demonstrating their influence. *Proceedings of the 2020 CHI Conference on Human Factors in Computing Systems*, vol. 194, pp. 1–13.

Nowak, K. L., & Rauh, C. (2005). The Influence of the avatar on online perceptions of anthropomorphism, androgyny, credibility, homophily, and attraction. *Journal of Computer-Mediated Communication, 11*(1), 153–178. https://doi.org/10.1111/j.1083-6101.2006.tb00308.x

Ogonji, M. M., Okeyo, G., & Wafula, J. M. (2020). A survey on privacy and security of Internet of Things. *Computer Science Review, 38*(100), 312. https://doi.org/10.1016/j.cosrev.2020.100312

Oulasvirta, A., Suomalainen, T., Hamari, J., Lampinen, A., & Karvonen, K. (2014). Transparency of intentions decreases privacy concerns in ubiquitous surveillance. *Cyberpsychology, Behavior and Social Networking, 17*(10), 633–638. https://doi.org/10.1089/cyber.2013.0585

Pagani, M., Racat, M., & Hofacker, C. F. (2019). Adding voice to the omni-channel and how that affects brand trust. *Journal of Interactive Marketing, 48*, 89–105. https://doi.org/10.1016/j.intmar.2019.05.002

Paluch, S., & Wittkop, T. (2020). Voice Marketing – Die Stimme der Zukunft? In M. Bruhn, C. Burmann, & M. Kirchgeorg (Eds.), *Marketing Weiterdenken* (pp. 510–520). Springer Gabler.

Peck, J., & Childers, T. L. (2003). Individual differences in haptic information processing: The "Need for Touch" scale. *Journal of Consumer Research, 30*(3), 430–442. https://doi.org/10.1086/378619

Pelau, C., Dabija, D.-C., & Ene, I. (2021). What makes an AI device human-like? The role of interaction quality, empathy and perceived psychological anthropomorphic characteristics in the acceptance of artificial intelligence in the service industry. *Computers in Human Behavior, 122*(106), 855. https://doi.org/10.1016/j.chb.2021.106855

Petrock, V. (2020, November 16). Voice assistant and smart speaker users 2020. *eMarketer*. Retrieved June 17, 2021, from https://www.emarketer.com/content/voice-assistant-and-smart-speaker-users-2020

Pijetlovic, D., & Mueller-Christ, G. (2022). HumanRoboLab: Experiments with chatbots in management education at universities. In L. Hornuf (Ed.), *Diginomics research perspectives: The role of digitalization in business and society*. Springer International Publishing.

Pitardi, V., & Marriott, H. R. (2021). Alexa, she's not human but ... Unveiling the drivers of consumers' trust in voice-based artificial intelligence. *Psychology and Marketing, 38*(4), 626–642. https://doi.org/10.1002/mar.21457

Polyakov, E. V., Mazhanov, M. S., Rolich, A. Y., Voskov, L. S., Kachalova, M. V., & Polyakov, S. V. (2018). Investigation and development of the intelligent voice assistant for the Internet of Things using machine learning. *Moscow Workshop on Electronic and Networking Technologies (MWENT)*, 1–5. https://doi.org/10.1109/MWENT.2018.8337236.

Qiu, L., & Benbasat, I. (2009). Evaluating anthropomorphic product recommendation agents: A social relationship perspective to designing information systems. *Journal of Management Information Systems, 25*(4), 145–182. https://doi.org/10.2753/MIS0742-1222250405

Rhee, C. E., & Choi, J. (2020). Effects of personalization and social role in voice shopping: An experimental study on product recommendation by a conversational voice agent. *Computers in Human Behavior, 109*(106), 359. https://doi.org/10.1016/j.chb.2020.106359

Schanke, S., Burtch, G., & Ray, G. (2020). Estimating the impact of "humanizing" customer service chatbots. *Information Systems Research, 32*(3), 736–751. https://doi.org/10.31235/osf.io/xud6z

Schweitzer, F., Belk, R., Jordan, W., & Ortner, M. (2019). Servant, friend or master? The relationships users build with voice-controlled smart devices. *Journal of Marketing Management, 35*(7–8), 693–715. https://doi.org/10.1080/0267257X.2019.1596970

Smith, K. T. (2018). Marketing via smart speakers: What should Alexa say? *Journal of Strategic Marketing, 28*(4), 350–365. https://doi.org/10.1080/0965254X.2018.1541924

Statista. (2019). *Share of internet users who are more concerned about their online privacy compared to a year ago as of February 2019, by country*. Retrieved July 7, 2021, from https://www.statista.com/statistics/373322/global-opinion-concern-online-privacy/.

Stewart, D. W. (2017). A comment on privacy. *Journal of the Academy of Marketing Science, 45*(2), 156–159. https://doi.org/10.1007/s11747-016-0504-7

Sundar, S. S. (2008). The MAIN model: A heuristic approach to understanding technology effects on credibility. In M. J. Metzger & A. J. Flanagin (Eds.), *Digital, media, youth, and credibility* (pp. 72–100). The MIT Press.

Taylor, S. E. (1979). Hospital patient behavior: Reactance, helplessness, or control? *Journal of Social Issues, 35*(1), 156–184. https://doi.org/10.1111/j.1540-4560.1979.tb00793.x

Thorat, S. A., & Jadhav, V. (2020). A review on implementation issues of rule-based chatbot systems. *SSRN Electronic Journal*.https://doi.org/10.2139/ssrn.3567047.

Toader, D.-C., Boca, G., Toader, R., Măcelaru, M., Toader, C., Ighian, D., & Rădulescu, A. T. (2020). The effect of social presence and chatbot errors on trust. *Sustainability, 12*(1), 256. https://doi.org/10.3390/su12010256

Tsai, J. Y., Egelman, S., Cranor, L., & Acquisti, A. (2011). The effect of online privacy information on purchasing behavior: An experimental study. *Information Systems Research, 22*(2), 254–268.

Tsai, W.-H. S., Liu, Y., & Chuan, C.-H. (2021). How chatbots' social presence communication enhances consumer engagement: The mediating role of parasocial interaction and dialogue. *Journal of Research in Interactive Marketing, 15*(3), 460–482. https://doi.org/10.1108/jrim-12-2019-0200

Tucker, C. E. (2014). Social networks, personalized advertising, and privacy controls. *Journal of Marketing Research, 51*(5), 546–562. https://doi.org/10.1509/jmr.10.0355

Vail, M. W., Earp, J. B., & Antón, A. I. (2008). An empirical study of consumer perceptions and comprehension of web site privacy policies. *IEEE Transactions on Engineering Management, 55*(3), 442–454. https://doi.org/10.1109/TEM.2008.922634

Van Dyke, T. P., Midha, V., & Nemati, H. (2007). The effect of consumer privacy empowerment on trust and privacy concerns in e-commerce. *Electronic Markets, 17*(1), 68–81.

Verhagen, T., van Nes, J., Feldberg, F., & van Dolen, W. (2014). Virtual customer service agents: Using social presence and personalization to shape online service encounters. *Journal of Computer-Mediated Communication, 19*(3), 529–545. https://doi.org/10.1111/jcc4.12066

Warnock, S., & Gantz, J. S. (2017). Gaming for respondents: A test of the impact of gamification on completion rates. *International Journal of Market Research, 59*(1), 117–138. https://doi.org/10.2501/IJMR-2017-005

Waytz, A., Heafner, J., & Epley, N. (2014). The mind in the machine: Anthropomorphism increases trust in an autonomous vehicle. *Journal of Experimental Social Psychology, 52*, 113–117. https://doi.org/10.1016/j.jesp.2014.01.005

Whang, C., & Im, H. (2020). "I like your suggestion!" The role of humanlikeness and parasocial relationship on the website versus voice shopper's perception of recommendations. *Psychology and Marketing, 38*(4), 581–595. https://doi.org/10.1002/mar.21437

Wiezorrek, J., & Dulle, M. (2021). I am willing to sell my data for ... Drivers of consumers' privacy valuation in e-commerce. *Proceedings of the European Marketing Academy (EMAC)*, 50th, Madrid.

Wirtz, J., Lwin, M. O., & Williams, J. D. (2007). Causes and consequences of consumer online privacy concern. *International Journal of Service Industry Management, 18*(4), 326–348. https://doi.org/10.1108/09564230710778128

Xu, H., Teo, H. H., Tan, B. C., & Agarwal, R. (2012). Research note: Effects of individual self-protection, industry self-regulation, and government regulation on privacy concerns: A study of location-based services. *Information Systems Research, 23*(4), 1342–1363. https://doi.org/10.1287/isre.1120.0416

Yam, K. C., Bigman, Y. E., Tang, P. M., Ilies, R., de Cremer, D., Soh, H., & Gray, K. (2020). Robots at work: People prefer – and forgive – service robots with perceived feelings. *The Journal of Applied Psychology*. https://doi.org/10.1037/apl0000834

Zhang, B., & Sundar, S. S. (2019). Proactive vs. reactive personalization: Can customization of privacy enhance user experience? *International Journal of Human–Computer Studies, 128*, 86–99. https://doi.org/10.1016/j.ijhcs.2019.03.002

Zhou, W., & Piramuthu, S. (2015). Information relevance model of customized privacy for IoT. *Journal of Business Ethics, 131*(1), 19–30. https://doi.org/10.1007/s10551-014-2248-y

Human Resource Management in a Digital Environment

Vera Hagemann and Katharina Klug

1 Introduction

Human resource management (HRM) concerns the functions and processes in organizations that focus on personnel and aim to attract, deploy, motivate, and optimize this resource (Rowold, 2015). These functions include such areas as HR marketing, personnel selection, personnel deployment planning, people development, leadership, management behavior, and workplace design, to name the most important. The responsibilities of HRM are therefore not new, but what has changed significantly over time are the implementations of these functions in organizations, given that the tasks, the ways of working, the requirements, and the relationships among employees and with managers have changed due to digitalization and automation. Digitalization in this context means the introduction of digital technologies into organizations in the sense of the digital transformation process (Petry, 2019). If, by contrast, individual functions or entire human activities are transferred to a system, the terms "automation" and "automatization" are used, often interchangeably. However, the term automatization refers to the process, while automation describes the result of this shift (Hauß & Timpe, 2000). A modern HRM must respond to these changes and adapt accordingly (Petry & Jäger, 2018).

The present chapter addresses current topics in HRM, such as mental health (Sect. 2) and how this can be assessed by HR. Factors influencing mental health include work design (Sect. 3) and leadership (Sect. 4). However, these topics are themselves also strongly influenced by digital transformation. Due to ongoing changes in demands on employees, the topic of people development (Sect. 5) is important to discuss. Similarly important, though still relatively in its infancy, is the field known as human resource analytics (Sect. 6), which is also reviewed in this

V. Hagemann (✉) · K. Klug
Faculty of Business Studies and Economics, University of Bremen, Bremen, Germany
e-mail: vhagemann@uni-bremen.de; kklug@uni-bremen.de

L. Hornuf (ed.), *Diginomics Research Perspectives*, Advanced Studies in Diginomics and Digitalization, https://doi.org/10.1007/978-3-031-04063-4_3

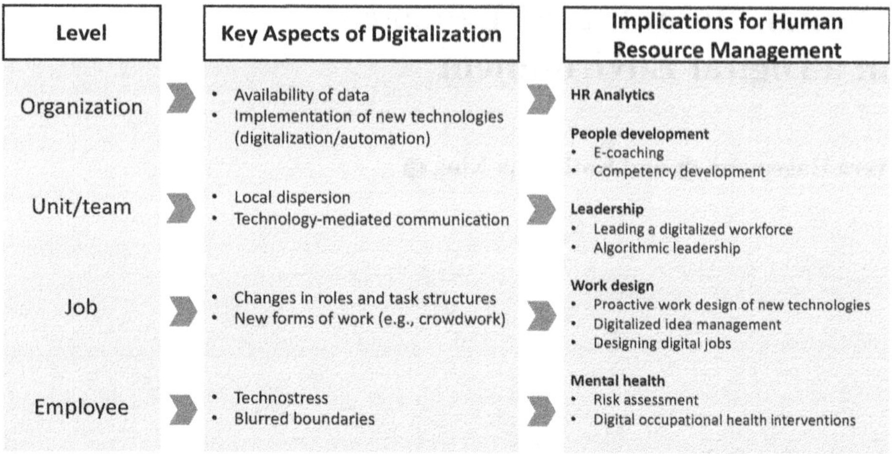

Fig. 1 Conceptual overview of key implications of digital transformation for human resource management at different levels of the organization

chapter. Figure 1 provides a conceptual overview of the key aspects and implications of digitalization for HRM at different levels in an organization.

2 Mental Health at Work

The digital transformation has brought employees' mental health to the forefront. Manual jobs have declined in favor of an expanding service and knowledge economy, while automation in the Fourth Industrial Revolution (known as "Industry 4.0") has also changed the cognitive demands placed on industrial workers interacting with smart technologies. As a result, stress and health at work pertain to psychosocial rather than physical issues for many workers today (de Jonge & Dormann, 2017).

The rapid expansion and accelerating development of information and communication technologies (ICTs), as well as digitalization of processes at work, create both opportunities and risks for employees' mental health. Among other advantages, ICTs allow for more flexibility in work hours and location to support employees in balancing their work and non-work roles and reduce stress (see telework, Sect. 3). But increased flexibility and constant connectivity also carry the risk of work intensification, blurred boundaries between work and private life, and specific stressors related to technology use (Demerouti et al., 2014). Modern HRM needs to respond to these challenges to protect employees' mental health at work through risk assessments and (digital) occupational health promotion.

2.1 Challenges: Technostress and Blurred Boundaries

Extensive use of technology on and off the clock can create a particular kind of stress experience known as "technostress" (La Torre et al., 2019; Riedl, 2013). Most definitions of technostress include physiological, psychological, and/or behavioral strain reactions to stressors related to the use and anticipated use of technology (Salanova et al., 2013). In line with the traditional job stress literature (de Jonge & Dormann, 2017), techno*stressors* (i.e., events and conditions eliciting stress reactions) can be distinguished from techno*strain*, which denotes an individual's response to the stressors. Technostrain includes experiences of anxiety, fatigue, skepticism, and inefficacy in relation to technology use at work (Salanova et al., 2013).

Several studies have linked technostress to physiological stress reactions, self-reported stress, exhaustion, and decreased job satisfaction (see La Torre et al., 2019 for a systematic review). The causes of technostress broadly relate to the two categories of information overload (i.e., having to process large amounts of information from multiple sources) and constant connectivity (i.e., accessing work and being accessible potentially everywhere and anytime; La Torre et al., 2019). Acute technostressors such as computer crashes can further be distinguished from chronic stressors such as availability expectations, requirements for continuous learning, or employee surveillance, although frequently occurring acute stressors can transform into chronic stressors (Riedl, 2013). A particular kind of technostress related to the unique challenges of nonverbal communication in videoconferencing ("Zoom fatigue") has gained media attention during the Covid-19 pandemic, although empirical research on the nature and relevance of this phenomenon is still in its infancy (see Fauville et al., 2021a, b; Shockley et al., 2021).

The framework of ICT demands introduced by Day et al. (2012) builds on the job demands–resources model (Demerouti & Bakker, 2011, see Sect. 2.2) and provides a validated, systematic operationalization of technostressors comprising eight categories: (1) hassles, meaning ICT malfunctions such as system crashes, freezes or data loss; (2) response expectations, or the pressure to respond quickly to work-related messages; (3) availability expectations, such as accessibility beyond regular hours or outside the office; (4) increased workload; (5) lack of control over technology; (6) ineffective communication, particularly misunderstandings in digital communication; (7) learning requirements to keep up with technological advancement; and (8) being monitored through technology. Collectively, ICT demands have been shown to relate to employee burnout and strain above and beyond classic job demands (Day et al., 2012).

ICT use can also blur the boundaries between work and non-work life. Availability expectations and work-related smartphone use after work have been shown to increase work–family conflict, obstruct recovery and impede well-being (Derks & Bakker, 2014; Dettmers et al., 2016). At the same time, employers may fear that cyberloafing (i.e., private browsing at work) and smartphone use impede employees' productivity and motivation. Empirical evidence in this area is ambiguous. For example, although employees who use social media during work more often than others report generally lower work engagement, a short social media break when energy levels are low can replenish engagement later on in the workday (Syrek et al., 2018). Another study suggests that cyberloafing may have simultaneous positive and negative effects on mental health through psychological detachment and fatigue, respectively (Wu et al., 2020). Interestingly, a profile analysis of employee groups with different patterns of smartphone use suggests that private smartphone use at work goes hand-in-hand with work-related smartphone use at home, indicating a general preference for more or less segmentation between life domains. Frequent smartphone use in both domains was associated with lower psychological detachment from work, a core element of recovery (Dora et al., 2019). The pervasiveness of ICT thus affects employees' mental health in various ways which are not yet fully understood. Nevertheless, existing research suggests specific risk factors for mental health that HRM needs to detect and address.

2.2 *Assessment of Mental Stress and Strain at (Digitalized) Work*

Digitalization changes not only the methods (see Sects. 2.3 and 6), but also the content of risk assessments. With respect to content, risk assessments ought to include specific characteristics of the digital working environment pertinent to mental health. The opportunities and challenges presented by digitalization of workplaces and processes make work easier and improve well-being, but they can also lead to increased mental stress and strain. Digitalized work has practical advantages for the workforce, such as relieving people of inhumane requirements through automation, but it can also lead to an increased mental workload due to changed job demands (Diebig et al., 2020; Hartwig et al., 2020). Technologies can help to simplify cognitive and physical actions through better planning and self-determined, flexible work design (Kraus et al., 2021; Schwarzmüller et al., 2018), but might also lead to more work in the same amount of time, as well as the need to react flexibly to changes in work processes, resulting in higher mental workload (Atanasoff & Venable, 2017; Hartwig et al., 2020; Klumpp et al., 2020a; Turel & Gaudioso, 2018). Changes in mental workload often lead to an increase in experienced mental stress and strain, with widespread consequences such as emotional exhaustion, job dissatisfaction, burnout symptoms, and fatigue (Fischer et al., 2021; Hartwig et al., 2020).

Conducting mental health risk assessments is not only mandatory for companies in Germany (§§ 5, 6 ArbSchG),[1] but is also supported by the numbers. The number of sick days due to mental illness has increased by 64.2%, since 2008. In 2018, the average annual duration of a mental illness was 26.3 days per case, which is more

[1] https://www.gesetze-im-internet.de/arbschg/

than two times the average of 11.8 days per case for other illnesses (Meyer et al., 2019).

Organizations and human resource management departments seeking to digitalize workplaces are thus faced with the various challenges of analyzing, evaluating, and mitigating a potential increase in mental workload for employees and leaders. In making digitalization a success from the employer and employee perspective, the first step must be assessment of work factors leading to mental stress and strain. After that, measures can be planned and implemented to counteract the stressful working conditions. Mitigation measures can be at the individual level and relate, for example, to personnel development programs (see Sect. 5), or at the organizational level, possibly relating to the design of workplaces and work processes (see Sect. 3).

In order to assess factors causing stress and strain and to analyze resources as potential starting points for remedial measures, it is helpful to have a theoretical model that can be used as a basis for orientation. One such model is the job demands–resources (JD–R) model, which provides a framework for understanding the relationships between demands and available resources at work (Demerouti & Bakker, 2011). The JD-R model states that each job may have specific risk factors associated with work-related stress (Bakker & Demerouti, 2007). The model emphasizes two essential underlying psychological processes causing the progression of either job-related stress or motivation. First, the model assumes that workplace demands, such as problems with new technologies or working with more and different technological devices, increase stress, affect employee health, and deplete employee energy. Second, the model assumes that work resources, such as time savings for certain tasks or technical support, offer motivational potential and thus lead to greater work engagement and higher performance. The model also postulates an interaction effect between work demands and resources, by which resources such as task variety, technical support, or work relief may buffer such negative consequences as work overload and problems with technical equipment (Demerouti & Bakker, 2011). The JD-R model provides a well-tuned framework for relating job demands to job resources and assessing impacts on employee mental stress and strain. Figure 2 provides an overview of the model as it has been empirically used in the measurement of mental stress and strain.

A large number of instruments for measuring mental stress and procedures for mental risk assessment are available (see GDA-Psyche, 2017 or Kauffeld, 2019 for comprehensive overviews). One example is Sandrock's (2017) Kompaktverfahren Psychische Belastung (KPB), which is a suitable instrument for measuring psychological stress in small and medium-sized companies, although it does not take psychological strain into account. The KPB can be used to restructure a critical work environment, but it reaches its limits when it comes to deriving measures for personnel development, since no information is collected about the employees. Contemporary aspects such as the digitalization and automation of work processes and the participation of employees are also not considered. A more recently developed screening tool is the digital stressors scale (Fischer et al., 2021), which captures possible negative effects of digitalization in the workplace, but is limited exclusively to these and does not allow a holistic assessment of mental stress and

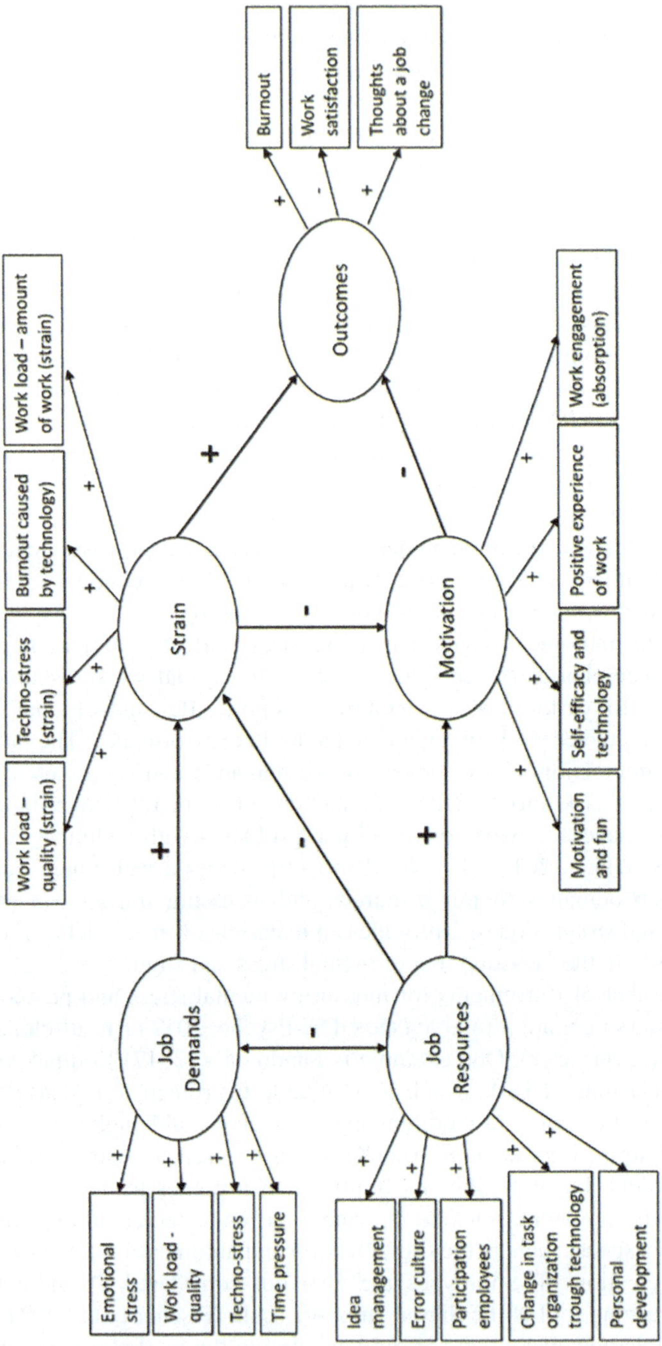

Fig. 2 The JD-R model assessing mental stress and strain (cf. Hagemann et al., 2021)

strain at work. This scale can nevertheless be used as a supplement to an already established instrument. A risk assessment screening instrument that is not only free of charge, but is applicable both online and offline, usable by HR specialists and non-professionals, and which is all-purpose and considers individual strain and digital aspects of work is the mental stress and strain assessment tool for employees and leaders (MESTAT) (Hagemann et al., 2021). Balancing the advantages and disadvantages of each method is essential to the validity of the first step in risk assessment, which is to measure mental stress and strain. A next step would be to identify and initiate appropriate mitigation measures.

2.3 Opportunities: Innovation in Occupational Health Promotion Through Online and Smartphone-Based Interventions

Digital technologies also offer opportunities to improve employees' mental health. The advantages of telework, for example, are discussed below in the context of work design (Sect. 3). The present section focuses on the potential of ICTs in implementing occupational health promotion (OHP) interventions. The wide range of intervention methods for improving employee well-being can be broadly categorized along two dimensions: (a) the level, that is, whether the intervention targets organizational structures or culture versus individual behavior; and (b) the focus, that is, whether the aim is to reduce negative experiences (e.g., stress management) or to enhance positive experiences (e.g., resource-oriented and positive psychology interventions)—although these distinctions are not always clear-cut in practice (Beehr, 2019; Hülsheger et al., 2020). The literature suggests that interventions should combine both stress management and resource enhancement, and that multimodal interventions targeting different levels are the most effective (for systematic reviews of OHP intervention research, see LaMontagne et al., 2007; Tetrick & Winslow, 2015).

Digitalized intervention programs utilize a wide range of methods and technologies such as web-based trainings, mobile applications, social media, serious games, virtual reality, videoconferencing, and instant messaging, each of which may be used alone or in combination with traditional face-to-face methods (Lehr & Boß, 2019; see also e-coaching in Sect. 5.1). A recurring problem in OHP programs is low participation, especially given the paradox that the most strained employees in need of intervention are the least likely to participate (Krick et al., 2019). Digital technologies may tackle this problem by making interventions more accessible and engaging. For example, online interventions reduce constraints regarding time, location and number of participants and provide anonymity, reducing potential stigma associated with seeking support (Ryan et al., 2017). Elements of gamification may incentivize participation, while virtual reality and simulations create a safe space to try out new behaviors. Smartphones or wearables can keep participants engaged through the use of alarms and reminders, as well as by providing automated feedback based on data collected in real time. Collecting such data also offers a convenient and reliable method for monitoring employee participation and well-being for process and outcome evaluations (Lehr & Boß, 2019; Stepanovic, 2020 see also HR analytics in Sect. 6).

Although research on organizational-level online programs remains limited (Ryan et al., 2017), emerging empirical evidence points to the effectiveness of individual-level online interventions. For example, a systematic review of online mental health trainings for teachers documents their effectiveness with regard to depressive symptoms, sleep quality, and sickness absence (Lehr & Boß, 2019). According to a meta-analysis, online mindfulness interventions are just as effective as their face-to-face counterparts (Bartlett et al., 2019). Shann et al. (2019) evaluated an online training for leaders' mental health competencies in a randomized control trial and reported that participants' depression-related stigma was significantly reduced 6 months later. Although this type of intervention can be categorized as individual-focused, training leaders is thought to also benefit their employees and thus have a wider organizational impact (see Kelloway & Barling, 2010). However, factors related to the work environment, organizational readiness, and support from HR were found to influence the leaders' transfer of training (Shann et al., 2019), which underlines the importance of addressing structural conditions to achieve sustainable change with digital interventions.

3 Work Design

Work design, defined as the content and organization of tasks, activities, responsibilities and relationships, is fundamentally linked to employee performance, motivation and well-being (Parker, 2014). Whether digitalization and automation have positive or negative effects on key work design characteristics (e.g., job autonomy, skill use and variety, feedback, and social relationships) depends in large part on how technologies are implemented (Parker & Grote, 2020). Work design has thus emerged as a crucial HRM field with regard to (a) ensuring that automation leads to improved job quality instead of decline and (b) the prevention and management of technology-specific demands such as technostressors or blurred boundaries (see Sect. 2). The present section discusses the role of prospective work design in the automation of tasks, digitalized idea management as a means to increase employee participation, and the management of demands and resources in telework and crowdwork.

3.1 Prospective Work Design in the Implementation of New Technologies

Despite widespread concern about artificial intelligence replacing people and jobs, in reality, it is usually tasks within broader job roles that are automated. Automation thus intensifies the interaction between humans and technology in organizations, affecting task structures and job characteristics of the employees working with technology—that is, their work design (Parker & Grote, 2020). Classic models of work design focus on motivational characteristics of jobs and tasks. The job characteristics model (JCM; Hackman & Oldham, 1976) identifies five essential job characteristics for employee motivation: autonomy (the degree of freedom over how to do one's job, often synonymous with job control); skill variety (the degree to which employees get to use different skills); task significance (the degree to which the job has an impact on other people); task identity (the degree to which a task is complete); and feedback (receiving information about one's performance). These characteristics motivate employees by creating experiences of meaningfulness, ownership, and knowledge of the results of one's work. Although work design research has expanded the list of job characteristics (e.g., social relations), mediating mechanisms, moderators, and relevant outcomes over the years, the validity of the core job characteristics for employee motivation, performance, and well-being still holds up (Humphrey et al., 2007; Parker, 2014). The JCM's job characteristics can be subsumed as resources in the job demands–resources model (Demerouti & Bakker, 2011), which additionally includes the potentially stressful aspects of work in terms of demands (see Sect. 2.2).

There is ongoing debate as to whether automation leads to an increase in job quality (e.g., more autonomy and flexibility, fewer tedious routine tasks) or a deterioration (e.g., being limited to monitoring technological systems and increased monotony). The skill-biased technological change perspective, for example, suggests a dichotomy between employees in high-skilled jobs with non-routine tasks reaping the benefits of automation, and those whose lower-skilled, routine jobs will change for the worse (Autor et al., 2003). Throughout this chapter, we reiterate how the digital transformation can both improve or worsen different aspects of people's jobs (see Sect. 2). For example, automating leadership tasks (Sect. 3.2) has the potential to relieve managers of administrative tasks, enabling them to focus on what is viewed as the more meaningful aspects of leadership that require human judgment or social skills (Kolbjørnsrud et al., 2016). But if managers leave administrative decisions (e.g., regarding shift schedules or task allocation) to algorithms, these may become impossible for employees to control (Kellogg et al., 2020), reducing their autonomy in turn.

The impact of automation on employees' job characteristics is extensive and more complex than we can discuss in detail here; instead, we refer the reader to the comprehensive review by Parker and Grote (2020). Their main message, which we seek to emphasize as well, is that the outcome of automation on work design is not unambiguously positive or negative and not deterministic either. Whether automation results in more versus less autonomy, active skill use versus a reduction to passive monitoring, or a relief from excessive demands versus increased workload, depends in large part on how the technology is designed and implemented. The choice and implementation of a specific technology involve decisions on different organizational levels about the distribution and coordination of tasks among humans and machines, which calls for involving work design experts in these processes early on. HRM therefore needs to assume a proactive role, not just in training employees to adapt (Sect. 5.2), but in ensuring that the technology above all serves human needs, in the sense of a prospective work design strategy (Parker & Grote, 2020).

3.2 Employee Participation Through Digitalized Idea Management

Acceptance of new technologies in the workplace is greater—and working with them less problematic—if employees participate in the change process and if the challenges of transformation are supported and shaped by all stakeholders in a partnership (Rogers, 2003). This can also promote identification with one's own work (Hackman & Oldham, 1976). Such engagement can be supported by idea management, which includes the collection, sorting, evaluation and utilization of suggestions for improvement (Kunert, 2014). The suggestion of new ideas and thus the direct participation of employees is promoted, thereby enabling specific knowledge about work processes, opportunities, and weaknesses to flow in.

The sort of participation discussed here is more meaningful than simple co-determination, such that a non-institutionalized and informal participation is possible, and opportunities arise to further develop the organization. This form of participation is similar to prosuming. Prosuming, a joint activity between consumer and producer, has gained particular importance in digital contexts (Ritzer & Jurgenson, 2010), with consumers of a product taking over individual sub-activities in the context of product creation. This is comparatively easy to achieve and has been successfully used in digital service contexts, especially with regard to the provision of data in online communication and advertising networks (Beer & Burrows, 2010). This concept is also suitable for considering employees in organizations because it can illustrate how they can participate in shaping their working conditions.

Participation can take place within the framework of a continuous improvement process (CIP) or in the company suggestion scheme (BVW) in the organization. The concept of a CIP is understood as an instrument of quality management and developed in the context of lean management considerations. The PDCA cycle (plan, do, check, act) is understood as the core element, which, as a form of implementation in quality circles, is intended to ensure that ideas for improvements are continuously taken up, evaluated and, if possible, implemented (Prashar, 2017). Employees play a central role in this, but methods such as the creation of quality teams and quality circles consisting of several employees are also used specifically to point beyond the perspective of individual employees (Blaga & Jozsef, 2014).

The BVW is a participative instrument for optimizing processes or products and pursues the goal of utilizing the ideas and innovation potential of employees. The suggestions for improvement are typically developed outside of actual working hours and can concern both smaller and larger changes. In contrast to CIP, the suggestions for improvement do not relate to the immediate tasks and duties of the employees submitting them (Crespo et al., 2009). The suggestions for improvement submitted by the employees are reviewed by superiors and/or experts, and the works council is also involved. If the suggestion is implemented, employees receive a portion of the resulting savings as a bonus under certain conditions. Due to the rather complex processes of a BVW, it tends to be perceived as sluggish and can have long reaction and processing times from the submission of a suggestion to its implementation (Crespo et al., 2009). In the long term, the lack of feedback or the long delays in providing feedback to employees on the proposals submitted leads to demotivation and to the fact that the BVW is often not practiced.

Digital idea management can and should be used to counteract this problematic circumstance. The development of digital idea management can be based on the two established concepts CIP and BVW, but seeking to combine their advantages and reduce the disadvantages. Ruiner et al. (2020) devised a comprehensive model of digital idea management, clearly presenting the progression from idea through processing, decision-making, and implementation to awarding. This method of idea management was developed as a responsive web app, enabling automatic adaptation of the application to the platform used (e.g., desktop PC or mobile device).

In practice, such digital idea management offers the opportunity for increased individualization, traceability, and transparency. For example, users of the app can see an overview of their own submitted proposals and also follow the review process live. This, in turn, can increase the motivation for further idea submissions from the prior experience of the transparent, fast, and appreciative review of previously submitted ideas, potentially leading to an overall and long-term increase in the number of ideas submitted. This can open up new innovation and value creation potential for the organizations.

3.3 Work Design in Different Forms of Digital Work

The expansion of ICTs has also changed the traditional structures in which people work. First, telework has afforded employees in traditional organizational structures more flexibility over when and where they work (Contreras et al., 2020; Gajendran & Harrison, 2007). Second, the gig economy has created new forms of work (e.g., crowdwork) that challenge the boundaries of employment relationships and traditional HRM practices (Duggan et al., 2020).

Telework (also known as telecommuting, remote work, or working from home) refers to "an alternative work arrangement in which employees perform tasks elsewhere [in most cases from home] that are normally done in a primary or central workplace, for at least some portion of their work schedule, using electronic media to interact with others inside and outside the organization" (Gajendran & Harrison, 2007, p. 1525). Telework is by no means new, but it is seeing a resurgence of interest by both researchers and practitioners in the wake of the Covid-19 pandemic, as organizations worldwide have had to move large parts of their workforces to remote work (Contreras et al., 2020; Rieth & Hagemann, 2021a).

Like most other aspects of digitalization, telework can have ambiguous effects on employee work design and well-being, many of which reflect different sides of the same coin (referred to as the "telework paradox;" Gajendran & Harrison, 2007). For example, working remotely increases employees' autonomy over where and when they work and saves commuting time, and can thereby facilitate integrating family demands into the workday. However, blurred boundaries can also lead to family interfering with work (with telework increasing the amount of household responsibilities assumed by the remote employee) and work interfering with family when constant connectivity and response expectations (see Sect. 2.1) lead to stress and extended working hours (Allen et al., 2015; Rieth & Hagemann, 2021a). As another example, employees tend to enjoy more autonomy, fewer interruptions, and higher productivity when working from home compared to the office (Anderson et al., 2015; Müller & Niessen, 2019; Tavares, 2017). However, working alone and uninterrupted also reduces contact with colleagues and supervisors, which can lead to social isolation and concerns about career prospects (Cooper & Kurland, 2002; Gajendran & Harrison, 2007; Golden et al., 2008). Research has suggested part-time telework as a desirable compromise, as benefits seem to attenuate and risks to aggravate when employees work more than about 2.5 days per week from home (Backhaus et al., 2020; Gajendran & Harrison, 2007). From an HRM perspective, establishing policies and guidelines with regard to communication, availability and response expectations, as well as training leaders in effectively managing remote employees (see Sect. 4.1), emerge as viable instruments to ensure good work design in telework.

New forms of digital work, such as crowdwork or platform-based work, are often subsumed under the "gig economy," which denotes short-term project-based or piece-rate work mediated by digital platforms (Duggan et al., 2020). This includes a range of heterogenous working arrangements and task types. Here, we focus on crowdwork, which refers to tasks that are offered by an individual or organization to an undefined group of workers and can be completed online. Crowdwork can be distinguished from app-work, where digital platforms match workers to clients for services that are carried out offline (e.g., transport and delivery; De Stefano, 2016; Duggan et al., 2020). Crowdwork in itself is heterogenous too: It includes contest-based models, where many workers complete the task but only one result is used and compensated, as well as "micro-tasking," where a large number of workers complete very small subtasks for low rates. Accordingly, work design in crowdwork can range from highly skilled, complex, and complete tasks (e.g., designing a logo) to simplistic, repetitive partialized tasks (e.g., classifying images; Huws et al., 2016).

Even though crowdwork is not yet widespread and few workers rely on it as their main source of income (Huws et al., 2016), it warrants discussion in the context of work design for two reasons. First, the historic origins of work design are rooted in criticism of the scientific management principles that characterized early industrial jobs (Parker, 2014). In micro-tasking, the partialized tayloristic job seems to reappear, as workers complete simplified, repetitive tasks at low rates (Parker &

Grote, 2020; Peinl & Bildat, 2017). Algorithmic management in general has been termed "scientific management 2.0" in this context (Schildt, 2017, p. 25). Platforms are often designed such that people work their way up; that is, a track record of good performance offers access to more interesting and better-paying tasks. Against this background, a recent study across different platforms found that intrinsic task qualities such as task identity, variety or feedback (Hackman & Oldham, 1976; see Sect. 3.1) relate more strongly to satisfaction among higher-paid crowdworkers than among those with lower pay, such that financial compensation seems to be a hygiene factor (Durward et al., 2020).

Second, crowdwork is portrayed as offering workers autonomy and flexibility because they are freelancers and not employees. But their true degree of autonomy may be questioned, for example, when the rates for microtasks are so low that people end up working constantly to earn enough, or when the platforms exert "soft controls" to nudge workers toward accepting tasks (Parker & Grote, 2020; see also algorithmic management in Sect. 4.2). The problem from an HRM perspective is that crowdworkers as "free agents" risk slipping through the cracks. Organizations utilize crowdwork by either outsourcing simplified tasks (micro-tasking) or benefiting from unpaid labor (contest-based crowdwork) without assuming responsibility for the crowdworkers, who are not their employees. Meanwhile, the platform companies' HRM usually caters to their core staff of platform developers. In turn, the management of crowdworkers in terms of task allocation, performance management and in some cases compensation is left to algorithms created by the core staff (Duggan et al., 2020).

4 Leadership and Digitalization

Due to their crucial role in coordinating work activities, organizational leaders (especially immediate supervisors) influence their employees' performance, motivation, and well-being (Judge & Piccolo, 2004; Schyns & Schilling, 2013). The two key challenges for leadership in digital transformation concern changes in competency requirements for leaders (see also Sect. 5.2) and the potential of automated leadership. First, organizational leaders operating in the context of rapid technological changes while supervising an increasingly autonomous and dispersed workforce need to be both technology- and people-oriented, pointing to technical and communication skills as important areas of leadership training and development (Cortellazzo et al., 2019). Second, some essential leadership tasks such as performance monitoring can be automated such that technology may complement but also potentially supplant the traditional job of an organizational leader.

4.1 Leadership Competencies in a Digital Environment

Leadership can be understood as "influencing and facilitating individual and collective efforts to accomplish shared objectives" (Yukl, 2012, p. 66). Although by this definition anyone can be a leader, the study of organizational leadership is usually concerned with the behavior and effectiveness of people in formal leadership roles (i.e., managers, supervisors; Kelloway & Barling, 2010). Accordingly, the focus of this section is on the impact of digitalization on leaders' behavior toward their employees rather than organizational management. A complete review of the various theories that have been proposed to explain leadership effectiveness is beyond the scope of this chapter (see Kelloway & Gilbert, 2017).

According to Yukl (2012), the range of leadership behaviors can be meta-categorized into task-oriented behavior (e.g., monitoring operations, problem-solving), relations-oriented behavior (e.g., supporting, developing), change-oriented behavior (e.g., advocating and envisioning change, facilitating learning), and external behavior (e.g., external monitoring, representing). Numerous studies have documented how constructive leadership (i.e., facilitating task achievement, supporting and motivating employees) is conducive to improvement in both performance and mental health (Montano et al., 2017), whereas laissez-faire and destructive leader behavior are associated with negative employee outcomes (Schyns & Schilling, 2013). Due to leaders' influential role in coordinating work activities, a large share of training resources in HRM is allocated to leadership development (Riggio, 2017). Against this background, the question is: What characterizes effective leadership in the digital age?

One of the main challenges for leadership is that virtual collaboration and technology-mediated communication increase the distance between leaders and employees. Though the degree of virtual teamwork can vary from face-to-face to fully mediated online collaboration across multiple locations, most organizational teamwork today is at least partly virtual (Rudolph et al., 2021). In virtual settings, it becomes more difficult for leaders to be aware of their employees' stress levels, as overtime and signs of strain can go unnoticed (Efimov et al., 2020; Kordsmeyer et al., 2020). Virtual teamwork can also feel isolating, and technology-mediated communication is prone to misunderstandings, increasing the risk of conflicts as a source of stress (Day et al., 2012; Rudolph et al., 2021). This means that team leaders have to put more deliberate effort into things that grow more naturally in face-to-face settings to establish trust and a good team climate (e.g., by checking in with individual employees, creating opportunities for informal exchange or setting up communication rules; Hoch & Kozlowski, 2014; Kordsmeyer et al., 2020). As increased distance also entails less control for the leader, research has shown that facilitating self- and shared leadership among team members may be more beneficial for performance and satisfaction than "traditional," hierarchical leadership styles in virtual work settings (Eisenberg et al., 2019; Hoch & Kozlowski, 2014).

Technology-mediated leadership is also referred to as "e-leadership" (Contreras et al., 2020). Originally introduced as "a social influence process mediated by [advanced information technology] to produce a change in attitudes, feelings, thinking, behavior, and/or performance with individuals, groups, and/or organizations" (Avolio et al., 2001, p. 617), e-leadership does not seem all that different from traditional understandings of leadership. Hence, many competencies emphasized for successful "e-leadership" to meet the challenges of virtual work, such as effective communication or social and teambuilding skills, are not new compared to traditional leadership competencies (Contreras et al., 2020). What is new is that leadership is mediated by technology, which means that leaders need to be proficient in using (communication) technology to effectively exert influence and manage their teams (Newman et al., 2020a). Accordingly, Cortellazzo et al. (2019) have observed a "renaissance" of technical competencies as an important additional field for leadership development.

4.2 *Automating Leadership Functions*

There is also the possibility of technology supplementing or even replacing organizational leaders. "Automated" or "algorithmic" leadership refers to algorithms assuming HR and managerial tasks such as hiring and compensation, performance appraisal, and the allocation of tasks (Duggan et al., 2020; Wesche & Sonderegger, 2019). For example, algorithmic management has been defined as "a system of control where self-learning algorithms are given the responsibility for making and executing decisions affecting labour, thereby limiting human involvement and oversight of the labour process" (Duggan et al., 2020, p. 119). Closer to Yukl's (2012) definition of leadership, Wesche and Sonderegger (2019) define automated leadership as "a process whereby purposeful influence is exerted by a computer agent over human agents to guide, structure, and facilitate activities and relationships in a group or organization" (Wesche & Sonderegger, 2019, p. 200), which illustrates that in contrast to e-leadership, technology is no longer the mediator but rather the leader itself in this scenario.

So far, the discussion of automated leadership in the literature has concentrated on theoretical reviews (e.g., Kellogg et al., 2020; Wesche & Sonderegger, 2019), while empirical measurement of repercussions for leaders, employees and HRM is still scarce. We can distinguish between platform-based gig work, where automated leadership is fully realized, and the introduction of automated leadership elements into traditional organizational structures with supervisors and employees. Platform- or app-based work has indeed eradicated human leaders and replaced them with algorithms: Although platforms like MTurk or Uber may be perceived as simply matching demand and supply, these systems also set incentives, allocate tasks, and reward, sanction and monitor workers' performance, thereby assuming HR- and leadership functions (Duggan et al., 2020; see also Sect. 3.2).

In more conventional organizational settings, leadership tasks can also be automated to assist in and complement the activities of human leaders. According to a corporate survey of leaders at different organizational levels, a viable scenario is that artificial intelligence takes over administrative tasks (e.g., scheduling shifts, compiling reports), freeing up leaders' resources to concentrate on tasks that require judgment, creativity or social skills (Kolbjørnsrud et al., 2016). From the employee perspective, experimental evidence suggests that people perceive automated leadership agents as less benevolent and overall less trustworthy, but also more transparent than human leaders (Höddinghaus et al., 2021), underlining the importance of considering employee attitudes and acceptance in the implementation of automated leadership (see also Abraham et al., 2019; Lee, 2018). More research is needed to guide HRM in successfully aligning automated leadership—as algorithms need data—with an organizational strategy for HR analytics (Sect. 6).

5 People Development

People development is central to HR maintaining the competitiveness of the company as well as the health and motivation of the staff. In this respect, digitalization has two effects on people's development. First, it can take place in a different way, in a digital form. On the other hand, the digitalization of work processes and the introduction of automation in the workplace are changing what is demanded of employees (Rieth & Hagemann, 2021b), and thus warrant changes in training and continuing education (Parker & Grote, 2020).

5.1 E-Coaching

Along with the proliferation of digital work, there is also a growing need on the side of employees for support that is flexible in terms of space and time, such as virtual or e-coaching. Just as information can now be quickly obtained, people want to receive personal feedback on their behavior or ideas directly, and to decide for themselves when to take the time for consultation (Kluge & Hagemann, 2016). Especially due to circumstances surrounding the Covid-19 pandemic, demand for online-based consulting products has increased dramatically, and providers of these solutions have had an immense competitive advantage.

Coaching is understood to be a "person-centered counseling and support process that can include professional and private content and is limited in time" (Rauen, 2001, p. 64). In this context, coaching seeks to provide "intensive and systematic facilitation of result-oriented problem and self-reflection as well as counseling of persons or groups to improve the achievement of self-congruent goals or to consciously change and develop oneself" (Greif, 2008, p. 59).

Not only can digital media be used directly in the coaching sessions, but the entire coaching process can benefit from digitalization at its various stages (Pascal et al., 2015). Digital media play an important role in the selection process of the appropriate coach, for example, with a good match between coach and client (e.g., in terms of certain personality variables) being a relevant predictor of coaching success (De Haan et al., 2013). The past limitation of geographic proximity between coach and client can now be lifted and time and location can be flexible. Clients can instead select their coaches based on whether the coach's experience is considered sufficient, whether relevant knowledge about the client's industry is available on the coach's side, or whether the coach holds certain certifications. In addition to a digital-based self-search, a data-based development of algorithms is also conceivable in order to optimally predict a match between coach and client for the success of the coaching (similar to the applications of chatbots discussed by Pijetlovic & Mueller-Christ, 2022 and Klein et al., 2022). Numerous providers of web-based coaching management systems have emerged to meet the various requirements of organizations, coaches, and clients. These web-based systems help all parties to optimally control the entire coaching process and to make it easier and clearer (e.g., with regard to the selection of the coach, the scheduling of appointments, or the tracking of the content of the coaching sessions). Evaluations, which are essential for the success of a coaching process, can be integrated into the coaching management systems or carried out separately. For this purpose, too, there are various commercial and freely available software solutions to distribute digital and online-based evaluation forms.

One of the most common cases of digitalization in coaching concerns the coaching relationship itself, which can proceed without personal contact between coach and client. We talk about distance coaching or e-coaching when, for example, e-mail exchanges, telephone, chat, or video telephony are used (Geißler & Kanatouri, 2015; Kluge & Hagemann, 2016). It is also possible that coaching sessions take place in virtual rooms where participants are represented by avatars (Heller & Koch, 2018). In this way, the relationship between coach and client, a factor that is essential for successful coaching, is supported through the use of new media that is adapted to the context (Berry et al., 2011). One way of classifying digital support in the coaching process can be as follows (Heller & Koch, 2018):

- Human versus machine: Does a machine (a bot, for example) generate coaching content exclusively, or does the client communicate with a human coach using digital media?
- Synchronous versus asynchronous: Do the coach and client communicate contemporaneously with each other, or is the answering of questions time-independent?
- Verbal versus written: Is there verbal communication or purely written communication, possibly with corresponding imagery?
- Avatar versus human: Will the process integrate the use of avatars as representatives of the participants?

An illustrative example of an e-coaching application within the production and logistics sector can be found in Klumpp et al. (2020b). This use case is an e-coaching system for employees and managers to expand self-efficacy as well as learning-, competence- and health-promoting work design and to enhance self-directed, flexible, and context-related learning with the support of digital media.

For the successful use of e-coaching, it is important for clients to have an affinity for computers and an expectation of internet self-efficacy. Even though computers and other electronic devices are part of daily life, people exhibit different attitudes toward their use and are sometimes averse to using computers and other technical devices. Computer aversion means "a negative affective state (discomfort or apprehension) relating to computer technology" (Schulenberg & Melton, 2008, p. 2621). A positive attitude toward the use of computers positively influences their acceptance in a coaching process. Internet self-efficacy is defined as "the belief in one's capabilities to organize and execute courses of internet actions required to produce given attainments" (Eastin & LaRose, 2000, p. 1). If this form of self-efficacy (i.e., the conviction that one can perform a certain action and meet challenges) is highly pronounced, people may have greater confidence in the e-coaching process; hence, the assessment of one's own skills influences the client's motivation and behavior in using these applications (cf. Bandura, 1986).

Computer affinity and self-efficacy are important client-side resources for dealing with the challenges and new demands within the digitalized coaching process. Overall, individuals with higher self-efficacy expectations and motivation to learn are more likely to seek out coaching situations and initiate processes for change (Kluge & Hagemann, 2018).

5.2 The Impact of Digitalization and Automation on Required Competencies

Existing task structures and work roles will be fundamentally changed by digitalization and automation (Härtwig & Sapronova, 2020). Organizations face new challenges and new competence requirements for employees (Cascio & Montealegre, 2016; Demerouti, 2020; Härtwig & Sapronova, 2020; Rieth & Hagemann, 2021b; Umbach et al., 2018). For organizations to be successful, it is essential that they systematically support the development and expansion of employees' competencies. This requires planning, implementation, and monitoring of employee competence development in alignment with the strategic goals of the organization (Kauffeld & Paulsen, 2018). In the context of such strategic competence management, it also is essential to consider future requirements that may arise (e.g., due to increasing automation) at an early stage in order to remain competitive.

The changed competence requirements as a result of automation have been analyzed primarily in the industrial sector (Grzybowska & Łupicka, 2017; Hecklau et al., 2016; Hirsch-Kreinsen, 2018). Occasionally, the focus is also on the consequences for logistics and retail (Böving et al., 2019; Umbach et al., 2018). Other organizations that are also strongly influenced by the automation of work processes are what are known as high-risk organizations (HROs). HROs are organizations for which mistakes can have serious consequences, and hence must maintain attentiveness and meet a high standard of reliability due to their acute responsibility toward other people and the environment. HROs include, for example, the police, fire departments, nuclear power plants, airlines, and medical care providers and make up a large proportion of the overall workforce. Teams working in such organizations are called high responsibility teams (Hagemann, 2011). HROs thus place very specific demands on high responsibility teams and are not comparable to other organizations (Hagemann et al., 2012).

HROs work with very complex technologies (Weick & Sutcliffe, 2007). In HROs in particular, the goals of automation are to increase safety and reliability in addition to the economic benefits. At the same time, automated systems entail new risks that can have far-reaching consequences, such as in the event of faulty execution or automation failure. In these critical moments, humans must be prepared to return to service and independently perform the functions previously outsourced to automation (Manzey, 2008;). Humans thus remain an important resource in organizations, although their role is changing fundamentally (Rieth & Hagemann, 2021b). Active control tasks are decreasing as automation increasingly performs them. Instead, humans must take on the role of system monitors and check whether the automation is working correctly. Thus, passive monitoring tasks become more important for humans (Manzey, 2008; Sheridan & Parasuraman, 2005). Consequently, one of the greatest challenges of human–machine interaction is that humans in their passive role must remain vigilant at all times, maintain appropriate situational awareness, and be able to intervene in the event of a malfunction (Manzey, 2008). However, it is often the case that the more reliably automation works, the more likely it is that there is an overconfidence in it—what is called one of the "ironies of automation" (Bainbridge, 1983). Automation is supposed to reduce the burden on humans; however, the more complex the processes and the more automated the tasks, the more challenging human intervention becomes in the event of a malfunction (Bainbridge, 1983). Another consequence of using automated systems can be the loss of necessary skills (Parasuraman et al., 2000).

With this in mind, it is especially important to train for skill retention (Frank & Kluge, 2019; Kluge et al., 2016; Parker & Grote, 2020).

6 Human Resource Analytics

Drastic changes in our working world are currently leading to HR seizing the opportunity to shed its dusty image and assume a new, decisive function in companies. The current changes are driven by a growing amount of both employee and company data (see Fieberg et al., 2022), and HR increasingly has the crucial role of advising the company on the basis of this data. The future of HRM, one could say, lies in understanding the data, analyzing it, and deriving recommendations from it for charting the future course of the organization.

The use of data and statistical analysis in HRM is central to the field of human resource analytics (HR analytics or HR-A) (Angrave et al., 2016; Marler & Boudreau, 2017). Through HR-A, managers of HR aim to collect, analyze, and process data relating to employees to provide a basis for decision-making on strategic business issues. Increasing amounts of available data and data analysis are gradually transforming what is still a widespread administrative role of HRM into a more strategic one, whereby key decision-making processes are data-driven and evidence-based. In addition to this strategic orientation of HR, which is ultimately seen as a competitive advantage for the company (McIver et al., 2018), decision-making processes that have often been perceived as subjective or intuitive can be approached more objectively. This in turn affects HR in all its functional areas, from HR marketing and personnel deployment planning to people development and staff retention (Isson & Harriott, 2016; Marler & Boudreau, 2017).

6.1 Application Options

There is great diversity in the possible designs of HR-A in practice. In personnel recruitment, for example, artificial intelligence software could be used as a complement to traditional interviews, not only to analyze the application documents in advance, but also to analyze the personality of the applicants by evaluating, say, nonverbal behavior or voice, thus providing additional data about the candidate (Chamorro-Premuzic et al., 2017). In the context of stress and burnout prevention, fitness trackers and smart keyboards could be used to collect data on employees' sleep patterns, heart rates, and keystrokes, with the goal of promoting employee health and preventing overwork. An interesting example is the project Marble by Lanwehr and Gober (2017). It should be noted that these examples may skirt the limits of incursion into personal space, highlighting the absolute care that must be taken with respect to ethics and data protection (see Hornuf & Mangold, 2022; Klein et al., 2022). Above all, the EU General Data Protection Regulation must be applied at all times (Binder, 2018).

In the area of professional development, information on which group of employees (e.g., analyzed via the stored curriculum vitae) would benefit most from an internal seminar or coaching session (e.g., tracked via the HR system) could be helpful in offering employees tailored solutions for their development and career. Based on this, advanced technologies could be equipped with smart learning analytics—learning systems that adapt to the respective learner in terms of difficulty and pace (Giannakos et al., 2016).

HR-A projects may also apply to areas of leadership, such as employee performance appraisals, using algorithms to make decisions based on such data as the number of hours worked, the rate of project completion, employee attitudes toward work and colleagues, and personal development potential. What is known about this so far is that, on average, employees perceive less fairness and show lower commitment when their performance is assessed by an algorithm instead of their leader, especially when it comes to qualitative performance data. Leader decisions supported by an algorithm have been found to be more accepted than decisions arrived at through an algorithm alone or with minimal intervention by the leader (Newman et al., 2020b).

In summary, HR-A plays a significant role in the overall employee journey in an organization. From the first point of contact, which can be before joining the company, through one's time in the company to leaving it, there are numerous touchpoints between the employee and the company and its managers. Whether it is applied to performance appraisal, motivation, employee retention, appraisal interviews, vacation planning, or promotions, HR-A can, if applied in smart projects, provide important insights for the company and shape these touchpoints in an optimal way.

6.2 Process Models for the Implementation of HR-A Projects

For an effective HR-A project, a strategically relevant question is needed at the beginning. This makes it clear to all stakeholders and the company that HR-A is not an end in itself, but serves to provide strategic value for the organization. This strategically relevant question forms the starting point and determines the course over which data is needed for the processing of the project. For example, it must be clarified to what extent existing data sources can be used or whether new data must be collected. The next step is to determine how the data can be analyzed. Because HR-A projects go through different phases, there are process flow models in which the individual phases are clearly presented. Although there are a large number of process models that describe the course of an HR-A project, the unifying logic behind all of these models is the necessity of starting out with a strategically relevant question.

A well-known example of such a process model is the I-CAN-Enable model established by Mühlbauer et al. (2018). In the first phase, *identify*, the research question and the analysis objective must be identified and defined. This central question can be brought to the HR department by the management or a specialist department of the company, or it can be developed independently by the HR department. In the second phase, *collect*, it must now be determined which data can be used to answer the question, where and how such data are available, and how they can be linked. The third phase, *analyze*, relates to the evaluation of the data. It is important to choose the right analysis method based on the question at hand and the quality of the data. The aim of the fourth phase, *navigate*, is to unleash the benefits of the HR-A project by automating the analysis routines and making them accessible to the relevant stakeholders in the company. Software-based solutions with interactive user interfaces should be used for this purpose. The solutions can be made widely available to employees from different areas in order to underpin the respective decision-making processes with empirical evidence. The fifth and final phase, *enable*, focuses on the derivation of action implications as well as the evaluation of the project. It is now important to incorporate the results into the decision-making process and then to continue to use the analytical procedures to check how the circumstances are changing. In this way, the best measure can be identified and, if necessary, rolled out company-wide.

Another process flow model that is similar in many respects to the previous model, but which offers a higher level of detail in the description of individual phases, is the people analytics *Prozessmodell* (PAP), with eight phases in total (Reindl & Krügl, 2017). After the first step of identifying the question, the PAP model emphasizes the important point that analyses in the context of HR-A projects should be hypothesis-driven, and their basis should lie in assumptions that make sense in terms of content. Theories or models known from the literature can be invoked for this purpose. This is followed by the concrete planning of the research design. In order to properly analyze the data in the next step, the PAP model recommends a thorough data cleaning beforehand. The analysis of the data is followed by visualizing and communicating the results. To ensure that evidence based on the data has an impact and can be used as a basis for decisions, this evidence must be presented and communicated in a coherent and transparent manner. Successful presentation often hinges on storytelling and good data visualization. After all, if the recommendations that result from the analysis are not understood, they will fail to elicit dialogue, and the insights will not lead to action within the organization (Welbourne, 2015). After the implementation of planned measures, the final step of an HR-A project is evaluation, that is, the review of whether and to what extent decisions made or measures derived were successful.

The potential benefits and process models outlined above make HR-A a powerful tool for human resource management, enabling HR work to be aligned with the requirements of the company in a targeted manner. Especially in view of the challenges that arise in the context of industry 4.0 requiring a high degree of agility with regard to HR decisions, such an approach is of great importance. By focusing on evidence and positioning itself as a strategic partner, HR-A is also helping to overcome the administrative image of HR work, strengthening its capabilities to face the challenges of the future.

7 Conclusion

Digital transformation affects almost every aspect of organizational life relevant for HRM, from organizational structures supporting leadership and collaboration to the people interacting with technology and their competencies, development, and well-being. Given this pervasiveness, it is beyond the scope of this discussion to detail all implications of technological change in all areas of HRM. Instead, this chapter provides an overview of recent developments and selected issues in the HRM fields of health management, leadership, work design, people development, and HR analytics, emphasizing employees' mental health as a vital outcome. It is the aim of this discussion to stimulate further exploration, both in research and in practice, of an active role of HRM for organizations' successful adaptation to their digital transformation.

References

Abraham, M., Niessen, C., Schnabel, C., Lorek, K., Grimm, V., Möslein, K., & Wrede, M. (2019). Electronic monitoring at work: The role of attitudes, functions, and perceived control for the acceptance of tracking technologies. *Human Resource Management Journal, 29*(4), 657–675. https://doi.org/10.1111/1748-8583.12250

Allen, T. D., Golden, T. D., & Shockley, K. M. (2015). How effective is telecommuting? Assessing the status of our scientific findings. *Psychological Science in the Public Interest, 16*(2), 40–68. https://doi.org/10.1177/1529100615593273

Anderson, A. J., Kaplan, S. A., & Vega, R. P. (2015). The impact of telework on emotional experience: When, and for whom, does telework improve daily affective well-being? *European Journal of Work and Organizational Psychology, 24*(6), 882–897. https://doi.org/10.1080/1359432X.2014.966086

Angrave, D., Charlwood, A., Kirkpatrick, I., Lawrence, M., & Stuart, M. (2016). HR and analytics: Why HR is set to fail the big data challenge. *Human Resource Management Journal, 26*(1), 1–11. https://doi.org/10.1111/1748-8583.12090

Atanasoff, L., & Venable, M. (2017). Technostress: Implications for adults in the workforce. *The Career Development Quarterly, 65*(4), 326–338. https://doi.org/10.1002/cdq.12111

Autor, D. H., Levy, F., & Murnane, R. J. (2003). The skill content of recent technological change: An empirical exploration. *The Quarterly Journal of Economics, 118*(3), 1279–1333.

Avolio, B. J., Kahai, S., & Dodge, G. E. (2001). E-leadership: Implications for theory, research, and practice. *The Leadership Quarterly, 11*(4), 615–668. https://doi.org/10.1016/j.cels.2020.12.004

Backhaus, N., Tisch, A., & Beermann, B. (2020). *Telearbeit, Homeoffice und Mobiles Arbeiten: Chancen, Herausforderungen und Gestaltungsaspekte aus Sicht des Arbeitsschutzes.*

Bainbridge, L. (1983). Ironies of automation. *Automatica, 19*(6), 775–779.

Bakker, A. B., & Demerouti, E. (2007). The job demands–resources model: State of the art. *Journal of Managerial Psychology, 22*(3), 309–328. https://doi.org/10.1108/02683940710733115

Bandura, A. (1986). *Social foundations of thought and action. A social cognitive theory*. Prentice-Hall.

Bartlett, L., Martin, A., Neil, A. L., Memish, K., Otahal, P., Kilpatrick, M., & Sanderson, K. (2019). A systematic review and meta-analysis of workplace mindfulness training randomized controlled trials. *Journal of Occupational Health Psychology, 24*(1), 108–126. https://doi.org/10.1037/ocp0000146

Beehr, T. A. (2019). Interventions in occupational health psychology. *Journal of Occupational Health Psychology, 24*(1), 1–3. https://doi.org/10.1037/ocp0000140

Beer, D., & Burrows, R. (2010). Consumption, prosumption and participatory web cultures: An introduction. *Journal of Consumer Culture, 10*, 3–12.

Berry, R., Ashby, J., Gnilka, P., & Matheny, K. (2011). A comparison of face-to-face and distance coaching practices: Coaches' perceptions of the role of the working alliance in problem resolution. *Consulting Psychology Journal: Practice and Research, 63*, 243–253.

Binder, J. (2018). Die europäische Datenschutz-Grundverordnung – Neue Anforderungen an den Datenschutz in der betrieblichen Praxis. In W. Appel & M. Wahler (Eds.), *Die digitale HR-Organisation. Wo wir stehen, was wir brauchen* (pp. 97–106). Wolters-Kluwer.

Blaga, P., & Jozsef, B. (2014). Human resources, quality circles and innovation. *Procedia Economics and Finance, 15*, 1458–1462.

Böving, H., Glaß, E., Haberzeth, E., & Umbach, S. (2019). Digitalisierte Arbeit und menschliche Initiative. Empirische Analysen aus Logistik und Einzelhandel. In R. Dobischat, B. Käpplinger, G. Molzberger, & D. Münk (Eds.), *Bildung 2.1 für Arbeit 4.0?* (pp. 141–160). Springer VS.

Cascio, W. F., & Montealegre, R. (2016). How technology is changing work and organizations. *Annual Review of Organizational Psychology and Organizational Behavior, 3*(1), 349–375.

Chamorro-Premuzic, T., Akhtar, R., Winsborough, D., & Sherman, R. A. (2017). The datafication of talent: How technology is advancing the science of human potential at work. *Current Opinion in Behavioral Sciences, 18*, 13–16. https://doi.org/10.1016/j.cobeha.2017.04.007

Contreras, F., Baykal, E., & Abid, G. (2020). E-leadership and teleworking in times of COVID-19 and beyond: What we know and where do we go. *Frontiers in Psychology, 11*, 3484. https://doi.org/10.3389/fpsyg.2020.590271

Cooper, C. D., & Kurland, N. B. (2002). Telecommuting, professional isolation, and employee development in public and private organizations. *Journal of Organizational Behavior, 23*(Spec. Iss), 511–532. https://doi.org/10.1002/job.145

Cortellazzo, L., Bruni, E., & Zampieri, R. (2019). The role of leadership in a digitalized world: A review. *Frontiers in Psychology, 10*(1), 938. https://doi.org/10.3389/FPSYG.2019.01938

Crespo, I., Bergmann, L., & Portmann, S. (2009). Kontinuierliche Verbesserungsprozesse. In U. Dombrowski, C. Herrmann, T. Lacker, & S. Sonnentag (Eds.), *Modernisierung kleiner und mittlerer Unternehmen* (pp. 169–178). Springer.

Day, A., Paquet, S., Scott, N., & Hambley, L. (2012). Perceived information and communication technology (ICT) demands on employee outcomes: The moderating effect of organizational ICT support. *Journal of Occupational Health Psychology, 17*(4), 473–491. https://doi.org/10.1037/a0029837

De Haan, E., Duckworth, A., Birch, D., & Jones, C. (2013). Executive coaching outcomes research: The contribution of common factors such as relationships, personality match, and self-efficacy. *Consulting Psychology Journal: Practice and Research, 65*(1), 40–57.

de Jonge, J., & Dormann, C. (2017). Why is my job so stressful? Characteristics, processes and models of stress at work. In N. Chmiel, F. Fraccaroli, & M. Sverke (Eds.), *An introduction to work and organizational psychology* (3rd ed., pp. 80–101). Wiley. https://doi.org/10.1002/9781119168058.ch5

De Stefano, V. (2016). The rise of the just-in-time workforce: On-demand work, crowdwork, and labor protection in the gig-economy. *Comparative Labor Law & Policy Journal, 37*(3), 471–504.

Demerouti, E. (2020). Turn digitalization and automation to a job resource. *Applied Psychology: An International Review*, 1–6. doi: https://doi.org/10.1111/apps.12270.

Demerouti, E., & Bakker, A. B. (2011). The job demands–resources model: Challenges for future research. *SA Journal of Industrial Psychology, 37*(2), 1–9. https://doi.org/10.4102/sajip.v37i2.974

Demerouti, E., Derks, D., Ten Brummelhuis, L. L., & Bakker, A. B. (2014). New ways of working: Impact on working conditions, work–family balance, and well-being. In C. Korunka & P. Hoonakker (Eds.), *The impact of ICT on quality of working life* (pp. 123–141). Springer. https://doi.org/10.1007/978-94-017-8854-0_8

Derks, D., & Bakker, A. B. (2014). Smartphone use, work–home interference, and burnout: A diary study on the role of recovery. *Applied Psychology, 63*(3), 411–440. https://doi.org/10.1111/j.1464-0597.2012.00530.x

Dettmers, J., Vahle-Hinz, T., Bamberg, E., Friedrich, N., & Keller, M. (2016). Extended work availability and its relation with start-of-day mood and cortisol. *Journal of Occupational Health Psychology, 21*(1), 105–118. https://doi.org/10.1037/a0039602

Diebig, M., Müller, A., & Angerer, P. (2020). Impact of the digitization in the industry sector on work, employment, and health. In T. Theorell (Ed.), *Handbook of socioeconomic determinants of occupational health. Handbook Series in Occupational Health Sciences* (pp. 305–319). Springer.

Dora, J., van Hooff, M. L. M., Geurts, S. A. E., Hooftman, W. E., & Kompier, M. A. J. (2019). Characterizing work-related smartphone use at home and private smartphone use at work using latent class analysis. *Occupational Health Science, 3*(2), 187–203. https://doi.org/10.1007/s41542-019-00040-6

Duggan, J., Sherman, U., Carbery, R., & McDonnell, A. (2020). Algorithmic management and app-work in the gig economy: A research agenda for employment relations and HRM. *Human Resource Management Journal, 30*(1), 114–132. https://doi.org/10.1111/1748-8583.12258

Durward, D., Blohm, I., & Leimeister, J. M. (2020). The nature of crowd work and its effects on individuals' work perception. *Journal of Management Information Systems, 37*(1), 66–95. https://doi.org/10.1080/07421222.2019.1705506

Eastin, M., & LaRose, R. (2000). Internet self-efficacy and the psychology of the digital divide. *Journal of Computer-Mediated Communication, 6*. https://doi.org/10.1111/j.1083-6101.2000.tb00110.x

Efimov, I., Harth, V., & Mache, S. (2020). Health-oriented self- and employee leadership in virtual teams: A qualitative study with virtual leaders. *International Journal of Environmental Research and Public Health, 17*(18), 1–19. https://doi.org/10.3390/ijerph17186519

Eisenberg, J., Post, C., & DiTomaso, N. (2019). Team dispersion and performance: The role of team communication and transformational leadership. *Small Group Research, 50*(3), 348–380. https://doi.org/10.1177/1046496419827376

Fauville, G., Luo, M., Muller Queiroz, A. C., Bailenson, J. N., & Hancock, J. (2021a). Zoom exhaustion & fatigue scale. *SSRN Electronic Journal*. https://doi.org/10.2139/SSRN.3786329

Fauville, G., Luo, M., Muller Queiroz, A. C., Bailenson, J. N., & Hancock, J. (2021b). Nonverbal mechanisms predict Zoom fatigue and explain why women experience higher levels than men. *SSRN Electronic Journal*. https://doi.org/10.2139/SSRN.3820035

Fieberg, C., Hesse, M., Loy, T., & Metko, D. (2022). Machine learning in accounting research. In L. Hornuf (Ed.), *Diginomics research perspectives: The role of digitalization in business and society*. Springer International Publishing.

Fischer, T., Reuter, M., & Riedl, R. (2021). The Digital stressors scale: Development and validation of a new survey instrument to measure digital stress perceptions in the workplace context. *Frontiers in Psychology, 12*, 607598. https://doi.org/10.3389/fpsyg.2021.607598

Frank, B., & Kluge, A. (2019). Is there one best way to support skill retention? Putting practice, testing and symbolic rehearsal to a test. *Zeitschrift für Arbeitswissenschaft (ZfA), 73*(2), 214–228. https://doi.org/10.1007/s41449-018-00136-9

Gajendran, R. S., & Harrison, D. A. (2007). The good, the bad, and the unknown about telecommuting: Meta-analysis of psychological mediators and individual consequences. *Journal of Applied Psychology, 92*(6), 1524–1541. https://doi.org/10.1037/0021-9010.92.6.1524

GDA-Psyche. (2017). Instrumente und Verfahren zur Gefährdungsbeurteilung psychischer Belastung. *Sicher Ist Sicher, 68*(4) https://www.gda-psyche.de/SharedDocs/Publikationen/DE/instrumente-und-verfahren-zur-gefaehrdungsbeurteilung-psychischer-belastung.pdf?__blob=publicationFile&v=2

Geißler, H., & Kanatouri, S. (2015). Coaching mit modernen Medien. In A. Schreyögg & C. Schmidt-Lellek (Eds.), *Die Professionalisierung von Coaching*. Springer.

Giannakos, M. N., Sampson, D. G., & Kidziński, Ł. (2016). Introduction to smart learning analytics: Foundations and developments in video-based learning. *Smart Learning Environments, 3*(1). https://doi.org/10.1186/s40561-016-0034-2

Golden, T. D., Veiga, J. F., & Dino, R. N. (2008). The impact of professional isolation on teleworker job performance and turnover intentions: Does time spent teleworking, interacting face-to-face, or having access to communication-enhancing technology matter? *Journal of Applied Psychology, 93*(6), 1412–1421. https://doi.org/10.1037/a0012722

Greif, S. (2008). *Coaching und ergebnisorientierte Selbstreflexion. Theorie, Forschung und Praxis des Einzel- und Gruppencoachings*. Hogrefe Verlag.

Grzybowska, K., & Łupicka, A. (2017). Key competencies for industry 4.0. *Economics and Management Innovations, 1*(1), 250–253.

Hackman, J. R., & Oldham, G. R. (1976). Motivation through the design of work: Test of a theory. *Organizational Behavior and Human Performance, 16*(2), 250–279. https://doi.org/10.1016/0030-5073(76)90016-7

Hagemann, V. (2011). *Trainingsentwicklung für High Responsibility Teams*. Papst Verlag.

Hagemann, V., Kluge, A., & Ritzmann, S. (2012). Flexibility under complexity: Work contexts, task profiles and team processes of high responsibility teams. *Employee Relations, 34*(3), 322–338.

Hagemann, V., Meinecke, J., Schaper, M., Debbing, C., Ruiner, C., Klumpp, M., & Hesenius, M. (2021). Mental stress and strain assessment in digital work: The measurement instrument MESTAT for employees and leaders. *German Journal of Work and Organizational Psychology*. https://doi.org/10.1026/0932-4089/a000387

Härtwig, C., & Sapronova, A. (2020). Keine Angst vor der Digitalisierung! Zum Stand digitalisierter Arbeitsanforderungen in verschiedenen Industriebranchen und Tätigkeitsfeldern sowie Zusammenhänge zwischen Belastung, Ressourcen und Beanspruchungsfolgen in Deutschland. *Zeitschrift für Arbeitswissenschaft*, 1–16.

Hartwig, M., Wirth, M., & Bonin, D. (2020). Insights about mental health aspects at intralogistics workplaces: A field study. *International Journal of Industrial Ergonomics, 76*, 102944. https://doi.org/10.1016/j.ergon.2020.102944

Hauß, Y., & Timpe, K.-P. (2000). Automatisierung und Unterstützung im Mensch-Maschine-System. In K.-P. Timpe, T. Jürgensohn, & H. Kolrep (Eds.), *Mensch-Maschine-Systemtechnik. Konzepte, Modellierung, Gestaltung, Evaluation* (pp. 41–62). Symposion Publishing.

Hecklau, F., Galeitzke, M., Flachs, S., & Kohl, H. (2016). Holistic approach for human resource management in industry 4.0. *Procedia CIRP, 54*, 1–6.

Heller, J., & Koch, A. (2018). Digitalisierung im coaching. In J. Heller, C. Triebel, B. Hauser, & A. Koch (Eds.), *Digitale medien im coaching* (pp. 1–4). Springer.

Hirsch-Kreinsen, H. (2018). Einleitung: Digitalisierung industrieller Arbeit. In H. Hirsch-Kreinsen, P. Ittermann, & J. Niehaus (Eds.), *Digitalisierung industrieller Arbeit* (pp. 13–32). Nomos Verlagsgesellschaft mb H & Co. KG.

Hoch, J. E., & Kozlowski, S. W. J. (2014). Leading virtual teams: Hierarchical leadership, structural supports, and shared team leadership. *Journal of Applied Psychology, 99*(3), 390–403. https://doi.org/10.1037/a0030264

Höddinghaus, M., Sondern, D., & Hertel, G. (2021). The automation of leadership functions: Would people trust decision algorithms? *Computers in Human Behavior, 116*, 106635. https://doi.org/10.1016/j.chb.2020.106635

Hornuf, L., & Mangold, S. (2022). Digital dark nudges. In L. Hornuf (Ed.), *Diginomics research perspectives: The role of digitalization in business and society*. Springer International Publishing.

Hülsheger, U. R., Hoppe, A., & Michel, A. (2020). Interventions to improve employee well-being. In L.-Q. Yang, R. Cropanzano, C. Daus, & V. Martinez-Tur (Eds.), *The Cambridge handbook of workplace affect* (pp. 214–226). Cambridge University Press.

Humphrey, S. E., Nahrgang, J. D., & Morgeson, F. P. (2007). Integrating motivational, social, and contextual work design features: A meta-analytic summary and theoretical extension of the work design literature. *Journal of Applied Psychology, 92*(5), 1332–1356. https://doi.org/10.1037/0021-9010.92.5.1332

Huws, U., Spencer, N. H., & Joyce, S. (2016). *Crowd work in Europe*. Preliminary results from a survey in the UK.

Isson, J. P., & Harriott, J. (2016). *People analytics in the era of big data: Changing the way you attract, acquire, develop, and retain talent* (1st ed.). Wiley.

Judge, T. A., & Piccolo, R. F. (2004). Transformational and transactional leadership: A meta-analytic test of their relative validity. *Journal of Applied Psychology, 89*(5), 755–768. https://doi.org/10.1037/0021-9010.89.5.755

Kauffeld, S. (2019). *Arbeits-, Organisations- und Personalpsychologie für Bachelor*. Springer.

Kauffeld, S., & Paulsen, H. F. K. (2018). *Kompetenzmanagement in Unternehmen. Kompetenzen beschreiben, messen, entwicklen und nutzen*. Kohlhammer.

Kellogg, K. C., Valentine, M. A., & Christin, A. (2020). Algorithms at work: The new contested terrain of control. *Academy of Management Annals, 14*(1), 366–410. https://doi.org/10.5465/annals.2018.0174

Kelloway, E. K., & Barling, J. (2010). Leadership development as an intervention in occupational health psychology. *Work & Stress, 24*(3), 260–279. https://doi.org/10.1080/02678373.2010.518441

Kelloway, E. K., & Gilbert, S. (2017). Does it matter who leads us? The study of organizational leadership. In N. Chmiel, F. Fraccaroli, & M. Sverke (Eds.), *An introduction to work and organizational psychology* (pp. 192–211). Wiley. https://doi.org/10.1002/9781119168058.ch11

Klein, K., Eisenbeiss, M., Dulle, M., Taherparvar, N., Wiemann, M., & Wiezorrek, J. (2022). Marketing in a digital world. In L. Hornuf (Ed.), *Diginomics research perspectives: The role of digitalization in business and society*. Springer International Publishing.

Kluge, A., & Hagemann, V. (2016). Neue und Soziale Medien in der Fertigung und der Personalentwicklung – am Beispiel von Industrie 4.0 und E-Coaching aus Sicht der AO-Psychologie. *Wirtschaftspsychologie, 18*(1), 5–21.

Kluge, A., & Hagemann, V. (2018). Lernen als grundlage von coaching. In S. Greif, H. Möller, & W. Scholl (Eds.), *Handbuch schlüsselkonzepte im coaching* (pp. 335–342). Springer.

Kluge, A., Frank, B., Maafi, S., & Kuzmanovska, A. (2016). Does skill retention benefit from retentivity and symbolic rehearsal? Two studies with a simulated process control task. *Ergonomics, 59*(5), 641–656.

Klumpp, M., Hagemann, V., & Schaper, M. (2020a). Assessment of cognitive strain in digital logistics work: Background, analysis and implications. In M. Freitag, H.D. Haasis, H. Kotzab, & J. Pannek (Eds.), *Proceedings of the 7th International Conference on Dynamics in Logistics* (LDIC 2020) (pp. 504–5515), : Springer Nature Switzerland. https://doi.org/10.1007/978-3-030-44783-0

Klumpp, M., Hesenius, M., Ruiner, C., & Hagemann, V. (2020b). Künstliche Intelligenz zur Unterstützung neuer Arbeitswelten in Produktion, Handel und Logistik. In R. Buchkremer, T. Heupel, & O. Koch (Eds.), *Künstliche Intelligenz in Wirtschaft und Gesellschaft* (pp. 155–167). Springer.

Kolbjørnsrud, V., Amico, R., & Thomas, R. J. (2016). How artificial intelligence will redefine management. *Harvard Business Review*, November, 1–6. doi:https://doi.org/10.1093/biomet/asm033.

Kordsmeyer, A. C., Mette, J., Harth, V., & Mache, S. (2020). Health-oriented leadership in virtual teamwork. *Zentralblatt fur Arbeitsmedizin, Arbeitsschutz und Ergonomie, 70*(2), 76–82. https://doi.org/10.1007/s40664-019-0347-4

Kraus, S., Schiavone, F., Pluzhnikova, A., & Invernizzi, A. C. (2021). Digital transformation in healthcare: Analyzing the current state-of-research. *Journal of Business Research, 123*, 557–567. https://doi.org/10.1016/j.jbusres.2020.10.030

Krick, A., Felfe, J., & Klug, K. (2019). Turning intention into participation in OHP courses? The moderating role of organizational, intrapersonal and interpersonal factors. *Journal of Occupational and Environmental Medicine, 61*(10), 779–799. https://doi.org/10.1097/JOM.0000000000001670

Kunert, S. (2014). Open Innovation im Ideenmanagement. In W. Scholl, F. Schmelzer, S. Kunert, S. Bedenk, J. Hüttner, J. Pullen, & S. Tirre (Eds.), *Mut zu Innovationen. Impulse aus Forschung, Beratung und Ausbildung* (pp. 191–199). Wiesbaden.

La Torre, G., Esposito, A., Sciarra, I., & Chiappetta, M. (2019). Definition, symptoms and risk of techno-stress: A systematic review. *International Archives of Occupational and Environmental Health, 92*(1), 13–35. https://doi.org/10.1007/s00420-018-1352-1

LaMontagne, A. D., Keegel, T., Louie, A. M., Ostry, A., & Landsbergis, P. A. (2007). A systematic review of the job-stress intervention evaluation literature, 1990–2005. *International Journal of Occupational and Environmental Health, 13*(3), 268–280. https://doi.org/10.1179/oeh.2007.13.3.268

Lanwehr, R., & Gober, P. (2017). Schutz persönlicher Daten am Arbeitsplatz - das Projekt Marble. In C. Reindl & S. Krügl (Eds.), *People Analytics in der Praxis: Mit Datenanalyse zu besseren Entscheidungen im Personalmanagement* (1st ed., pp. 94–97). Haufe-Lexware GmbH & Co. KG.

Lee, M. K. (2018). Understanding perception of algorithmic decisions: Fairness, trust, and emotion in response to algorithmic management. *Big Data and Society, 5*(1), 1–16. https://doi.org/10.1177/2053951718756684

Lehr, D., & Boß, L. (2019). Occupational e-Mental Health – eine Übersicht zu Ansätzen, Evidenz und Implementierung. In B. Badura, A. Ducki, H. Schröder, J. Klose, & M. Meyer (Eds.), *Fehlzeiten-Report 2019. Digitalisierung - gesundes Arbeiten ermöglichen* (pp. 155–178). Springer. https://doi.org/10.1007/978-3-662-59044-7_11

Manzey, D. H. (2008). Systemgestaltung und Automatisierung. In P. Badke-Schaub, G. Hofinger, & K. Lauche (Eds.), *Human Factors. Psychologie sicheren Handelns in Risikobranchen* (pp. 307–325). Springer Medizin Verlag.

Marler, J. H., & Boudreau, J. W. (2017). An evidence-based review of HR Analytics. *The International Journal of Human Resource Management, 28*(1), 3–26. https://doi.org/10.1080/09585192.2016.1244699

McIver, D., Lengnick-Hall, M. L., & Lengnick-Hall, C. A. (2018). A strategic approach to workforce analytics: Integrating science and agility. *Business Horizons, 61*(3), 397–407. https://doi.org/10.1016/j.bushor.2018.01.005

Meyer, M., Maisuradze, M., & Schenkel, A. (2019). Krankheitsbedingte Fehlzeiten in der deutschen Wirtschaft im Jahr 2018 – Überblick. In B. Badura, A. Ducki, H. Schröder, J. Klose, & M. Meyer (Eds.), *Fehlzeiten-Report 2019* (pp. 413–477). https://doi.org/10.1007/978-3-662-59044-7_27

Montano, D., Reeske, A., Franke, F., & Hüffmeier, J. (2017). Leadership, followers' mental health and job performance in organizations: A comprehensive meta-analysis from an occupational health perspective. *Journal of Organizational Behavior, 38*(3), 327–350. https://doi.org/10.1002/job.2124

Mühlbauer, D., Huff, J., & Süß, J. (2018). People analytics und arbeit 4.0. In S. Werther & L. Bruckner (Eds.), *Arbeit 4.0 aktiv gestalten* (pp. 107–132). Springer.

Müller, T., & Niessen, C. (2019). Self-leadership in the context of part-time teleworking. *Journal of Organizational Behavior, 40*(8), 838–898. https://doi.org/10.1002/job.2371

Newman, D. T., Fast, N. J., & Harmon, D. J. (2020a). When eliminating bias isn't fair: Algorithmic reductionism and procedural justice in human resource decisions. *Organizational Behavior and Human Decision Processes, 160*, 149–167. https://doi.org/10.1016/j.obhdp.2020.03.008

Newman, S. A., Ford, R. C., & Marshall, G. W. (2020b). Virtual team leader communication: Employee perception and organizational reality. *International Journal of Business Communication, 57*(4), 452–473. https://doi.org/10.1177/2329488419829895

Parasuraman, R., Sheridan, T. B., & Wickens, C. D. (2000). A model for types and levels of human interaction with automation. *IEEE Transactions on Systems, Man, and Cybernetics – Part A Systems and Humans, 30*(3), 286–297.

Parker, S. K. (2014). Beyond motivation: Job and work design for development, health, ambidexterity, and more. *Annual Review of Psychology, 65*(1), 661–691. https://doi.org/10.1146/annurev-psych-010213-115208

Parker, S., & Grote, G. (2020). Automation, algorithms, and beyond: Why workdesign matters more than ever in a digital world. *Applied Psychology: An International Review*. https://doi.org/10.1111/apps.12241

Pascal, A., Sass, M., & Gregory, J. (2015). I'm only human: The role of technology in coaching. *Consulting Psychology Journal: Practice and Research, 67*(2), 100–109.

Peinl, I., & Bildat, L. (2017). *Forschungsdesiderate: Bezahlte repetitive Crowdarbeit und Gesundheit*. https://doi.org/10.13140/RG.2.2.10139.46886.

Petry, T. (2019). Digital Leadership – Unternehmens- und Personalführung im digitalen Zeitalter. In T. Petry (Ed.), *Digital Leadership. Erfolgreiches Führen in Zeiten der Digital Economy* (2nd ed., pp. 23–126). Haufe.

Petry, T., & Jäger, W. (2018). *Digital HR*. Haufe.

Pijetlovic, D., & Mueller-Christ, G. (2022). HumanRoboLab: Experiments with chatbots in management education at universities. In L. Hornuf (Ed.), *Diginomics research perspectives: The role of digitalization in business and society*. Springer International Publishing.

Prashar, A. (2017). Adopting PDCA (plan-do-check-act) cycle for energy optimization in energy-intensive SMEs. *Journal of Cleaner Production, 145*, 277–293.

Rauen, C. (2001). *Coaching*. Hogrefe Verlag.

Reindl, C., & Krügl, S. (Eds.). (2017). People Analytics in der Praxis: Mit Datenanalyse zu besseren Entscheidungen im Personalmanagement (1. Auflage). Haufe-Lexware GmbH & Co. KG

Riedl, R. (2013). Mensch-Computer-Interaktion und Stress. *HMD Praxis Der Wirtschaftsinformatik, 50*(6), 97–106.

Rieth, M., & Hagemann, V. (2021a). The impact of telework and closure of educational and childcare facilities on working people during COVID-19. *German Journal of Work and Organizational Psychology, 65*(4), 202–214. https://doi.org/10.1026/0932-4089/a000370

Rieth, M., & Hagemann, V. (2021b). Veränderte Kompetenzanforderungen an Mitarbeitende infolge zunehmender Automatisierung – Eine Arbeitsfeldbetrachtung, *Gruppe. Interaktion. Organisation – Zeitschrift für Angewandte Organisationspsychologie, 52*(1), 37–49. https://doi.org/10.1007/s11612-021-00561-1

Riggio, R. E. (2017). *Introduction to industrial/organizational psychology* (7th ed.). Routledge. https://doi.org/10.4324/9781315620589

Ritzer, G., & Jurgenson, N. (2010). Production, consumption, prosumption: The nature of capitalism in the age of the digital "prosumer". *Journal of Consumer Culture, 10*, 13–36.

Rogers, E. M. (2003). *Diffusion of innovations*. Free Press.

Rowold, J. (2015). *Human resource management* (2. Auflage ed.). Springer.

Rudolph, C. W., Allan, B., Clark, M., Hertel, G., Hirschi, A., Kunze, F., Shockley, K., Shoss, M., Sonnentag, S., & Zacher, H. (2021). Pandemics: Implications for research and practice in industrial and organizational psychology. *Industrial and Organizational Psychology, 14*, 1–35. https://doi.org/10.1017/iop.2020.48

Ruiner, C., Hagemann, V., Hesenius, M., & Klumpp, M. (2020). Digitales Ideenmanagement als Mitbestimmung 4.0? Chancen und Herausforderungen der Partizipation von Beschäftigten in betrieblichen Veränderungsprozessen. In V. Bader & S. Kaiser (Eds.), *Arbeit in der Data Society – Zukunftsvisionen für Mitbestimmung und Personalmanagement* (pp. 243–262). Springer.

Ryan, C., Bergin, M., Chalder, T., & Wells, J. S. (2017). Web-based interventions for the management of stress in the workplace: Focus, form and efficacy. *Journal of Occupational Health, 59*(3), 215–236.

Salanova, M., Llorens, S., & Cifre, E. (2013). The dark side of technologies: Technostress among users of information and communication technologies. *International Journal of Psychology, 48*(3), 422–436.

Sandrock, S. (2017). Weiterentwicklung des KPB zur Gefährdungsbeurteilung psychischer Belastung. In Gesellschaft für Arbeitswissenschaft e.V., Dortmund (Ed.), *Frühjahrskongress 2017 in Brugg: Soziotechnische Gestaltung des digitalen Wandels – kreativ, innovativ, sinnhaft –* Beitrag A.1.8.

Schildt, H. (2017). Big data and organizational design: The brave new world of algorithmic management and computer augmented transparency. *Innovation: Management, Policy and Practice, 19*(1), 23–30. https://doi.org/10.1080/14479338.2016.1252043

Schulenberg, S. E., & Melton, A. M. A. (2008). The computer aversion, attitudes, and familiarity index: A validity study. *Computers in Human Behavior, 24*, 2620–2638.

Schwarzmüller, T., Brosi, P., Duman, D., & Welpe, I. M. (2018). How does the digital transformation affect organizations? Key themes of change in work design and leadership. *Management Revue, 29*(2), 114–138. https://doi.org/10.5771/0935-9915-2018-2-114

Schyns, B., & Schilling, J. (2013). How bad are the effects of bad leaders? A meta-analysis of destructive leadership and its outcomes. *The Leadership Quarterly, 24*(1), 138–158. https://doi.org/10.1016/J.LEAQUA.2012.09.001

Shann, C., Martin, A., Chester, A., & Ruddock, S. (2019). Effectiveness and application of an online leadership intervention to promote mental health and reduce depression-related stigma in organizations. *Journal of Occupational Health Psychology, 24*(1), 20–35. https://doi.org/10.1037/ocp0000110

Sheridan, T. B., & Parasuraman, R. (2005). Human–automation interaction. *Reviews of Human Factors and Ergonomics, 1*(1), 89–129.

Shockley, K. M., Gabriel, A. S., Robertson, D., Rosen, C. C., Chawla, N., Ganster, M. L., & Ezerins, M. E. (2021). The fatiguing effects of camera use in virtual meetings: A within-person field experiment. *Journal of Applied Psychology, 106*(8), 1137–1155. https://doi.org/10.1037/APL0000948

Stepanovic, S. (2020). Incentivizing the use of quantified self devices: The cases of digital occupational health programs and data-driven health insurance plans. *International Conference on Well-Being in the Information Society* (pp. 73–86).

Syrek, C. J., Kühnel, J., Vahle-Hinz, T., & De Bloom, J. (2018). Share, like, twitter, and connect: Ecological momentary assessment to examine the relationship between non-work social media use at work and work engagement. *Work and Stress, 32*(3), 209–227. https://doi.org/10.1080/02678373.2017.1367736

Tavares, A. I. (2017). Telework and health effects review. *International Journal of Healthcare, 3*(2), 30. https://doi.org/10.5430/ijh.v3n2p30

Tetrick, L. E., & Winslow, C. J. (2015). Workplace stress management interventions and health promotion. *Annual Review of Organizational Psychology and Organizational Behavior, 2*(1), 583–603. https://doi.org/10.1146/annurev-orgpsych-032414-111341

Turel, O., & Gaudioso, F. (2018). Techno-stressors, distress and strain: The roles of leadership and competitive climates. *Cognition, Technology & Work, 20*(2), 309–324. https://doi.org/10.1007/s10111-018-0461-7

Umbach, S., Böving, H., & Haberzeth, E. (2018). Kompetenzverschiebungen und menschliche Handlungsqualitäten im Digitalisierungsprozess. Ergebnisse aus Betriebsfallstudien in Einzelhandel und Logistik und Konsequenzen für die berufliche Weiterbildung. *Berufsbildung in Wissenschaft und Praxis, 47*(1), 16–19.

Weick, K. E., & Sutcliffe, K. M. (2007). *Managing the unexpected.* Jossey-Bass.

Welbourne, T. M. (2015). Data-driven storytelling: The missing link in HR data analytics. *Employment Relations Today, 41*(4), 27–33. https://doi.org/10.1002/ert.21471

Wesche, J. S., & Sonderegger, A. (2019). When computers take the lead: The automation of leadership. *Computers in Human Behavior, 101*, 197–209. https://doi.org/10.1016/j.chb.2019.07.027

Wu, J., Mei, W., Liu, L., & Ugrin, J. C. (2020). The bright and dark sides of social cyberloafing: Effects on employee mental health in China. *Journal of Business Research, 112*, 56–64. https://doi.org/10.1016/j.jbusres.2020.02.043

Yukl, G. (2012). Effective leadership behavior: What we know and what questions need more attention. *The Academy of Management Perspectives, 26*(4), 66–85. https://doi.org/10.5465/AMP.2012.0088

Virtual Business Incubators: A Support for Entrepreneurship in Rural Areas?

Jörg Freiling, Leon Marquardt, and Tatevik Reit

1 Introduction

There is growing evidence that accelerating value creation through entrepreneurial activities (Bosma et al., 2020) depends to a large extent on basing such activities on vibrant urban entrepreneurial hotspots like Silicon Valley or Tel Aviv (Startup Genome, 2020). In the case of rural environments, given a lack of support infrastructure, entrepreneurship can hardly reap its potential as a formidable driver of job creation, innovation, and economic growth (Dhahri & Omri, 2018; Ihugba et al., 2013). Rural regions have become increasingly decoupled from the high speed of innovation and digital transformation in bigger cities and urban agglomerations. This decoupling is reinforced by an unfortunate combination of poor socioeconomic environment and infrastructure, low population density, aging population, and distance from markets and services (Brown & Schafft, 2011; Easterlin et al., 2011; OECD, 2020). Policy makers in rural regions find themselves confronted with the question of how to fight this disadvantageous development (Müller, 2016; Ribeiro-Soriano, 2017), to stem the tide of migration to cities, and to close the gap between city and countryside. The obstacles to rural entrepreneurs are often insurmountable, forcing them to move their business to urban areas to access a supportive environment and to leave the rural region for good (Mack & Mayer, 2016; Roundy & Bayer, 2019). Given the difficulty faced by policy makers seeking to provide sufficient entrepreneurial resources in quantity and quality in rural regions, this chapter presents an alternative: supporting the activities of rural entrepreneurs by embedding virtual business incubators in their entrepreneurial environment. We focus on incubators rather than accelerators as a first development step to enhance the entrepreneurial support infrastructure in rural areas.

J. Freiling · L. Marquardt (✉) · T. Reit
Faculty of Business Studies and Economics, University of Bremen, Bremen, Germany
e-mail: freiling@uni-bremen.de; Leon.marquardt@uni-bremen.de; tatevik@uni-bremen.de

L. Hornuf (ed.), *Diginomics Research Perspectives*, Advanced Studies in Diginomics and Digitalization, https://doi.org/10.1007/978-3-031-04063-4_4

A virtual business incubator (VBI) is identical to its physical counterpart—providing support services such as networks, business training, and access to funding—but differs in its lacking of physical proximity and thus offering its services virtually (Barbero et al., 2012). In bridging this geographical distance, VBIs may pave the way for overcoming resource scarcity and the lack of support infrastructure in rural areas (Zinke et al., 2018), thereby preventing potential entrepreneurs from migrating into cities (Haugh, 2020). This may hold particularly if the VBI design takes into consideration the distinct challenges of rural entrepreneurship, i.e., the lack of density and interconnectedness, limited access to upfront infrastructure, the fewer and more tenuous connections of rural entrepreneurs, and the specific market structure of rural regions (Brown & Schafft, 2011; Dabson, 2001).

The literature to date on VBIs is lacking an examination of resource transfer opportunities for rural regions. This chapter thus seeks to explore the possibilities for VBIs to facilitate entrepreneurial activities in these regions by identifying the specific traits and challenges of rural entrepreneurs and strategies for VBIs to address them. To generate insights on the mechanisms for bridging entrepreneurial resources through VBIs, this study builds on an explorative grounded theory approach, extending the work of Charmaz (2014) as a research design to generate in-depth knowledge without neglecting the contextual setting. At the core of this study is the analysis of empirical data collected through semi-structured interviews with rural entrepreneurs and representatives of virtual business incubators.

2 Conceptual Background

2.1 Entrepreneurship in Rural Areas

More recent scholarship has emphasized the importance of context in exploring and explaining entrepreneurship (Welter, 2011; Zahra, 2007), specifically the enabling and constraining influence of environment on entrepreneurial behavior (Johns, 2006). Entrepreneurial activities may run more smoothly (Welter et al., 2019) in case of a supporting institutional (Polanyi, 2001), social (Granovetter, 1985), or spatial embeddedness (Steyaert & Katz, 2004). Accordingly, entrepreneurship scholars have increasingly focused on exploring the context of entrepreneurial activities to investigate its impact on the extent and quality of these activities (e.g., Autio et al., 2014; Nijkamp, 2003). Such studies commonly address entrepreneurial activities in metropolitan regions (e.g., Audretsch & Belitski, 2017; Mason & Brown, 2014; Spigel, 2016) and do not sufficiently consider the emergence of entrepreneurship in rural settings. As an urban versus rural context of venturing seems to matter in terms of the run of events and the outcome of venturing, it is important to distinguish the peculiarities of rural areas relevant to entrepreneurship issues.

There is broad ongoing debate about the essence of rurality (Pato & Teixeira, 2016). Some approaches build on "hard" measures such as geographic scope, population density, and local economic structures, while others build on "soft" measures such as characteristics of social networks within a community (du Plessis et al., 2001; Labrianidis, 2006; Stathopoulou et al., 2004). More recent terminological approaches to rurality reflect changing perceptions of rural regions stemming from declining dependence on traditional agriculture and forestry, acknowledging the economic transformation to multi-sectoral activities (Galvão et al., 2020; Pato & Teixeira, 2016). Rural areas nevertheless continue to be characterized by fewer and less-connected resource endowments in terms of infrastructure, financial capital, and human capital, stemming from and resulting in increased resource deprivation (Lavesson, 2018; Lekhanya & Visser, 2016). Rurality is also often associated with a high degree of remoteness and, therefore, a low level of market access (Sternberg, 2009). Although the rural context has inherent shortcomings that may complicate entrepreneurial activities, some individuals do recognize and exploit entrepreneurial opportunities that stem from this context.

Even though research on rural entrepreneurship is gaining currency among entrepreneurship scholars (Pato & Teixeira, 2016), it remains a niche topic in entrepreneurship research (McElwee & Smith, 2014), leading to the absence of a uniform understanding. The variety of real-life phenomena in the realm of rural venturing leads to the considerable heterogeneity (Ward & Brown, 2009). In one of the earliest efforts to conceptualize rural entrepreneurship, Wortman (1990) defines it as "the creation of a new organization that introduces a new product, serves or creates a new market, or utilizes a new technology in a rural environment" (p. 330). Kalantaridis and Bika (2006) highlight spatial characteristics as determinants for rural entrepreneurship and describe it as an entrepreneurial activity emerging in "places characterized by large open spaces, small population settlements relative to the national context" (p. 111). Thus, rural entrepreneurship is distinguished by its spatial components (Korsgaard et al., 2015a).

While it is broadly understood that context constitutes the meaningful peculiarities of rural entrepreneurship, scholars have increasingly pointed to its content dimension by highlighting the personal traits of rural entrepreneurs. Rural entrepreneurs are found to be individuals having an intimate relationship with and emotional attachment to their (rural) home region and hence are also committed to developing it by means of their entrepreneurial action (Korsgaard et al., 2015b; McElwee & Atherton, 2011). Scholars point out the difference between rural entrepreneurship and entrepreneurship in rural areas, with the former being highly socially and economically determined by the rural setting (Akgün et al., 2010; Müller & Korsgaard, 2018) and the latter being entrepreneurial activity located in a rural area but with less engagement and lower levels of embeddedness (McElwee & Smith, 2014).

Both the specific context and the content have an impact on the process dimension of organizational phenomena (Pettigrew, 1987). Due to the different profiles of entrepreneurs and their distinct support constellations, processes often take longer and reveal a variety of interaction profiles among founders and external stakeholders (Korsgaard et al., 2015a).

The dimensions of context, content, and processes thus suggest a specific profile of rural entrepreneurship—one of rurally socialized and/or committed entrepreneurs capitalizing on the strengths and coping with specific challenges of rural regions.

Alongside the personal traits of rural entrepreneurs, research has addressed *location-specific advantages* in rural areas. These result from beneficial physical, social, and economic features that can bear entrepreneurial opportunities (Stathopoulou et al., 2004). For example, rural areas usually feature less competition, lower operating costs, proximity to spatial resources (Korsgaard et al., 2021), and often a higher level of social cohesion within their community (Müller, 2016; Pallares-Barbera et al., 2004). Entrepreneurs can also benefit from more personal networks and a sense of community within rural areas (Freire-Gibb & Nielsen, 2014). Kalantaridis and Bika (2006) argue that rural entrepreneurs also benefit from rural human capital through greater employee stability and loyalty.

Further studies in entrepreneurship research deal with obstacles to rural entrepreneurship. For example, the small population size and limited local demand hinder rural entrepreneurs from reaching economies of scale compared to urban regions with higher densities of population, potentially resulting in higher production costs (Dabson, 2001). Related to this are higher distribution and marketing costs to enter external, distant markets (Lekhanya, 2018; Sternberg, 2009). The small population size also limits the number of potential interpersonal interactions that are important for entrepreneurial survival (Francis & Sandberg, 2000). Rural areas are often associated with deep-rooted, cohesive social networks, which often serve entrepreneurs as important sources for resources (Rooks et al., 2016). Baumgartner et al. (2013), however, stress that these kinds of social settings constrain information flows through interactions often limited to family, friends, and close acquaintances. A lack of diversity of relationships may hinder crucial processes for venture development, such as outside-the-box thinking (Perry-Smith & Mannucci, 2015). Such social surroundings can also limit the emergence of entrepreneurial behavior due to the fear of social exclusion resulting from potential failure, among other possibilities. This often leads to an underdeveloped entrepreneurial culture, which has an important impact on the emergence of entrepreneurial behavior (Spigel & Harrison, 2018), and which is reflected in a less encouraging attitude toward entrepreneurial action in rural areas (Honig & Dana, 2008). Additionally, entrepreneurial ventures are often confronted with difficulties in finding access to skilled and educated human capital (Deller et al., 2019). Closely related to this is lack of knowledge due to the shortage of human capital and the absence of knowledge spillovers from other firms and universities (Audretsch & Lehmann, 2005).

In summary, research has shown that rural entrepreneurs face challenges in the low availability of entrepreneurial resources due to remoteness from vibrant entrepreneurial hotspots and, therefore, a lack of access to their agglomeration effects. Rural areas also lack the necessary network diversity, network dynamics, and entrepreneurial support infrastructure that characterize thriving entrepreneurial ecosystems, particularly in urban regions (Haugh, 2020). To tackle these regional issues, digital solutions and their ability to span geographical boundaries (Nambisan, 2017) seem promising. Research concerning such opportunities to foster entrepreneurship is nevertheless still in its infancy (Sussan & Acs, 2017). This chapter thus seeks to explore how VBIs can help overcome entrepreneurial disadvantages arising from geographic isolation.

2.2 *Virtual Business Incubators*

Our knowledge-based economy has decreased the importance of physical work spaces through the emergence of virtual networks and virtual value creation (Cakula et al., 2013). This general development has been reinforced considerably by the COVID-19 pandemic and resulting physical proximity restrictions (Engels, 2020). These trends have galvanized the development of entrepreneurial support systems, as seen in the rising number of VBIs (Hausberg & Korreck, 2020). VBIs are described in the context of physical incubators as follows: "A business incubator is a service provider that offers a comprehensive package of services (more than one) designed to support, facilitate and accelerate the growth of starting businesses. A VBI does this with services and tools that are—at least to a significant extent—independent of the location of the service provider and/or the users of these services" (Triodos Bacet, 2011, p. 22). VBIs are thus similar to their physical counterparts when it comes to the services they provide, but are decisively distinct with regard to physical space. Owing to their virtual character, VBIs are able to bundle and provide international resources in the form of expert knowledge and advice, a network of entrepreneurs and investors from all over the world, international virtual training programs, and online access to financing and funding without requiring physical proximity (Triodos Bacet, 2011; Tsai et al., 2009).

Interestingly, research on VBIs began even before they actually existed. Nowak and Grantham (2000) introduced a conceptual model of a virtual incubator, which should be Internet-based and possess formalized control systems, a market focus, distributed resources, management expertise, and a focus on human resources and human capital. They stress the relevance of VBIs for fragmented industries such as the IT sector, as VBIs bundle distributed resources and make them available to entrepreneurs who otherwise could not access them. Barbero et al. (2012) emphasize that VBIs facilitate the early strategic alliance formation between individuals, groups, and institutions that could not have taken place physically due to geographical distances. VBIs thus have clear relevance to the circumstances of incubatees from remote areas, who are mostly fragmented and often seek to overcome their lack of access to relevant business resources by migrating to startup hubs in larger cities (Dabson, 2001).

von Zedtwitz (2003) adds that, unlike physical business incubators, VBIs do not focus on a specific industry or a geographical area, but rather center on entrepreneurial needs. In further comparison with physical business incubators, VBIs enjoy significantly higher market reach and larger social networks through their location independence. Thus, incubatees are provided access to their relevant market and a network of fellow entrepreneurs, investors, and advisors without having to leave their environment. Another essential quality of VBIs is their flexibility in providing an exact match between entrepreneurial needs and VBI resources. Many entrepreneurs struggle to find specific advice for their business in their environment. This challenge could be met by the huge entrepreneurial and expert networks of VBIs, whose databases enable entrepreneurs to find resource providers fitting their specific needs (von Zedtwitz, 2003).

Carayannis and von Zedtwitz (2005) emphasize the relevance of VBIs in less-developed entrepreneurial economies as they bridge divides in knowledge, digitalization, socioeconomic policy, and culture, and increase accessibility and availability of financial, human, intellectual, and social capital. However, despite their large networks, the interaction between entrepreneurs in VBIs is relatively low and left to the entrepreneurs' initiative (von Zedtwitz, 2003). This means that the crucial benefit of location-independent connections and resources would be reserved for those entrepreneurs who actively pursue such resources from the VBI.

Despite its history of more than 20 years, the VBI literature is still in its infancy. The most relevant papers date to the 2000s, when VBIs and their potential were not as established as they are today and thus could not be examined in their current breadth of context. Their growing practical relevance and increasing number further point to the merits of continued research. VBIs' lack of location dependencies and their capacities to bundle and match resources make them particularly interesting in the context of rural entrepreneurship, as they address its particular challenges while conserving its inherent benefits.

3 Method

3.1 Research Design

This study follows the social constructivist approach adopted by Charmaz (2014), acknowledging that the observations are closely interrelated with the context, socially constructed, and subject to the interpretations of the authors. Considering that rural entrepreneurship is highly dependent on the context where it occurs, this study does not aim to generalize the findings but to observe and analyze the interviewees' perceptions and experiences to understand the respective setting through a single case study (Yin, 2017). Since there is little knowledge on how VBIs can support entrepreneurs in rural areas, this qualitative approach appears suitable to explore resource interaction opportunities.

3.2 Data Selection and Collection

This study applies its design in one of the most rural regions in Germany—Lower Saxony—as a unit of analysis reflective of the context described above. Lower Saxony was selected as it is the second-largest federal state in Germany with a rather low population density containing urban centers, but more importantly a lot of rural areas (Statistisches Bundesamt, 2021). Interestingly, Lower Saxony is one of the top five federal states in terms of foundations, and hence ranks above the average rate for Germany (Bundesverband Deutsche Startups, 2020). Furthermore, Lower Saxony is notable for a high number of startup support initiatives at the state and regional levels.

Primary data sources are in-depth interviews with founders in rural areas as well as interviews with employees of VBIs. The former were identified via the personal network of the authors and the online platform "startup.niedersachsen."[1] VBI employees were identified through web search. These data sources allow a comprehensive view of the support of entrepreneurial activities in rural regions, directly addressing the primary aims of this research. Following theoretical sampling principles suggested by Glaser and Strauss (1967) for data selection, potential interviewees had to fulfill certain criteria. For entrepreneurs, the requirements were to have a business located in a town or municipality with a population of fewer than 20,000 and located more than 30 km away from a major urban center, or else to have grown up in such a place. Incubators had to have a program that consisted largely of digital elements. Potential interviewees were then contacted via email or LinkedIn. In total, six interviews were conducted between April and September 2021, meeting the requirement of a qualitative single case study (Eisenhardt, 1989).

The primary data consist of six interviews with five entrepreneurs located in rural areas and two managers of VBIs (see Table 1). The secondary data result from the screening and analysis of public statistics and the websites and social media channels of the interviewees to gather further information regarding governmental initiatives, business backgrounds, and the incubation programs. The interviews lasted between 30 and 100 min, were held virtually via Zoom (as necessitated by the COVID-19 pandemic), and conducted in German as the preferred language of the interviewees. The empirical data were generated using a semi-structured interview guide based on open-ended questions. The first part of the interview guide facilitated storytelling and focused on personal backgrounds, founding and business processes, and perceptions of the rural context. The second part focused on perceived resource shortcomings as well as resource mobilization and interaction. The interview recordings were then transcribed using the InqScribe[2] and MAXQDA.[3]

[1] See: https://startup.nds.de/

[2] See: https://www.inqscribe.com/

[3] See: https://www.maxqda.de/

Table 1 Interviewee profiles

Interviewee	Business	Comments
Entrepreneur 1	Platform	Platform to support farmers and ensure fair dealing for them and their goods
Entrepreneur 2		
Entrepreneur 3	Coworking space	Professional experience in a corporate incubator program
Entrepreneur 4	Platform	Tourism platform to connect travelers with alternative camping sites
Entrepreneur 5	Platform	Platform for the referral of craftsmen
Expert 1	Virtual business incubator	Focusing on individuals associated with a university
Expert 2	Virtual business incubator	Focusing on digital innovation

3.3 Data Analysis

In a grounded theory approach, coding refers to a multistage analysis in which the researchers process the data into codes, concepts, and categories that the researchers continuously validate, develop, and relate to each other (Strauss & Corbin, 2010; Strübing, 2014). Coding is thus an iterative, creative, and interactive process of understanding and interpreting text passages, which means that the researcher takes an active part through labeling and constructing the data (Breuer, 2010). According to Charmaz (2014), coding in grounded theory research consists of two types: initial coding and focused coding.

During the initial coding, the researchers created codes by defining and labeling the collected data while remaining open and allowing topics to emerge by staying close to the data (Charmaz, 2014). Following this coding strategy, the transcripts were coded with MAXQDA and resulted in a total of 702 initial codes. The number of codes for each interview ranged from 65 to 130. During the coding procedure, the researchers used the most significant and frequent codes to sift the empirical focused data and categorize the data "incisively and completely" (Charmaz, 2014). The initial codes were processed into eleven categories. Through further analysis (similar to axial coding) and discussions between the researchers involved, these categories were synthesized and related to each other, resulting in three categories (see Sect. 4.2).

3.4 Research Validity

Qualitative research requires the fulfillment of quality criteria, particularly when many investigations using other than statistical research methods are generally referred to as qualitative studies without further quality requirements (Ali & Yusof, 2011). In order to ensure data rigor, different triangulation methods have been applied. Data triangulation has been used by collecting and analyzing primary data in the form of semi-structured interviews and secondary data in the form of blogs, websites, social media content, and newspaper articles concerning the interviewees and the conceptual research topics as suggested by Yin (2017) and Eisenhardt (1989). Method triangulation has been applied by considering interviews as well as secondary documents and observations. Furthermore, all researchers were involved in the development of the interview guides and the collection and analyses of the data. The authors individually developed codes and categories and discussed the results with each other for purposes of investigator triangulation (Guion et al., 2011). Regular discussions among the researchers relating to the challenges and outcomes of the research were held in order to eliminate researcher bias as much as possible. This method of peer debriefing has been additionally deepened through discussion of relevant codes and methods for categorization (Krefting, 1991).

4 Findings

4.1 Case Description

This section presents the personal background of the five entrepreneurs and their businesses to provide information regarding their motivation to locate their entrepreneurial ventures in rural areas. The backgrounds of the two VBI employees are then presented. These descriptions are based on the first part of the interviews and the complementary secondary data.

The venture of Entrepreneur 1 and Entrepreneur 2 is located in a rural area between Hamburg and Bremen. Both founders have an academic background—one in energy and environmental management and the other in renewable raw materials and renewable energies. After traveling around Europe together, they founded their business in July 2019. Their venture provides a platform that aims to connect farmers and end consumers to nurture sustainable agriculture. Similar to well-known crowdfunding concepts, regional agricultural businesses are financially supported in their transformation from traditional to organic sustainable farming and the expansion of their direct marketing. In return for financial support, end consumers receive products and/or services from the farms of the region. The founders' goal is to promote sustainable ecological agriculture in Germany. With their business, they have participated in a physical accelerator program and in a virtual incubation program.

With a degree in management and entrepreneurship, Entrepreneur 3 started her business in the middle of Lower Saxony. Afterward, she was employed by a PR agency and then for several years as communication manager in a corporate incubator program that provides coworking facilities, funding, and other support to startups. Four years ago, during her pregnancy, Entrepreneur 3 and her husband decided to move to the husband's hometown to be able to raise their children in a calmer environment. With a friend from this town, she opened a coworking space. Their services include the provision of coworking facilities with high-speed Internet. They also offer their premises for rent for hosting various courses such as local yoga classes and educational courses. More recently, they have begun using their facilities to host community events. With their venture, the founders want to facilitate the compatibility of life in the countryside with career success. Entrepreneur 3 also supports the local community by sharing her expertise regarding marketing and entrepreneurship.

Entrepreneur 4 founded his business in the southwest of Lower Saxony. Prior to his entrepreneurial career, he studied tourism management. Following his study program, he completed an internship at a startup active in alternative tourism in Hamburg, where he gained his first experience with startup processes. Driven by his passion for nature and his startup experience, Entrepreneur 4 developed his idea of a tourism marketplace. Since 2020, this C2C platform has enabled camping tourists to book camping sites on the private premises of locals far from crowded camping spots. He chose his place of operation because he knows the place very well, having grown up there and maintaining his local personal networks. He also appreciates the beauty of this place and perceives it as a good place to start offering camping sites within this region. He is responsible for quality management and maintains contact with the hosts, takes care of the website and service optimizations, and expands his network of hosts. Through his business, Entrepreneur 4 seeks to minimize the distance between city and country lifestyles.

Entrepreneur 5 is located in the middle of Lower Saxony. Before launching his venture, he did an apprenticeship as a mechatronics engineer and studied international industrial engineering. During an internship abroad, he gained experience in an AI startup. Entrepreneur 5 then worked as an operating engineer for a couple of years. While employed, he helped a friend launch a startup, which triggered his desire to start his own business. Together with a friend, he worked on the idea of an online platform that connects craftsmen and customers, which they launched in August 2020. At the time of the interview, Entrepreneur 5 explained that he no longer operates from his rural hometown since he wanted to live in a bigger city. Further, he argues that he benefits from operating in the city due to the high number of craftsmen in his physical proximity.

Expert 1 works in a VBI associated with a university. This VBI provides its services to students, graduates, scientists, and other employees associated with the university. It supports these groups in turning their business ideas into business plans. The VBI developed out of a campus initiative launched by a research institute in 2015. Expert 1 is working there as a startup manager, and is responsible for startups that have been granted business startup funding. Additionally, he conducts first consultations to nascent teams and guides them, starting with their idea phase through to the founding of their business and beyond, for as long as they remain affiliated with the university. He is also involved in improving the VBI's virtual support platform and organizing its startup podcast.

Expert 2 works for a VBI funded by public entities. It started operating in 2019 and aims to foster entrepreneurs focusing on digital innovation. Entrepreneurs must meet three requirements to participate in the incubation program. First, the venture has to be based on a digital business model. Second, it needs to be innovative. Third, it needs to be scalable in the long term. After acceptance, entrepreneurs can receive free coaching and access a network of startups, established firms, and universities. Expert 2 has a background in political science with a focus on governance. She previously worked as a networker for educational institutions. Within the VBI, she supervises and supports the founders in general matters but also in its networking activities.

4.2 How Virtual Business Incubators Can Support Entrepreneurship in Rural Areas

The empirical findings (translated for this volume by the authors) reveal that rural entrepreneurs in Lower Saxony face a variety of challenges when launching and operating their ventures. They also show how VBIs seek to lift barriers stemming from geographical isolation. Through comparing and synthesizing these two bodies of data, three distinct categories emerged that illuminate how VBIs specifically support entrepreneurs in rural areas: (1) balancing time shortages, (2) extending entrepreneurial networks, and (3) providing an entrepreneurial community and culture.

4.2.1 Balancing Time Shortages

Empirical data reveals how challenging the early business phase is. The entrepreneurs are all in the early stages of their business venturing and share the experience of time constraints.

The majority emphasize that they are on their own or have only a small team they can rely on, and are thus subject to a busy daily schedule, as Entrepreneur 5 describes: "There are only two of us trying to push this business idea and [his colleague] also has another job. My day is therefore filled with many tasks and appointments." Entrepreneur 3 points to severe time constraints as she has to take care of her family: "It is sometimes very challenging to juggle the kids, family and all the different tasks that come up every day. So, it's not unusual for me to work at home in the evening as well."

The entrepreneurs commonly agreed that they usually do not have enough time to participate in any entrepreneurship-related events in distant cities. Considering that VBIs provide their services virtually, travel time to incubator facilities is no longer required. However, as Entrepreneur 2 points out, participation in such virtual events is still not entirely possible due to scheduling problems: "We always had that in the evening, when you have actually already worked all day and your head is actually already empty. Actually, I think it's exciting to have something like that in the morning, but of course, it's super difficult to coordinate, because there are a lot of people who are working or doing whatever, going to university or something." As Expert 2 describes: "[. . .] the fluctuation is greater and the expectation is also greater, because if [incubatees] say, 'no, that doesn't fit [my schedule], what kind of rubbish is that, not worth my time,' then they just leave again." In this regard, Entrepreneur 1 appreciates asynchronous elements during her participation in a VBI, as she explains: "[. . .] that means you could download [the recording] afterwards, if you don't have time or couldn't watch the call." Expert 2 further stresses: "I think anything [virtually synchronous] over one to two hours should not be done [. . .] because there is also no longer virtual attention span [. . .] then it becomes critical." The majority of the founders showed great interest in virtual events and saw the great advantage of being able to participate in them regardless of location. It also came through that they appreciate being able to try out new formats of events. Nevertheless, they are sometimes confronted with incompatible schedules due to other duties. Therefore, they praised the advantages of content being accessible independent of time.

Ongoing and steadily increasing digitalization has changed the context of entrepreneurship, which has become less bound and less predefined. In that regard, entrepreneurial processes and outcomes tend to be less timely and geographically restrained, while at the same time being more collective (Nambisan, 2017). The VBI literature reflects this development, documenting how VBIs offer location-independent support services to geographically dispersed entrepreneurs (Tsai et al., 2009). Scholars emphasize that entrepreneurs can utilize these services in a flexible and cost-efficient manner better suited to today's entrepreneurial activities (Byarugaba, 2016). However, the VBI literature does not go much further than the geographical dimension and associated time savings when addressing increased flexibility. The empirical data shows that the interviewees have limited time capacity to engage in additional events due to the fact that they mostly act alone and have more pressing duties. They commonly see the value of taking part in VBI events remotely, but argue that it does not completely lift their time constraints. Rather, their observations indicate that the possibility of making use of time-independent content is promising in terms of improving the entrepreneurial circumstances in rural areas. Therefore, VBIs should provide suitable elements in asynchronous formats to provide access that is not only detached from the geographic location but also from time constraints. By doing so, VBIs can offer components of e-learning programs that are considered beneficial to entrepreneurial learning (Radović-Marković et al., 2017).

4.2.2 Extending Entrepreneurial Networks

Scholars examining entrepreneurship in rural areas commonly identify a lack of the resources necessary to enable productive entrepreneurship. During the analysis of the collected data, a similar pattern became evident, leading to the emergence of the second category. The interviewees in this sample express a lack of resources in their surroundings. Interestingly, resources were not addressed on an individual basis but related to the absence of entrepreneurial networks.

As Entrepreneur 5 describes: "What happens during the founding process is that you are faced with problems that you have to solve somehow and you look for people around you who have that kind of knowledge in this field, but these are rare here." He stresses that you "have to have people who already have the experience to just be in exchange, to avoid making every possible mistake that there is. And that saves time, money and a lot of nerves, of course." Entrepreneur 5 describes how he had "put a lot of time and effort into the business plan and all that and then it was just rejected [. . .] it would have been nice to have somebody experienced in submitting funding proposals." This highlights that the interviewees have experienced difficulties due to knowledge and relational constraints within their local communities. They especially acknowledge that other entrepreneurs could have eased the process of launching their businesses but were not present or available in their community.

Having faced similar challenges, Entrepreneur 4 explains how moving back to the city is not an option: "[This is] my hometown. I grew up here [. . .] and of course, I also have a network because I lived here until I graduated [. . .] so the networks are actually my friends, [. . .] that's how it is in the country [. . .] You know each other, you appreciate each other. And in the city . . . it's exactly the opposite." In contrast, Entrepreneur 5 explains why he left the rural area after launching his business: "I moved here because I wanted a bit to live in a larger city, no longer in such a small village. Why we located our business here in the region is simply because here we can talk with the craftsmen more easily and are simply on the spot and we just wanted to test it out here." Here, we observed that these entrepreneurs give a different value to their personal and business networks. Nevertheless, VBIs support entrepreneurs in building a business network by connecting them with coaches, mentors, investors, and, more importantly in these cases, fellow entrepreneurs (Carayannis & von Zedtwitz, 2005). This is illustrated by Entrepreneur 1, who takes part in a virtual business incubation program: "Can you actually see and implement the business model in a different way? I have to say that I now understand companies much better. I now understand, [fellow entrepreneurs] have this business model and have launched this business this certain way and [. . .] so it's really helpful." Aligning with Entrepreneur 4 and Entrepreneur 5, she highlights that being part of this incubation model is very beneficial in terms of peer learning within the incubation program, emphasizing that "[. . .] you can do that online, too. I don't see any limits there." Expert 1 described this process from the VBI's perspective: "When we talk to the founders, I try to recommend people from my network—experts or other entrepreneurs –and say, 'talk to him, talk to him.' If I had met them live on-site, then I could have just taken them by the hand and just gone over there. Now I email or call the person beforehand and tell him or her what it is all about [. . .] so it still works nearly the same way." VBIs connect their incubatees with people and organizations that can support their venturing processes. The virtual setting was not perceived as a constraint for this purpose.

Given the absence of entrepreneurial networks witnessed by the interviewees, it was observed that VBIs can compensate for these deficiencies. Considering the motive of Entrepreneur 5 to leave the countryside given the inability to access crucial resources (i.e., craftsmen) that his business model depends on, it is questionable whether VBIs would have been able to prevent him from relocating his business due to its large geographic scope. Expert 2 describes applying a narrower geographic scope and focusing on connecting people mostly at the state level: "[. . .] together with a [state-wide] partner [. . .]—and that's our big benefit here—we offer a very strong network of regional business representatives and also the universities." Expert 1 adds: "We have a number of founders who said that, thanks to the support they have received from us and the fact that we have helped them to build up their network, they have said that they will stay here. [. . .] they say, 'oh yes, we have built up our network here and we have made a name for ourselves here and now we can also earn money here. If we now pack our bags and go to Hamburg, no one will know us.' And for some, that's really the reason to stay here, and then to launch their business here, in the more rural area." Considering the statements of Expert 1 and Expert 2, it can be concluded that VBIs are able not only to bridge entrepreneurial resources at the individual level by connecting distant actors to facilitate virtual resource mobilization, but also to foster the development of entrepreneurial networks at the regional level by connecting local actors with each other to facilitate regional resource mobilization.

Economic action is embedded in social structures (Granovetter, 1985). Networks thus play a crucial role in the emergence and persistence of entrepreneurial behavior (Lafuente et al., 2007). The presence of dynamic entrepreneurial networks enables information flows and provides access to knowledge, capital, and labor (Malecki, 2018). In the rural context, however, the number of actors and consequently the size of one's potential network are a lot smaller. As a result, entrepreneurs in rural areas accumulate and make use of much less social capital than urban entrepreneurs (Bauernschuster et al., 2010). This is supported by the empirical data of this study—the entrepreneurs all expressed difficulties in launching their businesses due to the rural social structures. Notably, they did not relate this to financial capital or human capital, but rather their access to regional businesses and other entrepreneurs for knowledge-sharing purposes. The VBIs in this study thus represent a promising intermediary organization. Not only do they match entrepreneurs with coaches, mentors, and other resource providers to support their business ventures, but interviewees also emphasized the value of connecting incubatees with one another to mutually learn from experience. The VBI literature has demonstrated how these organizations provide entrepreneurs with access to business and knowledge networks. In this study, the VBIs also develop their own virtual entrepreneurial networks that help incubatees to succeed with their ventures. These entrepreneurs tend to stay in the region because they are able to become more regionally embedded. In this sense, it seems that geographical scope does matter in the virtual setting, a finding that has not been discussed in VBI scholarship.

4.2.3 Providing An Entrepreneurial Community and Culture

Closely related to the entrepreneurial networks described in the previous section, the empirical data reveals that the interviewees were not just challenged by the low levels of resource endowment in the rural setting but also by the lack of a supportive entrepreneurial community and culture.

The entrepreneurs lament that the local community has no entrepreneurial mindset. Entrepreneur 5, for example, describes the community's lack of "ability to look beyond the end of their nose, out of the village, out of the country [. . .] My friends and family are generally so focused on such things [. . .] such a limited way of thinking. That's even more common in the countryside." Accordingly, Entrepreneur 4 states that "It's very unusual to do something new here," adding that "Everywhere it's already being destroyed at the core. So, that is somehow the mindset. I think it's due to the . . . yes, I think it's just a country thing. It's always been that way and it always will be that way and change is always something that is critically eyed, unfortunately." Starting a business in the countryside is perceived as strange by the local culture, with entrepreneurial behavior being viewed critically not only during the founding process, but even earlier at the idea phase. Reflecting on her experience working in an urban business incubator program, Entrepreneur 3 explains: "Of course [people in the countryside] are clearly more risk-averse than in the city," indicating rural skepticism about founding a business and the risks it entails. The interviewees engaged in entrepreneurial activities *despite* the absence of an entrepreneurial mindset and the associated support and encouragement. This can be especially challenging in terms of initiating the founding process, as Entrepreneur 5 explains: "[. . .] basically you have to google it all, find necessary information and then just look if it is also applicable to your situation. [When it works out,] it gives an insane motivational boost that you do not get in this wasteland." Entrepreneur 4 adds: "it's good that the internet exists; it gives you cool examples of other founders that made it through very similar difficulties, but it definitely takes a lot of [one's own] initiative and action." Entrepreneur 4 describes that it would have been easier if "it was simply a 'hey, someone wants to start a business, let's support him' mindset in the community—that would certainly be an incredibly important factor for me, if I could utilize their knowledge and experience. Above all I would not have felt so foreign and alone sometimes and doubted so much myself and my project." Both founders stressed that they had to rely on the Internet not only to access crucial information but, more importantly, for emotional support. In line with the problems perceived due to the lack of a local entrepreneurial spirit, Entrepreneur 2 shares that the program of the VBI is important to them since it made them realize that they "[. . .] are not so exotic, there are people who think like us. It is really, really great that [the VBI] bundles these people, that you don't think that you're alone and that you're fighting alone. That really pushed us." In this sense, the VBI's program is not just important in terms of transferring resources but also as a source of motivation (Zedtwitz & Grimaldi, 2006). Additionally, they describe that they grew closer together with participants from other enterprises and take care of them, as Entrepreneur 1 stated: "Because he says he can't cope with [all the tasks] otherwise.

He just does everything, but forgets about himself. That's why we said ... I ask him every two weeks, 'how is your well-being?'" This illustrates that the VBI's program can also nurture the development of a caring community. Not only do the interactions between incubatees contribute to this supporting community, but also the VBI's team plays an important role. As Expert 2 describes her position: "it's not just a consulting job; somehow it's really rather an accompanying job [. . .] like a kind of [incubator-]mom. You're there, you're just always there, you listen, you have your ears open, and you always have to be on the lookout for the incubatees." It is clear that interactions in a VBI's program are based not only on professional but also interpersonal relationships.

In entrepreneurship studies, culture has been identified as an important determinant for entrepreneurial activities (Saxenian, 1994). It represents the extent to which entrepreneurial behavior is valued at the regional or community level (Fritsch & Wyrwich, 2014), and reflects the local norms and beliefs that make entrepreneurial action acceptable or even desirable (Kibler et al., 2015). This is closely connected to the cognitive dimension of social networks (Inkpen & Tsang, 2005; Kibler et al., 2014). In rural settings, resource sharing is mostly based on shared values (Rooks et al., 2016); therefore, regional culture exerts even greater influence than in other contexts. This also relates to the emotional support that entrepreneurs receive from their local community. Such support is crucial because emotional state impacts an entrepreneur's ability to engage in nascent entrepreneurial activities, as well as the ability to absorb information effectively and efficiently (Baron et al., 2012; Domurath & Patzelt, 2016; Patzelt & Shepherd, 2011). The entrepreneurs in this study perceive their region and community as closed-minded concerning creating something new, constantly questioning perceptions of their entrepreneurial actions by the local community. As a result, they have faced difficulties in keeping up their motivation and have even felt isolated as a result. By connecting entrepreneurs virtually, VBIs can create a space for these like-minded individuals to meet and relieve them of the feeling of being on the outside. In this sense, VBIs can provide a substitute community that is based on the same shared values and, by doing so, render emotional support to entrepreneurs in rural regions. This could not only positively affect established entrepreneurial ventures, but could also improve the likelihood of others engaging in entrepreneurial activities in regions without a supportive culture.

5 Discussion

The aim of this study is to clarify how VBIs can support entrepreneurial activities in rural regions. The answer to this research question is manifold, but begins with the pivotal role of context (Welter et al., 2019; Zahra et al., 2014). Given the distinctive nature of starting a business in rural settings (Freire-Gibb & Nielsen, 2014; Kalantaridis & Bika, 2006; Korsgaard et al., 2021; Müller, 2016; Pallares-Barbera et al., 2004), tailoring VBI program content to the context of rural venturing may bring VBIs into a favorable position compared to similar virtual or physical institutions. Certain challenges rural entrepreneurs are confronted with could be a focal point of program deployment. Avoiding wasting the precious time of rural entrepreneurs appears to be a feature these entrepreneurs particularly appreciate. VBIs are in an outstanding position to shorten certain processes, to offer them flexibly, or even to make them obsolete. The associated savings of such scarce resources may contribute considerably to supporting entrepreneurial activities in rural regions.

A second strong support function of VBIs relates to the core resources of venturing. While past scholarship provides extensive catalogs of valuable resources for venture development (Freiling & Baron, 2017), this study emphasizes the crucial role of social capital and helps specify what kinds of social capital rural entrepreneurs appreciate. Rural entrepreneurs express a strong relationship and commitment to their home region, as familiarity with the situation where they have lived leads to a certain socialization that makes them feel comfortable. Rural entrepreneurs are thus dependent to a large extent on their strong and long-lasting relationships. Nevertheless, they need help from outside their rural home, which is often physically hard to achieve. By virtue of their location independence, VBIs are uniquely positioned to overcome this obstacle. Networks can be made broader and richer by bridging physical distances to resources outside the rural area.

This second supportive function is in many ways interconnected with a third function relating to entrepreneurial spirit and culture. While it may be impossible to characterize the countryside in a uniform manner, there are certain aspects that make a difference between urban and rural areas (Rooks et al., 2016). Rural areas tend to be much more conservative in terms of behavior and thinking. This is reinforced by the simple fact that new developments, particularly of the disruptive kind, reach urban areas earlier and with greater magnitude. In rural regions, however, belief in the value of the established context is quite strong, and while this does not prevent entrepreneurial activities, it does make them harder to set in motion. The absence of entrepreneurial support infrastructure reinforces this situation and the related rigidities. VBIs connect different communities and facilitate a certain entrepreneurial communion among the incubatees. This study also reveals that other entrepreneurs and their behavior have a strong influence on rural entrepreneurs in softening the rigidities that inhibit their development.

6 Conclusion

VBIs provide entrepreneurs support for their business development. Their particular benefits lie in their lack of location dependency and their large pool of resources consisting of experts, mentors, and entrepreneurs. These characteristics meet rural entrepreneurs' challenges of remoteness and lack of access to entrepreneurial resources. However, rural entrepreneurs can be faced with specific conditions that have to be considered in tailoring a VBI program to the needs of rural entrepreneurs.

In this section. These conditions will be discussed in the context of this research's implications, together with its limitations, and prospects for future research.

6.1 Limitations

Efforts, such as the measures taken for qualitative rigor, have been made to present this research as objectively and precisely as possible. However, as a qualitative study, it is still exposed to some limitations.

Although triangulation methods have been applied, there is still the possibility that the researchers influenced the results through their subjective perceptions, interpretations, and biases. This might have happened partially due to the fact that the rural entrepreneurial environment in its empirical context was relatively new to the researchers. Past scholarship has suggested spending an extended period of time (approximately 4 months to 1 year) in the research field while collecting data in order to gain the participants' trust, make oneself familiar with the situation, and thus achieve more trustworthy results (Morse et al., 2002). Due to COVID-19, the different geographical contexts of the interviewees, and restricted time capacities, we did not spend the suggested time in the interviewees' environment. This exposes this research to the risk that interviewees might have said what they thought the researchers wanted to hear due to the lack of familiarity (Brink, 1993).

Additionally, the data rests more or less on snapshots taken from the informants. To fulfill the aims of the research with greater depth and breadth, a more evolutionary lens would be useful.

6.2 Implications

This study shows that there is a particular need for the development of VBIs for rural entrepreneurs to overcome the challenges which hinder entrepreneurial development in rural areas. However, these VBIs should be tailored to rural founders' specific entrepreneurial needs in order to exploit their full potential.

Given that rural founders are often early-stage entrepreneurs with existing full-time jobs, the rural VBI should pay attention to offering enough digitally asynchronous content and make synchronous content available to its incubatees later in their engagement. In this context, the synchronous services of the VBI should be planned in a flexible way, giving the incubatees the opportunity to arrange extracurricular appointments individually or in small groups.

Furthermore, supportive rural entrepreneurial communities are a much needed but lacking resource in the countryside. Therefore, the rural VBI should make sure not to focus only on providing international networks, but to also create and offer a regional community of rural entrepreneurs for mutual emotional support.

6.3 Future Research

This research provides novel insights by embedding VBIs in the rural entrepreneurial context. In order to extend these outcomes, future research should focus on revealing further specific needs of rural entrepreneurs and how the VBI program can be continuously adapted to make it as effective as possible.

The results further show that regional communities are essential for rural entrepreneurs. In this context, future studies should investigate whether for regional purposes it would be more effective for VBIs to develop local communities and their interaction physically on-site and thus become hybrid business incubators.

The specialization of VBIs on local circumstances proved to be relevant for the incubators' and the entrepreneurs' success. It would be interesting to see if—and, if so, how—this context applies to other geographical, cultural, and educational environments. Future research might thus consider VBI support in economically underdeveloped regions, to migrant and refugee entrepreneurs, or in university and school contexts.

References

Akgün, A. A., Nijkamp, P., Baycan, T., & Brons, M. (2010). Embeddedness of entrepreneurs in rural areas: A comparative rough set data analysis. *Tijdschrift voor Economische en Sociale Geografie, 101*(5), 538–553. https://doi.org/10.1111/j.1467-9663.2010.00630.x

Ali, A. M., & Yusof, H. (2011). Quality in qualitative studies: The case of validity, reliability and generalizability. *Issues In Social And Environmental Accounting, 5*(1), 25. https://doi.org/10.22164/isea.v5i1.59

Audretsch, D. B., & Belitski, M. (2017). Entrepreneurial ecosystems in cities: Establishing the framework conditions. *Journal of Technology Transfer, 42*(5), 1030–1051. https://doi.org/10.1007/s10961-016-9473-8

Audretsch, D. B., & Lehmann, E. E. (2005). Does the knowledge spillover theory of entrepreneurship hold for regions? *Research Policy, 34*(8), 1191–1202. https://doi.org/10.1016/j.respol.2005.03.012

Autio, E., Kenney, M., Mustar, P., Siegel, D., & Wright, M. (2014). Entrepreneurial innovation: The importance of context. *Research Policy, 43*(7), 1097–1108. https://doi.org/10.1016/j.respol.2014.01.015

Barbero, J. L., Casillas, J. C., Ramos, A., & Guitar, S. (2012). Revisiting incubation performance: How incubator typology affects results. *Technological Forecasting and Social Change, 79*(5), 888–902. https://doi.org/10.1016/j.techfore.2011.12.003

Baron, R. A., Hmieleski, K. M., & Henry, R. A. (2012). Entrepreneurs' dispositional positive affect: The potential benefits – and potential costs – of being "up". *Journal of Business Venturing, 27*(3), 310–324. https://doi.org/10.1016/j.jbusvent.2011.04.002

Bauernschuster, S., Falck, O., & Heblich, S. (2010). Social capital access and entrepreneurship. *Journal of Economic Behavior and Organization, 76*(3), 821–833. https://doi.org/10.1016/j.jebo.2010.09.014

Baumgartner, D., Pütz, M., & Seidl, I. (2013). What kind of entrepreneurship drives regional development in European non-core regions? A literature review on empirical entrepreneurship research. *European Planning Studies, 21*(8), 1095–1127. https://doi.org/10.1080/09654313.2012.722937

Bosma, N., Hill, S., Ionescu-Somers, A., Kelley, D., Levie, J., & Tarnawa, A. (2020). *Global entrepreneurship monitor 2019/2020 global report.*

Breuer, F. (2010). Der Forschungsstil der grounded theory. In *Reflexive grounded theory* (pp. 39–114). VS Verlag für Sozialwissenschaften. https://doi.org/10.1007/978-3-531-92580-6_2

Brink, H. I. L. (1993). Validity and reliability in qualitative research. *Curationis, 16*(2), 35–38

Brown, D. L., & Schafft, K. A. (2011). *Rural people and communities in the 21st century: Resilience and transformation* (2nd ed.). Polity Press.

Bundesverband Deutsche Startups. (2020). *Deutscher Startup Monitor 2020.*

Byarugaba, B. (2016). The role of virtual business incubation services in enterprise development: A critical analysis of international best practices. *International Journal of Technology and Management, 1*(1), 1–14. http://ijotm.utamu.ac.ug

Cakula, S., Jakobsone, A., & Motejlek, J. (2013). Virtual business support infrastructure for entrepreneurs. *Procedia Computer Science, 25*, 281–288. https://doi.org/10.1016/j.procs.2013.11.034

Carayannis, E. G., & von Zedtwitz, M. (2005). Architecting gloCal (global-local), real-virtual incubator networks (G-RVINs) as catalysts and accelerators of entrepreneurship in transitioning and developing economies: Lessons learned and best practices from current development and business incubation. *Technovation, 25*(2), 95–110. https://doi.org/10.1016/S0166-4972(03)00072-5

Charmaz, K. (2014). *Constructing grounded theory* (2nd ed.). sage.

Dabson, B. (2001). Supporting rural entrepreneurship. *Rural Development Paper Series* (pp. 1–13).

Deller, S., Kures, M., & Conroy, T. (2019). Rural entrepreneurship and migration. *Journal of Rural Studies, 66*, 30–42. https://doi.org/10.1016/j.jrurstud.2019.01.026

Dhahri, S., & Omri, A. (2018). Entrepreneurship contribution to the three pillars of sustainable development: What does the evidence really say? *World Development, 106*, 64–77. https://doi.org/10.1016/j.worlddev.2018.01.008

Domurath, A., & Patzelt, H. (2016). Entrepreneurs' assessments of early international entry: The role of foreign social ties, venture absorptive capacity, and generalized trust in others. *Entrepreneurship: Theory and Practice, 40*(5), 1149–1177. https://doi.org/10.1111/etap.12164

du Plessis, V., Beshiri, R., Bollman, R. D., Canada, S., Clemenson, H., Chartrand, D., Vani, R., Hillary, N., Burroughs, R., Mogan, A., Bourque, L., Beaulieu, M., & Bourdeau, J. (2001). *Rural and Small Town Canada Analysis Bulletin*, 3(3). Analysis Bulletin Catalogue no. 21-006-XIE.

Easterlin, R. A., Angelescu, L., & Zweig, J. S. (2011). The impact of modern economic growth on urban-rural differences in subjective well-being. *World Development, 39*(12), 2187–2198. https://doi.org/10.1016/j.worlddev.2011.04.015

Eisenhardt, K. M. (1989). Building theories from case study research. *The Academy of Management Review, 14*(4), 532. https://doi.org/10.2307/258557

Engels, B. (2020). *Corona: Stresstest für die Digitalisierung in Deutschland.* Institut der deutschen Wirtschaft (IW). http://hdl.handle.net/10419/215503www.econstor.eu

Francis, D. H., & Sandberg, W. R. (2000). Friendship within entrepreneurial teams and its association with team and venture performance. *Entrepreneurship Theory and Practice, 25*(2), 5–26. https://doi.org/10.1177/104225870002500201

Freiling, J., & Baron, T. (2017). A resource-based view of entrepreneurial ecosystems. In *Technologie, Strategie und Organisation* (pp. 65–84). Springer Fachmedien Wiesbaden. https://doi.org/10.1007/978-3-658-16042-5_4

Freire-Gibb, L. C., & Nielsen, K. (2014). Entrepreneurship within urban and rural areas: Creative people and social networks. *Regional Studies, 48*(1), 139–153. https://doi.org/10.1080/00343404.2013.808322

Fritsch, M., & Wyrwich, M. (2014). The long persistence of regional levels of entrepreneurship: Germany, 1925–2005. *Regional Studies, 48*(6), 955–973. https://doi.org/10.1080/00343404.2013.816414

Galvão, A. R., Mascarenhas, C., Marques, C. S. E., Braga, V., & Ferreira, M. (2020). Mentoring entrepreneurship in a rural territory: A qualitative exploration of an entrepreneurship program for rural areas. *Journal of Rural Studies, 78*, 314–324. https://doi.org/10.1016/j.jrurstud.2020.06.038

Glaser, B. G., & Strauss, A. L. (1967). *The discovery of grounded theory: Strategies for qualitative research*. Aldine Publishing Company.

Granovetter, M. (1985). Economic action and social structure: The problem of embeddedness. *American Journal of Sociology, 91*(3), 481–510.

Guion, L. A., Diehl, D. C., & McDonald, D. (2011). Triangulation: Establishing the validity of qualitative studies. *EDIS, 2011*(8), 3. https://doi.org/10.32473/edis-fy394-2011

Haugh, H. (2020). Call the midwife! Business incubators as entrepreneurial enablers in developing economies. *Entrepreneurship and Regional Development, 32*(1–2), 156–175. https://doi.org/10.1080/08985626.2019.1640480

Hausberg, J. P., & Korreck, S. (2020). Business incubators and accelerators: A co-citation analysis-based, systematic literature review. *Journal of Technology Transfer, 45*(1), 151–176. https://doi.org/10.1007/s10961-018-9651-y

Honig, B., & Dana, L. P. (2008). Communities of disentrepreneurship: A comparative cross-national examination of entrepreneurial demise. *Journal of Enterprising Communities: People and Places in the Global Economy, 2*(1), 5–20. https://doi.org/10.1108/17506200810861221

Ihugba, O. A., Odii, A., & Njoku, A. C. (2013). Theoretical analysis of entrepreneurship challenges and prospects in Nigeria. *International Letters of Social and Humanistic Sciences*. https://doi.org/10.18052/www.scipress.com/ILSHS.16.21

Inkpen, A. C., & Tsang, E. W. K. (2005). Social capital networks, and knowledge transfer. *Academy of Management Review, 30*(1), 146–165. https://doi.org/10.5465/AMR.2005.15281445

Johns, G. (2006). The essential impact of context on organizational behavior. *Academy of Management Review, 31*(2), 386–408. https://doi.org/10.5465/AMR.2006.20208687

Kalantaridis, C., & Bika, Z. (2006). Local embeddedness and rural entrepreneurship: Case-study evidence from Cumbria, England. *Environment and Planning A: Economy and Space, 38*(8), 1561–1579. https://doi.org/10.1068/a3834

Kibler, E., Kautonen, T., & Fink, M. (2014). Regional social legitimacy of entrepreneurship: Implications for entrepreneurial intention and start-up cehaviour. *Regional Studies, 48*(6), 995–1015. https://doi.org/10.1080/00343404.2013.851373

Kibler, E., Fink, M., Lang, R., & Muñoz, P. (2015). Place attachment and social legitimacy: Revisiting the sustainable entrepreneurship journey. *Journal of Business Venturing Insights, 3*, 24–29. https://doi.org/10.1016/j.jbvi.2015.04.001

Korsgaard, S., Ferguson, R., & Gaddefors, J. (2015a). The best of both worlds: How rural entrepreneurs use placial embeddedness and strategic networks to create opportunities. *Entrepreneurship and Regional Development, 27*(9–10), 574–598. https://doi.org/10.1080/08985626.2015.1085100

Korsgaard, S., Müller, S., & Tanvig, H. W. (2015b). Rural entrepreneurship or entrepreneurship in the rural: Between place and space. *International Journal of Entrepreneurial Behaviour and Research, 21*(1), 5–26. https://doi.org/10.1108/IJEBR-11-2013-0205

Korsgaard, S., Müller, S., & Welter, F. (2021). It's right nearby: How entrepreneurs use spatial bricolage to overcome resource constraints. *Entrepreneurship and Regional Development, 33*(1–2), 147–173. https://doi.org/10.1080/08985626.2020.1855479

Krefting, L. (1991). Rigor in qualitative research: the assessment of trustworthiness. *American Journal of Occupational Therapy, 45*(3), 214–222. https://doi.org/10.5014/ajot.45.3.214

Labrianidis, L. (2006). Fostering entrepreneurship as a means to overcome barriers to development of rural peripheral areas in Europe. *European Planning Studies, 14*(1), 3–8. https://doi.org/10.1080/09654310500339067

Lafuente, E., Vaillant, Y., & Rialp, J. (2007). Regional differences in the influence of role models: Comparing the entrepreneurial process of rural Catalonia. *Regional Studies, 41*(6), 779–796. https://doi.org/10.1080/00343400601120247

Lavesson, N. (2018). How does distance to urban centres influence necessity and opportunity-based firm start-ups? *Papers in Regional Science, 97*(4), 1279–1303. https://doi.org/10.1111/pirs.12289

Lekhanya, L. M. (2018). The digitalisation of rural entrepreneurship. In *Entrepreneurship: Trends and challenges*. InTech. doi:https://doi.org/10.5772/intechopen.75925.

Lekhanya, L. M., & Visser, K. (2016). Risks and factors contributing towards rural entrepreneurial orientation growth of business in an emerging economy. *Risk Governance and Control: Financial Markets and Institutions, 6*(4), 72–83. https://doi.org/10.22495/rcgv6i4art10

Mack, E., & Mayer, H. (2016). The evolutionary dynamics of entrepreneurial ecosystems. *Urban Studies, 53*(10), 2118–2133. https://doi.org/10.1177/0042098015586547

Malecki, E. J. (2018). Entrepreneurs, networks, and economic development: A review of recent research. *Advances in Entrepreneurship, Firm Emergence and Growth, 20*, 71–116. Emerald Group Publishing Ltd. doi:https://doi.org/10.1108/S1074-754020180000020010.

Mason, C., & Brown, R. (2014). Entrepreneurial ecosystems and growth oriented entrepreneurship. *Final Report to OECD, Paris, 30*(1), 77–102.

McElwee, G., & Atherton, A. (2011). *Rural entrepreneurship. In World encyclopedia of entrepreneurship* (pp. 377–384). Edward Elgar Publishing Ltd.. https://doi.org/10.4337/9781839104145.00070

McElwee, G., & Smith, R. (2014). Researching rural enterprise. In *Handbook of research on entrepreneurship: What we know and what we need to know* (pp. 307–334). Edward Elgar Publishing Ltd.. https://doi.org/10.4337/9780857936929.00022

Morse, J. M., Barrett, M., Mayan, M., Olson, K., & Spiers, J. (2002). Verification strategies for establishing reliability and validity in qualitative research. *International Journal of Qualitative Methods, 1*(2), 13–22.

Müller, S. (2016). A progress review of entrepreneurship and regional development: What are the remaining gaps? *European Planning Studies, 24*(6), 1133–1158. https://doi.org/10.1080/09654313.2016.1154506

Müller, S., & Korsgaard, S. (2018). Resources and bridging: The role of spatial context in rural entrepreneurship. *Entrepreneurship and Regional Development, 30*(1–2), 224–255. https://doi.org/10.1080/08985626.2017.1402092

Nambisan, S. (2017). Digital entrepreneurship: Toward a digital technology perspective of entrepreneurship. *Entrepreneurship: Theory and Practice, 41*(6), 1029–1055. https://doi.org/10.1111/etap.12254

Nijkamp, P. (2003). Entrepreneurship in a modern network economy. *Regional Studies, 37*(4), 395–405. https://doi.org/10.1080/0034340032000074424

Nowak, M. J., & Grantham, C. E. (2000). The virtual incubator: Managing human capital in the software industry. *Research Policy, 29*(2), 125–134. https://doi.org/10.1016/S0048-7333(99)00054-2

OECD. (2020). *OECD regions and cities at a glance 2020*. https://doi.org/10.1787/959d5ba0-en

Pallares-Barbera, M., Tulla, A. F., & Vera, A. (2004). Spatial loyalty and territorial embeddedness in the multi-sector clustering of the Berguedà region in Catalonia (Spain). *Geoforum, 35*(5), 635–649. https://doi.org/10.1016/j.geoforum.2004.03.004

Pato, M. L., & Teixeira, A. A. C. (2016). Twenty years of rural entrepreneurship: A bibliometric survey. *Sociologia Ruralis, 56*(1), 3–28. https://doi.org/10.1111/soru.12058

Patzelt, H., & Shepherd, D. A. (2011). Negative emotions of an entrepreneurial career: Self-employment and regulatory coping behaviors. *Journal of Business Venturing, 26*(2), 226–238. https://doi.org/10.1016/j.jbusvent.2009.08.002

Perry-Smith, J., & Mannucci, P. V. (2015). Social networks, creativity, and entrepreneurship. In C. Shalley, M. A. Hitt, & J. Zhou (Eds.), *The Oxford handbook of creativity, innovation, and entrepreneurship*. Oxford University Press. https://doi.org/10.1093/oxfordhb/9780199927678.013.0016

Pettigrew, A. M. (1987). Context and action in the transformation of the firm. *Journal of Management Studies, 24*(6), 649–670. https://doi.org/10.1111/j.1467-6486.1987.tb00467.x

Polanyi, K. (2001). *The great transformation: The political and economic origin of our time* (2nd ed.). Beacon Press.

Radović-Marković, M., Marković, D., Simović, V., Medić, Z., & Zivadinović, J. (2017). E-learning as a tool for empowering entrepreneurship. *Journal of Women's Entrepreneurship and Education, 3–4*, 65–72.

Ribeiro-Soriano, D. (2017). Small business and entrepreneurship: Their role in economic and social development. *Entrepreneurship and Regional Development, 29*(1–2) 1–3. Routledge. doi:https://doi.org/10.1080/08985626.2016.1255438.

Rooks, G., Klyver, K., & Sserwanga, A. (2016). The context of social capital: A comparison of rural and urban entrepreneurs in Uganda. *Entrepreneurship: Theory and Practice, 40*(1), 111–130. https://doi.org/10.1111/etap.12107

Roundy, P. T., & Bayer, M. A. (2019). To bridge or buffer? A resource dependence theory of nascent entrepreneurial ecosystems. *Journal of Entrepreneurship in Emerging Economies, 11*(4), 550–575. https://doi.org/10.1108/JEEE-06-2018-0064

Saxenian, A. L. (1994). *Regional advantage: Culture and competition in silicon valley and Route 128*. Harvard University Press.

Spigel, B. (2016). Developing and governing entrepreneurial ecosystems: The structure of entrepreneurial support programs in Edinburgh, Scotland. *International Journal of Innovation and Regional Development, 7*(2), 141. https://doi.org/10.1504/ijird.2016.077889

Spigel, B., & Harrison, R. (2018). Toward a process theory of entrepreneurial ecosystems. *Strategic Entrepreneurship Journal, 12*(1), 151–168. https://doi.org/10.1002/sej.1268

Startup Genome. (2020). *The global startup ecosystem report GSER 2020*.

Stathopoulou, S., Psaltopoulos, D., & Skuras, D. (2004). Rural entrepreneurship in Europe: A research framework and agenda. *International Journal of Entrepreneurial Behaviour & Research, 10*(6), 404–425. https://doi.org/10.1108/13552550410564725

Statistisches Bundesamt. (2021). Bundesländer mit Hauptstädten nach Fläche. *Bevölkerung und Bevölkerungsdichte am, 31*(12), 2020. https://www.destatis.de/DE/Themen/Laender-Regionen/Regionales/Gemeindeverzeichnis/Administrativ/02-bundeslaender.html

Sternberg, R. (2009). Regional dimensions of entrepreneurship. *Foundations and Trends in Entrepreneurship, 5*(4), 211–340. https://doi.org/10.1561/0300000024

Steyaert, C., & Katz, J. (2004). Reclaiming the space of entrepreneurship in society: Geographical, discursive and social dimensions. *Entrepreneurship and Regional Development, 16*(3), 179–196. https://doi.org/10.1080/0898562042000197135

Strauss, A. L., & Corbin, J. M. (2010). *Grounded theory - Grundlagen qualitativer Sozialforschung*. Beltz.

Strübing, J. (2014). Was ist 'gute' Grounded Theory? Konsequenzen einer pragmatistischen Epistemologie für Qualitätssicherung und Gütekriterien. In *Grounded theory* (pp. 79–95). VS Verlag für Sozialwissenschaften. https://doi.org/10.1007/978-3-531-19897-2_6

Sussan, F., & Acs, Z. J. (2017). The digital entrepreneurial ecosystem. *Small Business Economics, 49*(1), 55–73. https://doi.org/10.1007/s11187-017-9867-5

Triodos Bacet. (2011). *Lessons on virtual business incubation services: Case studies*. moz-extension://be12dd89-ee52-4e36-8fcb-a8f3376912c2/enhanced-reader.html?openApp&pdf=https%3A%2F%2Fwww.infodev.org%2Fsites%2Fdefault%2Ffiles%2Fresource%2FInfodevDocuments_1145.pdf

Tsai, F. S., Hsieh, L. H. Y., Fang, S. C., & Lin, J. L. (2009). The co-evolution of business incubation and national innovation systems in Taiwan. *Technological Forecasting and Social Change, 76*(5), 629–643. https://doi.org/10.1016/j.techfore.2008.08.009

von Zedtwitz, M. (2003). Classification and management of incubators: Aligning strategic objectives and competitive scope for new business facilitation. *International Journal of Entrepreneurship and Innovation Management, 3*(2), 176–196. https://doi.org/10.1504/IJEIM.2003.002227

Ward, N., & Brown, D. L. (2009). Placing the rural in regional development. *Regional Studies, 43*(10), 1237–1244. https://doi.org/10.1080/00343400903234696

Welter, F. (2011). Contextualizing entrepreneurship: Conceptual challenges and ways forward. *Entrepreneurship Theory and Practice, 35*(1), 165–184. https://doi.org/10.1111/j.1540-6520.2010.00427.x

Welter, F., Baker, T., & Wirsching, K. (2019). Three waves and counting: The rising tide of contextualization in entrepreneurship research. *Small Business Economics, 52*(2), 319–330. https://doi.org/10.1007/s11187-018-0094-5

Wortman, M. S. (1990). Rural entrepreneurship research: An integration into the entrepreneurship field. *Agribusiness, 6*(4), 329–344.

Yin, R. K. (2017). *Case study research and applications: Design and methods*. Sage.

Zahra, S. A. (2007). Contextualizing theory building in entrepreneurship research. *Journal of Business Venturing, 22*(3), 443–452. https://doi.org/10.1016/j.jbusvent.2006.04.007

Zahra, S. A., Wright, M., & Abdelgawad, S. G. (2014). Contextualization and the advancement of entrepreneurship research. *International Small Business Journal: Researching Entrepreneurship, 32*(5), 479–500. https://doi.org/10.1177/0266242613519807

Zedtwitz, M., & Grimaldi, R. (2006). Are service profiles incubator-specific? Results from an empirical investigation in Italy. *Journal of Technology Transfer, 31*(4), 459–468. https://doi.org/10.1007/s10961-006-0007-7

Zinke, G., Ferdinand, J.-P., Groß, W., Möring, J. L., Nögel, L., Petzolt, S., Richter, S., Robeck, M. S., & Wessels, J. (2018). *Trends in der Unterstützungslandschaft von Start-ups – Inkubatoren, Akzeleratoren und andere*. moz-extension://be12dd89-ee52-4e36-8fcb-a8f3376912c2/enhanced-reader.html?openApp&pdf=https%3A%2F%2Fwww.startupbw.de%2Ffileadmin%2Fuser_upload%2Ftrends-in-der-unterstuetzungslandschaft-von-start-ups.pdf

Digital Dark Nudges

Lars Hornuf and Sonja Mangold

1 Introduction

Websites and apps with fraudulent designs that lead users to inadvertently commit to contracts and subscriptions or to divulge more personal data than they actually want are widespread in the digital economy. Companies are increasingly resorting to dubious design practices such as manipulative coloring or font size of buttons and confusing language in order to increase profits and to obtain and monetize as much user data as possible. Such business tactics, which are often at the expense of consumers and direct competitors, have been termed by academics as digital "dark nudges" and "dark patterns" (Brignull, 2010, 2013; Luguri & Strahilevitz, 2021; Reisch, 2020). A uniform definition of manipulative digital designs does not yet exist (Martini et al., 2021). According to the pioneering definition by Brignull (2013), digital dark nudges are the "dark side of design" that has been crafted "with great attention to detail, and a solid understanding of human psychology, to trick users into do things they wouldn't otherwise have done."

1.1 Manifestations of Digital Dark Nudges

There is a great deal of variation in the use of digital dark nudges. Based on the available literature (Gray et al., 2018; Luguri & Strahilevitz, 2021; Martini et al., 2021; Mathur et al., 2019), five archetypes can be distinguished as Fig. 1 shows. The first is *pressure* to take or not to take a certain action. This includes repeated aggressive inquiries even though users have already declared their intent—also

L. Hornuf (✉) · S. Mangold
Faculty of Business Studies and Economics, University of Bremen, Bremen, Germany
e-mail: hornuf@uni-bremen.de; smangold@uni-bremen.de

L. Hornuf (ed.), *Diginomics Research Perspectives*, Advanced Studies in Diginomics and Digitalization, https://doi.org/10.1007/978-3-031-04063-4_5

Pressure	Operational Constraint	Obstruction	Sneaking	Misleading
to (not) take a certain action	Users actually have no decision-making option	tries to dissuade users from certain actions by placing obstacles in their way.	imposes additional purchases of goods or services without initially noticing	uses graphic design to divert attention from certain information
Includes:	**Includes:**	**Includes:**	**Includes:**	**Includes:**
Nagging Confirmshaming	Forced Enrollment Forced Continuity	Preselection Click Fatigue Roach Motel	Sneak in the shopping cart Hidden Subscription	Trick questions Misdirection

Fig. 1 Five archetypes of digital dark nudging strategies (based on Martini et al., 2021)

known as "nagging"—which are often accompanied by indications of an alleged scarcity of goods. Another example is known as "confirmshaming," for example, where rejection buttons are formulated to embarrass users into acceptance. The second type is *operational constraint*, in which the user actually has no decision-making option, or an alternative decision is linked to undesirable conditions. An example of this practice is known as "forced enrollment," in which the use of a service is made dependent on the user accepting further conditions that are not required for the provision of the service. "Forced continuity" is another common practice, in which free or low-cost trial subscriptions are automatically renewed, but for a fee or at an increased price. Third, *obstruction* seeks to discourage users from performing certain actions by placing obstacles in their path. This includes pre-selecting checkboxes for the least privacy-friendly options. Another example is "click fatigue," in which the click paths to various options are designed with different lengths so that users often choose the simpler option and, for example, accept all cookies. A "roach motel" is a strategy whereby signing up or subscribing is much easier than canceling. Fourth, *sneaking* forces users to make additional purchases of goods or services without initially realizing it, for example, when an additional item ends up in the shopping cart unintentionally. Similarly, with hidden subscriptions, users are signed up for a recurring fee under the guise of a one-time fee or a free trial. Fifth, *misleading* uses graphic design to divert attention from certain information or to subvert users' usual design expectations. One example is trick questions (e.g., using a double negative) that lead to consumers no longer recognizing the significance of their choices. Also common are misdirection strategies whereby conspicuous graphic elements distract from the content.

1.2 Behavioral Science Background

One of the fundamental questions of legal theory is what assumptions about human behavior should be made (Eidenmüller, 2011). The legislature may assume that citizens are fundamentally rational in pursuing their subjective goals and interests. If so, digital dark nudges would not be effective, and business strategies built on these practices would be essentially worthless. Behavioral science has nevertheless shown that people systematically make mistakes and act predictably irrationally in certain situations (Ariely, 2010; Kahneman, 2012). Therefore, the law must intervene and protect consumers from business practices such as digital dark nudges.

Nudges are broadly defined as mechanisms that aim to steer human behavior in a certain direction without prohibiting certain decision options and without fundamentally changing existing economic incentives (Thaler & Sunstein, 2009). Hence, nudges have often been viewed by behavioral and legal scholars as something positive that helps people make better decisions. Most prominently, Thaler and Sunstein (2009) put the concept of nudging on the global political agenda, arguing that a choice architecture cannot be avoided and therefore nudges should be implemented "that are most likely to help and least likely to inflict harm" (p. 74).

Digital dark nudging strategies do not have such positive intentions. What they have in common with positive nudges is that they use behavioral knowledge about human decision-making. Psychologists and particularly behavioral economists have discovered a veritable zoo of different behavioral anomalies that can be exploited. Scholars such as Todd and Gigerenzer (2007) have shown that heuristics, which are simple decision algorithms or mental shortcuts, can work very efficiently in specific environments and enable humans to make better decisions. They refer to the *recognition heuristic* as one such positive decision support system. For example, if people recognize one tennis player but not the other, then the recognized one is the one more likely to win (Gigerenzer, 2008). However, an extensive literature also shows that humans suffer from biases in their decision-making. For example, default bias refers to the tendency for a human to generally accept the default option in a strategic interaction, potentially because switching involves costs and cognitive effort (Altman, 2017). Amazon has used default bias in their business practices by setting "Subscribe and Save" as the default for some products, with the goal of luring customers into this option. Knowledge about behavioral science has hence become a decisive source of competitive advantage in the digital economy (Luca & Bazerman, 2020).

2 Driving Factors and Risk Potential

Numerous studies have shown that dark nudges are used in a wide variety of industries and have a considerable control effect on the behavior of internet users (Luguri & Strahilevitz, 2021; Mathur et al., 2019; Utz et al., 2019). As a result of fierce competitive pressure in the global digital economy, companies are increasingly investing in tricky interface designs in order to increase user numbers and to raise profit margins (Rieger & Sinders, 2020). With the help of field experiments, which primarily take place in the form of A/B testing,[1] the effects of design variants on user behavior are examined, and the respective designs are optimized (Luca & Bazerman, 2020). Big tech companies such as Alibaba, Amazon, Facebook, and Google have billions of users and have almost inexhaustible possibilities to test which designs have the desired effect on consumer behavior. But even smaller companies can buy huge datasets from third-party providers to exploit the individual weaknesses of users (Perlroth, 2021). Big data analytics also opens up new and dangerous potential for creating and applying personalized digital dark nudges (Reisch, 2020; Martini et al., 2021; Weinzierl, 2020).

Such designs can portend increased risks for vulnerable consumer groups. The costs of fraudulently solicited purchases and subscriptions hit socially disadvantaged consumers particularly hard. Older "digital immigrants" are also at risk of being manipulated more frequently and effectively. Similarly, inexperienced users such as children and adolescents may be easily controlled, deceived, and seduced into unwanted actions such as sensitive data disclosure (Bogenstahl, 2019).

Manipulative design practices pose challenges for the legal system, as well as blunting the efforts of benevolent companies in the digital economy.[2] Companies that use digital dark nudges may violate data protection law, can be prosecuted under competition law, or might even risk criminal prosecution for fraud. Often, however, misleading designs operate in a gray area that is legally difficult to grasp, which is discussed in more detail below. Deceptive companies are constantly using new and increasingly sophisticated digital dark nudges, which makes it difficult for the legislature to control this phenomenon in a problem-oriented manner. Moreover, it is often much more difficult for consumers and competitors to enforce the law in cross-border digital markets (see in general Calliess, 2006; with regard to digital dark nudges Reisch, 2020).

3 Relevant Problem Areas

3.1 Case 1: Manipulative Design of Cookie Banners

One of the most common examples of digital dark nudges involves design tricks related to cookie banners. The purpose of cookies is to store information related to

[1] A/B testing is a method in which two variants of an app or website are tested and compared. The goal is usually to evoke or increase a specific user action.

[2] Manipulative designs by private actors often aim at excessive data collection. Klein et al. (2022) discuss privacy concerns in digital marketing and Kinra et al. (2022) analyze data privacy challenges of social media analytics. Karpa et al. (2022) study data privacy risks caused by authoritarian states.

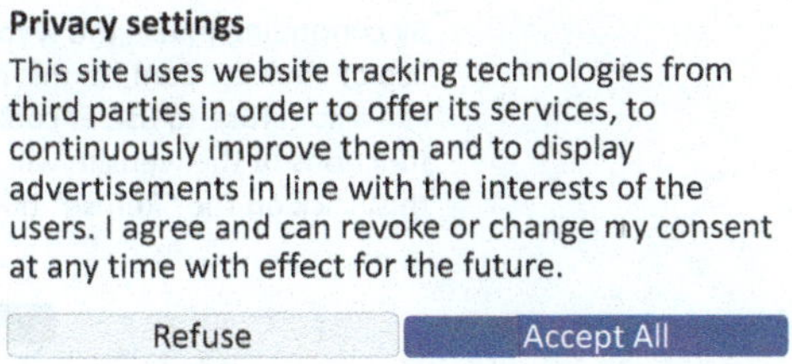

Fig. 2 Digital dark nudging in the form of deceptive color design

a website locally on a user's digital device for a certain period of time. During the next visit, the information is transmitted back to the server of the company the user wishes to engage with. Cookies thus enable companies to individualize their websites for users by authenticating them when they return to the website. Since 2002, the Privacy and Electronic Communications Directive (also known as the ePrivacy Directive or, more colloquially, the "cookie directive") has regulated minimum standards for cookies in EU member states. After its amendment in 2009, the directive has made cookies subject to prior consent, which has led to an increasing use of dark nudges to get customers to consent to cookies (Hausner & Gertz, 2021; Utz et al., 2019). Through manipulative design variations, companies use deceptive consent queries to persuade consumers to agree to cookie settings that will disclose as much personal data as possible to create comprehensive individual user profiles, for example, for targeted advertising purposes. In other business models, user profiles are created to calculate default probabilities and make credit decisions (Dorfleitner et al., 2021). Problematic design practices with cookie notices occur in various forms, including the graphic design of buttons, hidden privacy-friendly options, or through specific default settings.

3.1.1 Practical Examples

Dark nudges in cookie banners often appear in the form of manipulative color designs of individual buttons. Figure 2 shows a typical example of such tricky design variants.[3] The "accept all" button graphically clearly stands out with a colored background to encourage the user to agree to comprehensive web tracking; in contrast, not upstaging the pale gray "reject" button. This type of influence is a dark nudge in the form of *misleading*. By choosing based on different colors, consumers can be tempted to disclose more data than they presumably want.

Figure 3 shows another common variant of the manipulative design of cookie banners. The provider makes the unrestricted use of its website conditional on the granting of consent for web tracking. In this way, users are effectively forced to consent to the use of cookies. This example is a conditional dark nudge that can be classified in the category of *operational constraint*.

[3] All figures are based on website designs and privacy practices by real companies in 2021.

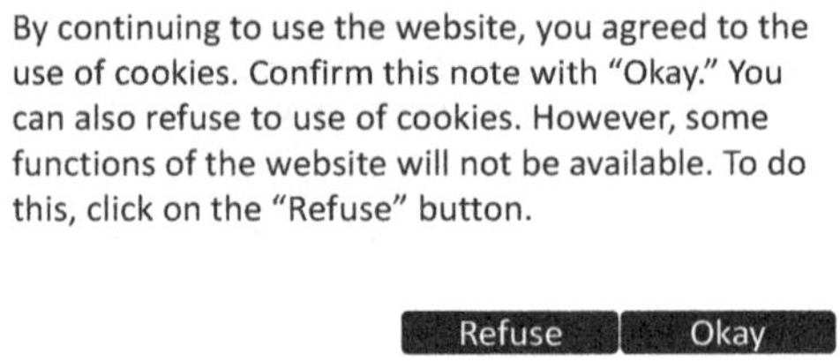

Fig. 3 Digital dark nudging in the form of operational constraint

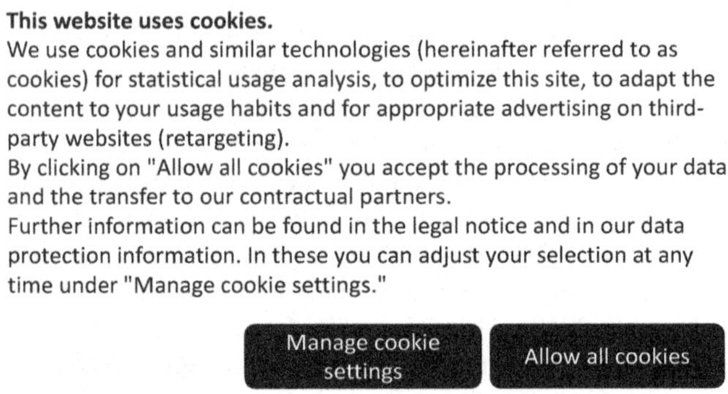

Fig. 4 Digital dark nudging in the form of click fatigue

An example of obstruction designs is the use of *click fatigue*, which makes the refusal of consent to web tracking dependent on further, cumbersome actions. Such a case is shown in Fig. 4. The website provider moves the rejection option to a settings menu, whereby users on the first level cannot see how many steps are necessary to ultimately refuse their consent. The desire of users to visit the website without interruption regularly leads to their consent to web tracking instead of clicking on the "settings" button.

Studies have shown that big tech companies often use several digital dark nudges at the same time, for example, by using a combination of manipulative color design, misleading language, and hiding privacy-friendly options to urge users to accept the lowest possible data privacy settings (Norwegian Consumer Council, 2018). Facebook currently encourages users to accept web tracking for advertising purposes by highlighting the "accept all" button and uses click fatigue by presenting the alternative as a commitment to "manage" settings.

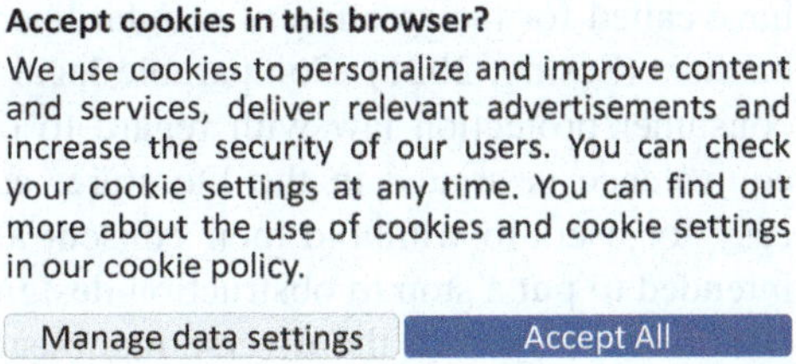

Fig. 5 Digital dark nudging in the form of manipulative color design and click fatigue

3.1.2 Legal Aspects and Gaps in Privacy Protection

Digital dark nudges in cookie banners can be legally problematic, especially from a data privacy perspective.[4] European and German privacy laws[5] generally require that users give their voluntary, specific, informed consent to the use of tracking and advertising cookies. The requirements for consent are laid down in the General Data Protection Regulation (GDPR),[6] which became binding in all EU member states in May 2018. If there is no valid consent, the use of cookies is illegal. It can be argued that data protection law currently prohibits some forms of dark digital nudges in cookie banners, but by no means covers all of them (Loy & Baumgartner, 2021; Sesing, 2021). European and German jurisprudence[7] recently put a stop to obstruction and preselection nudges in particular. Consequently, the website visitor's assent to the use of cookies through pre-selected check boxes is not permitted—consent must be given actively and expressly.

The question of whether and to what extent it is permissible to induce users to give their consent by different button designs is legally controversial. According to the prevailing view of the literature, highlighting the "accept all" or "reject" buttons in a different color, as exemplified in Fig. 2, does not lead to such a strong steering effect that it would negate voluntary consent (Loy & Baumgartner, 2021). The question of whether it is permissible to make the unrestricted use of a website dependent on consent to tracking has also not been clearly answered (Sesing, 2021). The example of conditional nudging shown in Fig. 3 is therefore in a legal gray area. Click fatigue strategies that make the rejection of all cookies more cumbersome than accepting all cookies are widely viewed as illegal in case law and literature (Loy & Baumgartner, 2021). The examples of digital dark nudges illustrated in Figs. 4 and 5 should therefore be impermissible.

It can be argued that data protection law *de lege lata* only prohibits some forms of manipulative designs. In order to close legal protection gaps, legal scholars

---

[4] Illegal cookie practices can also have consequences under competition law.

[5] See Art. 5 (3) ePrivacy Directive; § 15 (3) Telemedia Act (Telemediengesetz, TMG) and the pending Section 25 (1) Telecommunications Telemedia Data Protection Act (Telekommunikation - Telemedien - Datenschutzgesetz, TTDSG).

[6] See Art. 4 No.11, Art. 7 GDPR.

[7] See European Court of Justice (ECJ) (2019), Case C-673/17 ("Planet49"); Federal Court of Justice (BGH) (2020), case file number I ZR 7/16.

have called for the creation of standardized specifications for the design of cookie banners (Sesing, 2021). Comparable legal requirements already exist in European consumer protection law with regard to consumers' revocation rights. The legal equivalence is argued in the literature, according to which it should be just as easy for users to withhold their consent as it is to give it (Sesing, 2021). This is intended to put a stop to obstruction designs in the form of click fatigue strategies. However, in view of the diverse manifestations of digital dark nudges in cookie banners, it is questionable whether individual legal amendments are sufficient. It must also be taken into account that existing regulations are often not complied with. The German consumer protection authorities recently warned numerous companies about impermissible cookie consent management.[8] In the summer of 2021, the non-governmental organization, None of Your Business, led by the Austrian data protection activist Max Schrems, filed complaints with data protection authorities against digital dark nudges in cookie banners.[9] Hence there are significant legal and practical gaps in privacy protection that remain to be resolved.

3.2 *Case 2: Subscription Traps*

The second type of digital dark nudging we examine is subscription traps.[10] Subscription traps lead consumers to unwanted enrollment or renewal of subscriptions through manipulative design techniques. The forms of such subscription traps on the internet are diverse (Gray et al., 2018; Martini et al., 2021; Rieger & Sinders, 2020). For example, users are tempted to take out a subscription because only then can they use the service or certain functions. These *forced enrollment* strategies fall into the category of *operational constraints*. *Forced continuity* nudges are also common. After a trial period, an annual membership is automatically commenced, or a subscription is automatically extended. Another business practice is to make the termination of a membership more difficult by obscuring or concealing such functions. This is another example of the *roach motel* described above, whereby it is much easier for users to take out a subscription than to cancel it. Companies may also try to trick consumers into automatically subscribing to services through deceptive designs. This type of digital dark nudging is known as *hidden subscription*.

---

[8] More information on these topics can be found here: https://www.vzbv.de/pressemitteilungen/jedes-zehnte-cookie-banner-ist-klar-rechtswidrig (last accessed on November 10, 2021).

[9] For more detail, see: https://noyb.eu/de/noyb-reicht-422-formelle-dsgvo-beschwerden-gegen-cookie-banner-wahnsinn-ein (last accessed on November 10, 2021).

[10] According to the consumer advice center in Bremen, most of the complaints from consumers in connection with digital dark nudges—in addition to manipulative cookie designs—concern subscription tricks and traps.

3.2.1 Practical Examples

This section presents three illustrated cases of subscription tricks related to digital dark nudges. In the first case, as exemplified in Fig. 6, the company uses a "freemium" business model to acquire business customers. The basic product is offered free of charge, while the full product and extended functions are only available for a fee. Users also typically experience payment barriers for certain services. In this way, users are seduced into upgrading from the free version to a paid subscription. This strategy can be classified as digital dark nudging in the form of *forced enrollment*.

In the second case, exemplified in Fig. 7, the bold and large highlighted website design promises a free trial subscription. If you click on the "contract details" below in small print, you will find out that the subscription is automatically converted into an annual subscription, provided that users do not object in writing up to 7 days before the end of the trial phase. The company is trying to increase sales by taking advantage of availability bias and the expected non-timely cancelation of membership by consumers. This strategy is an example of digital dark nudging in the form of *forced continuity*. Alternatively, highlighting the cost-free nature of the trial subscription compared to the costs incurred later in small letters can be regarded as a *hidden subscription* strategy.

In the third case, as exemplified in Fig. 8, the termination of a subscription is made more difficult by the company, which does not offer a termination option on the website. Instead, it asks the customer to first contact customer support via telephone. This is another example of a subscription trap in the form of *forced continuity*.

Fig. 6 Subscription trick in the form of forced enrollment

Fig. 7 Subscription trick in the form of forced continuity and hidden subscription

Fig. 8 Subscription trick in the form of forced continuity

3.2.2 Legal Protection Instruments and Protection Gaps

Subscription traps on the internet are pertinent to several areas of law. In particular, consumer law, general contract law, and fair-trading law put a stop to the corresponding strategies of manipulative influence on consumers by companies, at least in part (Martini et al., 2021). In the event of an act of deception, a criminal liability for fraud[11] can be triggered. This is the case, for example, when the design of a website intentionally conceals the fact that a user is entering into a paid subscription[12] and offers the possibility of penalties in the form of hidden subscription strategies under certain circumstances.

A consumer protection instrument that can also come into play relates to rights of withdrawal.[13] Rights of withdrawal are not specifically directed against digital dark nudging, but they do allow consumers to nullify a contract that has been entered into under the influence of deceptive design strategies. The right of withdrawal is particularly relevant for distance contracts.[14] Accordingly, consumers in online trading are entitled to revoke contracts within a certain period without giving reasons. However, there is doubt in the literature whether existing rights of withdrawal are used in practice (Martini et al., 2021; Rieger & Sinders, 2020).

[11] Section 263 of the Criminal Code (Strafgesetzbuch).

[12] See also BGH, judgment of March 5, 2014 – case file number 2 StR 616/12.

[13] Section 355 of the German Civil Code (Bürgerliches Gesetzbuch, BGB).

[14] See Section 312 c, 312g BGB.

Subtle tricky design practices are often not noticed or are simply accepted by consumers.

Subscription traps in which subscriptions or trial periods are automatically extended for a fee without the consumer being transparently informed during the ordering process are specifically addressed by information obligations under consumer law.[15] According to the so-called "button solution,"[16] the customer must always confirm online orders with a button that does not contain anything other than the words "order with obligation to pay" or another clear formulation. If the labeling requirements are not complied with, no contract will be formed.[17] Case law has interpreted the provision strictly.[18] For example, the phrase "test now for free" was considered insufficient if the first month of a contract is free, but a contractual relationship that is subject to a fee follows, and the only way to prevent this from coming about is by canceling the contract. The case of *forced continuity* nudging, which we have exemplified in Fig. 7, can thus be classified as legally problematic.

Another lever against subscription tricks is the obligation for companies to set up a cancelation button,[19] which is provided for in a Germain law regarding fair consumer contracts that is scheduled to become binding at the end of May 2022.[20] According to this law, a termination button must be available on the website in the case of online subscriptions and must be labeled with the words "terminate contracts here" or an alternative, unequivocal formulation.[21] This reduces the hurdles for consumers to give notice of termination. In this way, *forced continuity* strategies that make cancelation of subscriptions difficult, as shown in Fig. 8, can be counteracted.

The general contractual instruments of contestation[22] and *culpa in contrahendo*[23] also offer certain protections against influencing tactics by companies in connection with subscription traps. However, here too there is the problem, mentioned above, that consumers often do not become aware of or are indifferent to subtle digital dark nudging and therefore waive the exercise of their rights.

Subscription traps in the context of digital dark nudging can also be impermissible from the point of view of unfair competition law (Martini et al., 2021). For example, hidden subscription tricks may violate No. 21 of the Annex to Section 3 (3) of the Act Against Unfair Competition (*Gesetz gegen den unlauteren Wettbewerb*, UWG). Accordingly, the offer of a product or service must not be indicated as free or similar if costs are still to be borne. *Roach motel* cases in which it is

[15] Section 312 j (2) seq. BGB.

[16] Section 312 j (3) BGB.

[17] Section 312 j (4) BGB, cf. Weiss (2013).

[18] See, for example, Munich Regional Court I, decision of June 11, 2013–33 O 12678/13.

[19] See Section 312k BGB.

[20] Act for Fair Consumer Contracts (Gesetz für faire Verbraucherverträge) of 10 August 2021, Federal Law Gazette Volume 2021 Part 1 No. 53, 3433 ff.

[21] Section 312 k (2) BGB.

[22] Sections 119, 123 BGB.

[23] Sections 280 (1), 311 (2), 241 (2) BGB.

much easier for users to take out a subscription than to cancel may not be allowed under German law as they constitute an "aggressive business act."[24] Accordingly, it is forbidden for companies to create obstacles that prevent consumers from exercising their contractual rights such as termination rights. Subscriptions and continued subscriptions obtained through digital dark nudging can also violate the prohibitions of misleading under fair-trading law.[25] Consumer associations have already successfully taken legal action against competition violations in connection with internet subscription traps.[26]

In summary, it is evident that existing laws only cover individual cases of digital dark nudging in the context of subscription tricks. Specific consumer protection norms still have weaknesses in factual terms of enforcement (Spindler et al., 2015). Additional legislative actions seem warranted.

4 Overcoming Digital Dark Nudging

In the following section, we take a brief look at current regulatory approaches to combat digital dark nudging. Finally, we shortly discuss which measures could be suitable and effective to curb the problem of manipulative design tricks.

4.1 State and Private Regulatory Responses

In Germany, there is currently no specific law to combat digital dark nudging. A first comprehensive proposal to prohibit companies from using manipulative website designs arose in the USA in 2019 with the "Deceptive Experiences to Online Users Reduction Act" (DETOUR Act).[27] The topic is nevertheless increasingly moving into the focus of German and European legislators. In its current consumer agenda,[28] the European Commission has expressly declared its commitment to fighting manipulative design practices in the digital economy. The Council of the European Union recently called for targeted improvements against digital dark

[24] Cf. Section 4a (2) no. 4 UWG.

[25] See Sections 5, 5a UWG.

[26] See, for example, higher regional court (OLG) Koblenz, ruling of December 22, 2010-9U 610/10.

[27] More information can be found at: https://www.congress.gov/bill/116th-congress/senate-bill/1084/text (last accessed on November 17, 2021).

[28] See European Commission, Communication from the Commission to the European Parliament and the Council of 13th November 2020, New Consumer Agenda, COM(2020) 696 final.

nudging[29] as part of the planned comprehensive EU regulatory package for online platforms.[30]

Calls for specific improvements, particularly in consumer and fair-trading law, have become louder in the public discourse (Bogenstahl, 2019). Antitrust law is seen as a possible lever to effectively counter the use of manipulative design tactics by powerful tech companies (Day & Stemler, 2020). Some voices in the literature even suggest the introduction of legal limits and transparency requirements with regard to methods such as A/B tests, which make digital dark nudging effective (Martini et al., 2021). However, legal limits to A/B tests raise the question of what the correct default design should be in each case (Luca & Bazerman, 2020) and whether nudges should not be used for consumers' benefit (Sunstein, 2015).

It is also questionable whether legal amendments are sufficient to master the problem of deceptive design tactics in the digital economy. Companies are constantly using new and increasingly sophisticated forms of digital dark nudges. In doing so, legal gray areas are often used that the legislature has not provided for. Statutory law often lags behind rapidly changing economic and technical developments. In addition, there are legal enforcement difficulties for consumers, especially if the company is based outside of Europe. The power and information asymmetry between companies and consumers, which has served as justification for active consumer protection policy within the national framework, is especially problematic in the cross-border digital economy (Adam & Micklitz, 2017).

Against this background, it is worthwhile to consider complementary strategies of private self-regulation and ethical self-restraint in the digital economy. The first initiatives have already been implemented. For example, with the Advertising and Marketing Communications Code,[31] the International Chamber of Commerce created a globally applicable self-regulatory framework designed to protect consumers from unethical digital marketing practices and excessive data collection. The Interactive Advertising Bureau's Europe Transparency & Consent Framework,[32] a standard for the digital advertising industry, aims to promote global compliance with consumer data protection regulations in accordance with the GDPR and the ePrivacy Directive. The US Association for Computing Machinery (ACM) has also taken on the topic of digital dark nudging and formulated professional ethical standards in the field of IT with the ACM Code of Ethics.[33]

---

[29] See for more information: https://marketresearchtelecast.com/dark-patterns-eu-countries-want-to-ban-psychological-tricks-with-the-digital-services-act/204974/ (last accessed on November 18, 2021).

[30] The proposed regulation includes the "Digital Services Act" (DSA) and the "Digital Markets Act" (DMA). The regulations include liability rules and transparency requirements for online platforms (cf. Gielen & Uphues, 2021). While the DSA applies to all providers, the DMA addresses big, powerful platforms.

[31] Online available at: https://iccwbo.org/content/uploads/sites/3/2020/03/icc-advertising-and-marketing-communications-code-german-final.pdf (last accessed on November 18, 2021).

[32] More information is available at: https://iabeurope.eu/transparency-consent-framework/ (last accessed on November 18, 2021).

In addition to self-binding activities of the digital economy, rulemaking by public–private standardization bodies can help to find problem-specific solutions against digital dark nudging (Bogenstahl, 2019). For example, the International Organization for Standardization has created the ISO 9241 norm, which has been adopted in Germany as DIN EN ISO 9241, and which contains quality requirements and guidance for user-friendly user experience and user interface design.[34]

4.2 Outlook

We have shown in this chapter that digital dark nudging has become a significant and growing problem in the internet economy. Companies in numerous industries use manipulative design tactics to suggestively influence consumers and thereby increase profits. The legislature has already taken first steps to better protect consumers and internet users. In view of increasingly dynamic economic and technical development, mere prohibitions and legal measures often fall short. Proactive, more comprehensive strategies therefore appear to be indicated to counter consumer-hostile practices in the digital world. These should include problem-related self-regulation approaches in digital industry. In addition, ethical aspects should be more closely integrated into education and training for professions in the field of IT and web design (Bogenstahl, 2019). Civil society organizations such as non-governmental organizations and consumer associations can increase public pressure and thus help curb fraudulent design practices by companies. Further research is nevertheless required in order to gain better knowledge about the effectiveness of tailor-made law in relation to digital dark nudging.

Literature

Adam, L., & Micklitz, H. W. (2017). Verbraucher und Online-Plattformen. In H. W. Micklitz, L. A. Reisch, G. Joost, & H. Zander-Hayat (Eds.), *Verbraucherrecht 2.0. – Verbraucher in der digitalen Welt* (pp. 45–102). Nomos.

Altman, M. (2017). Aspects of smart decision-making. In *Handbook of behavioural economics and smart decision-making* (pp. 155–156). Edward Elgar Publishing.

Ariely, D. (2010). *Predictably irrational: The hidden forces that shape our decisions*. Harper Collins Publishers.

Bogenstahl, C. (2019). *Dark patterns – Mechanismen (be)trügerischen Internetdesigns*. Retrieved November 10, 2021, from https://www.tab-beim-bundestag.de/de/pdf/publikationen/themenprofile/Themenkurzprofil-030.pdf

---

[33] Available online at: https://www.acm.org/code-of-ethics (last accessed on November 18, 2021).

[34] For more information, see: https://www.iso.org/standard/60476.html (last accessed on November 18, 2021).

Brignull, H. (2010). *Dark patterns: Dirty tricks designers use to make people do stuff.* Retrieved November 10, 2021, from https://90percentofeverything.com/2010/07/08/dark-patterns-dirty-tricks-designers-use-to-make-people-do-stuff/index.html

Brignull, H. (2013). *Dark Patterns: Inside the interfaces designed to trick you.* Retrieved February 7, 2022, from https://www.theverge.com/2013/8/29/4640308/dark-patterns-inside-the-interfaces-designed-to-trick-you

Calliess, G.-P. (2006). *Grenzüberschreitende Verbraucherverträge.* Mohr Siebeck.

Day, G., & Stemler, A. (2020). Are dark patterns anticompetitive? *Alabama Law Review, 72*(1), 1–46.

Dorfleitner, G., Hornuf, L., & Kreppmaier, J. (2021). *Promise not fulfilled: Fintech data privacy, and the GDPR.* CESifo Working Paper No. 9359. https://ssrn.com/abstract=3950094

Eidenmüller, H. (2011). Liberaler Paternalismus. *Juristen Zeitung, 66*(17), 814–821.

European Commission. (2020). Communication from the Commission to the European Parliament and the Council of 13.11.2020. *New Consumer Agenda*, COM(2020) 696 final. https://eur-lex.europa.eu/legal-content/DE/ALL/?uri=COM:2020:696:FIN

Gielen, N., & Uphues, S. (2021). Digital Markets Act und Digital Services Act. *Europäische Zeitschrift für Wirtschaftsrecht,* 627–637.

Gigerenzer, G. (2008). *Gut feelings: The intelligence of the unconscious.* Penguin Books.

Gray, C. M., Kou, Y., Battles, B., Hoggatt, J., & Toombs, A. L. (2018). The dark (patterns) side of UX design. *Conference Paper. Conference: CHI'18: Proceedings of the 2018 CHI Conference on Human Factors in Computing Systems.* Montréal, QU. Retrieved November 10, 2021, from https://www.researchgate.net/publication/322916969_The_Dark_Patterns_Side_of_UX_Design

Hausner, P., & Gertz, M. (2021). *Dark patterns in the interaction with cookie banners.* Preprint retrieved from https://arxiv.org/pdf/2103.14956.pdf.

Kahneman, D. (2012). *Thinking, fast and slow.* Penguin Books.

Karpa, D., Klarl, T., & Rochlitz, M. (2022). Artificial intelligence, surveillance and big data. In L. Hornuf (Ed.), *Diginomics research perspectives: The role of digitalization in business and society.* Springer International Publishing.

Kinra, A., Kotzab, H., & Siekmann, F. (2022). Social media analytics in operations and supply chain management: Opportunities, challenges and paradoxes. In L. Hornuf (Ed.), *Diginomics research perspectives: The role of digitalization in business and society.* Springer International Publishing.

Klein, K., Eisenbeiss, M., Dulle, M., Taherparvar, N., Wiemann, M., & Wiezorrek, J. (2022). Marketing in a digital world. In L. Hornuf (Ed.), *Diginomics research perspectives: The role of digitalization in business and society.* Springer International Publishing.

Loy, C., & Baumgartner, U. (2021). Consent-Banner und Nudging. Tracking-Mechanismen: Wie viel "Anstupsen" ist erlaubt? *Zeitschrift für Datenschutz,* 404–408.

Luca, M., & Bazerman, M. H. (2020). *The power of experiments: Decision making in a data-driven World.* MIT Press.

Luguri, J., & Strahilevitz, L. (2021). Shining a light on dark patterns. *Journal of Legal Analysis, 13*(1), 43–109. Retrieved November 10, 2021, from https://papers.ssrn.com/sol3/papers.cfm?abstract_id=3431205#

Martini, M., Drews, Ch., Seeliger, P., & Weinzierl, Q. (2021). Dark patterns. Phänomenologie und Antworten der Rechtsordnung. *Zeitschrift für Digitalisierung und Recht,* 47–74.

Mathur, A., Acar, G., Friedman, M. J., Lucherini, E., Mayer, J., Chetty, M., & Narayanan, A. (2019). *Dark patterns at scale: Findings from a crawl of 11K shopping websites.* Preprint retrieved from https://arxiv.org/pdf/1907.07032.pdf

Norwegian Consumer Council. (2018). *Deceived by design: How tech companies use dark patterns to discourage us from exercising our rights to privacy*. Retrieved November 10, 2021, from https://fil.forbrukerradet.no/wp-content/uploads/2018/06/2018-06-27-deceived-by-design-final.pdf

Perlroth, N. (2021). *This is how they tell me the world ends: The cyberweapons arms race*. Bloomsbury Publishing.

Reisch, L. A. (2020). *Nudging hell und dunkel: Regeln für digitales Nudging*. Preprint retrieved from https://link.springer.com/content/pdf/10.1007/s10273-020-2573-y.pdf

Rieger, S., & Sinders, C. (2020). *Dark patterns: Design mit gesellschaftlichen Nebenwirkungen*. Retrieved November 10, 2021, from https://www.stiftung-nv.de/sites/default/files/dark.patterns.pdf

Sesing, A. (2021). Cookie-Banner – Hilfe, das Internet ist kaputt! *Multimedia und Recht* (pp. 544–549).

Spindler, G., Thorun, Ch., & Blom, A. G. (2015). Die Evaluation der Button-Lösung. Ergebnisse einer empirischen Studie. *Multimedia und Recht (MMR)* (pp. 3–7).

Sunstein, C. R. (2015). *Why nudge? The politics of libertarian paternalism*. Storrs Lectures on Jurisprudence.

Thaler, R. H., & Sunstein, C. R. (2009). Nudge: Improving decisions about health, wealth, and happiness. Penguin Books.

Todd, P. M., & Gigerenzer, G. (2007). Environments that make us smart: Ecological rationality. *Current Directions in Psychological Science, 16*(3), 167–171. https://doi.org/10.1111/j.1467-8721.2007.00497.x

Utz, C., Degeling, M., Fahl, S., Schaub, F., & Holz. T. (2019). (Un)informed consent: Studying GDPR consent notices in the field. *Proceedings of the 2019 ACM SIGSAC Conference on Computer and Communications Security, CCS 2019*, London, November 11–15, 2019. https://doi.org/10.1145/3319535.3354212

Weinzierl, Q. (2020). Dark Patterns als Herausforderung für das Recht. Rechtlicher Schutz vor der Ausnutzung von Verhaltensanomalien. *Neue Zeitschrift für Verwaltungsrecht* – Extra. 39. Jahrgang, Band 5, 1–11.

Weiss, A. (2013). Die Untiefen der "Button"-Lösung. *Juristische Schulung* (pp. 590–594).

Machine Learning in Accounting Research

Christian Fieberg, Matthies Hesse, Thomas Loy, and Daniel Metko

1 Introduction

Artificial intelligence (AI), as a generic term for machine learning (ML), is already an indispensable part of our daily personal and business lives. Consumers enjoy personalized film and music recommendations on various platforms as well as the help of their voice-activated digital assistants. Businesswise, manufacturers trust in automatic quality control systems to detect defective parts, banks predict credit default probabilities to mitigate risks, doctors retrieve second opinions from artificial intelligence systems in critical on-demand situations, and retailers optimize their stocks on predicted demand (Kashyap, 2017). All of this is thanks to ML. The widespread use of ML seems ever-increasing and does not stop at accounting and empirical accounting research. Empirical accounting research consists of two main areas: (1) financial accounting and auditing and (2) management accounting. Financial accounting, also referred to as external accounting or financial reporting, is the communication of complex, aggregated business transactions to a wide set of internal and external stakeholders, such as investors, creditors, suppliers, customers, and employees. Depending on the jurisdiction, taxable income might also be deferred from the profit and loss statement contained in an overall (annual) financial statement. In contrast, auditing is the process of validating these financial statements such that they comply with the respective generally accepted accounting principles (GAAP). Management accounting, also referred to as internal accounting, has a greater focus on value-creation by, for example, estimating costs, setting budgets, or evaluating future project profitability. It is especially useful for strategic decision-makers inside firms.

C. Fieberg · M. Hesse · T. Loy (✉) · D. Metko
Faculty of Business Studies and Economics, University of Bremen, Bremen, Germany
e-mail: cfieberg@uni-bremen.de; hessem@uni-bremen.de; thomas.loy@uni-bremen.de; metko@uni-bremen.de

L. Hornuf (ed.), *Diginomics Research Perspectives*, Advanced Studies in Diginomics and Digitalization, https://doi.org/10.1007/978-3-031-04063-4_6

We identify the current state of use of ML along these main lines of accounting research. Specifically, we find that in financial accounting and auditing, ML is used in such areas as fraud detection and bankruptcy prediction. Additionally, we find that ML remains a rather niche topic in management accounting. We contribute to the literature by providing a compact overview of ML and its use in various areas of accounting research. We also identify research opportunities, such as (1) more extensive use of deep learning to process structured and unstructured data more efficiently and (2) use of ML as a white-box application (i.e., explainable ML) in contrast to the proverbial black-box of ML. In the first part of this chapter, we provide a brief introduction to ML by clarifying its meaning, showing popular techniques and presenting exemplary use cases. With this knowledge, the reader can easily follow the subsequent discussion, where we outline the use of ML in empirical accounting research. This allows us to appraise the current state of ML and to identify potential avenues for future research.

2 Machine Learning

2.1 Cutting through the Fog

The term artificial intelligence (AI) has long since become a buzzword. In the popular press, it often goes hand-in-hand with such terms as business analytics, big data, business intelligence, data analytics, data mining, statistical learning, machine learning (ML), and deep learning. Although these terms are used very frequently and seemingly interchangeably, we aim to disentangle them before taking a deeper look at the techniques behind ML and its application in the narrower context of accounting research.

Business analytics refers to the analysis of data (i.e., data analytics) within a business. Business data mostly meet the criteria of the term big data, with its three main characteristics: *volume*, *velocity*, and *variety*. Volume refers to the amount of data, velocity to the speed of the data generation and processing, and variety to the number of different data types (i.e., structured, unstructured, and semi-structured data) (Lee, 2017). Structured data is the kind that can be found in traditional, relational databases, whereas unstructured data are not standardized for efficient processing. Examples of unstructured data are texts, photos, audio, and audio-visual data. Semi-structured data are not standardized in the pure sense of a relational database, but still structured. An example would be financial statements in which unstructured data (e.g., texts contained in a footnote disclosure or in the Management Discussion & Analysis (MD&A) section) are electronically tagged using the eXtensible Business Reporting Language (XBRL), making them retrievable automatically (e.g., Hoitash & Hoitash, 2018). Business analytics is then used to analyze the business-generated data to support decision-making.

While business analytics has a rather descriptive character, business intelligence focuses primarily on prediction tasks. Business intelligence uses data analytics—or, more specifically, data mining—to detect patterns and gain knowledge from the data (Mishra et al., 2016). Data mining uses statistical learning and machine learning, both of which are predictive toolboxes. Statistical learning is an emergent field from statistics, while machine learning has a long history within computer science (James et al., 2013). Whereas statistical learning makes predictions based on statistical assumptions, machine learning acts in a purely data-driven way—the "machine" learns relationships within the data itself (i.e., self-learning) and predicts an outcome. Finally, deep learning is a subcategory of ML in which a neural network with many hidden layers at its core allows for deeper insights into the input–output relation structure. In other words, deep learning is more flexible in detecting hidden patterns than "classical" ML techniques such as decision trees, support vector machines or neural networks with only one hidden layer. Throughout this chapter, we will subsume both statistical learning and machine learning under the term ML for readability purposes.

2.2 *Supervised and Unsupervised Learning Techniques*

ML can generally be categorized into supervised, unsupervised, semi-supervised, and reinforcement learning (e.g., Géron, 2017). For the sake of brevity, this chapter focuses on supervised and unsupervised learning, but the concept of semi-supervised learning is introduced along the way.

With supervised learning, the main idea is to discover and approximate the relation between given input and output variables. In statistics, these input and output variables are called independent and dependent variables. Within ML, they are referred to as features and targets.[1] One difference between (classical) statistics and ML is that statisticians aim to derive inferences while ML engineers aim to predict the targets as accurately as possible. As this chapter is about ML in accounting research and, therefore, largely focuses on prediction tasks, ML notation is employed throughout this chapter. In terms of data, supervised learning is only applicable if each observation contains a number of features as well as corresponding target(s). Supervised learning is subdivided into regression and classification, depending on the targets' data type. A regression algorithm is used if targets are continuous, while a classification algorithm requires categorical targets.

Figure 1 shows some popular algorithms. Algorithms marked in light gray are only able to learn linear approximation functions (in the context of regression) or decision boundaries (in the context of classification). Examples of approximation functions and decision boundaries are provided in the following section. The

[1] Sometimes, targets are synonymously referred to as "labels," "annotations," "responses," or simply "outputs."

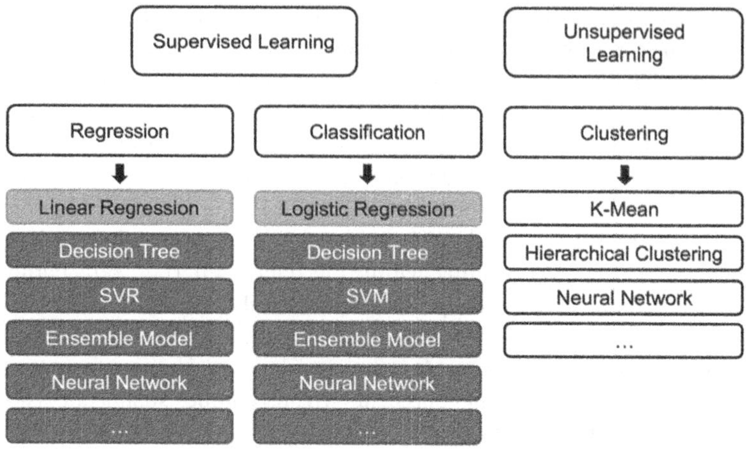

Fig. 1 Exemplary algorithms of supervised and unsupervised learning

algorithms presented in dark gray can be adapted such that they are able to learn linear or non-linear relations within the data. Support vector regression (SVR), support vector machines (SVMs), and neural networks are, for example, applicable in both linear and non-linear prediction tasks, with slight adjustments. Decision trees and more complex variations such as random forests and gradient-boosted trees, combined within ensemble models (i.e., combinations of predictions of individually poor performing models—so-called "weak learners"), are inefficient in learning linear relations. The advantage of linear algorithms is that the results are easier to interpret. On the other hand, algorithms with non-linear learning abilities are more flexible and can therefore detect non-linearities with ease, but are also prone to overfit. Overfitting means that a model performs well on data used in the training process (i.e., training data) but poorly on novel (i.e., test) data.

Most real-world data is available in unstructured form and a corresponding target is mostly not assigned (Lee, 2017). Without these feature–target pairs, supervised learning techniques are infeasible. However, unsupervised learning can extract meaningful information from unstructured data. Figure 1 summarizes some popular unsupervised learning algorithms. In general, unsupervised learning techniques cluster unstructured data to either draw conclusions or to assign targets which can then be used for supervised learning. Lastly, semi-supervised learning combines supervised and unsupervised learning by having a small set of feature–target pairs and a big set of features not assigned to targets (for example, to boost predictive performance). Here, a model is trained on the small set of available feature–target pairs in the first step. This model is then used to predict targets for the big set of features initially not assigned to targets. The model can then be retrained with all feature–target pairs (for an application in credit card fraud detection, see Melo-Acosta et al. 2017).

2.3 The Machine Learning Research Process

ML research consists of six distinct phases: (1) data extraction, (2) data preprocessing, (3) data analysis, (4) data mining, (5) result evaluation and (6) result interpretation. Although data mining (i.e., the actual use of ML algorithms) is only a fraction of the entire research process, finding the most suitable ML algorithm and applying it properly can be tedious and time-consuming. Specifically, the selection of an ML algorithm is not trivial. There is no generally superior ML algorithm, as algorithmic performance depends solely on the given data (Goodfellow et al., 2016). Because supervised learning has been most commonly applied within accounting research, the discussion below is confined to supervised learning. Unsupervised learning is used rather sporadically or as a first step in a two-step research approach combined with supervised learning (e.g., to assign unstructured data to targets which are then used as features for a supervised learning task; Brown et al., 2020). Every supervised learning technique approximates a function $f(.)$ that maps the features X onto the corresponding target y:

$$y \approx f(X).$$

In a regression task, y takes on a continuous value. In a binary classification task, y is restricted to two values (e.g., zero and one). In the latter, it is convenient to write y as a probability of X, $p(X)$. To visualize the mapping process of ML techniques with linear and non-linear learning abilities, Figs. 2 and 3 present examples of regression and classification, respectively.

Figure 2a illustrates a regression example with 100 observations, with feature values presented on the x-axis and target values on the y-axis. As one can see, the dots follow an inverted parabola (i.e., a non-linear pattern). Therefore, it is no surprise that an ML algorithm that is only able to learn linear relations between features and targets does not approximate the patterns in the data very well—see

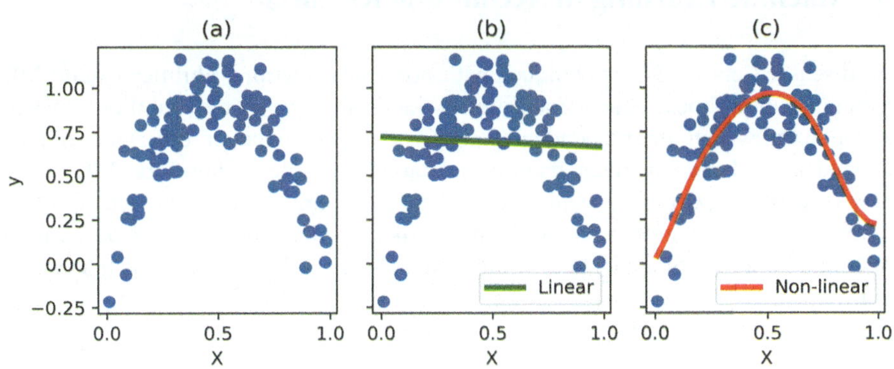

Fig. 2 Regression example with 100 observations, feature values on the x-axis and the corresponding targets on the y-axis

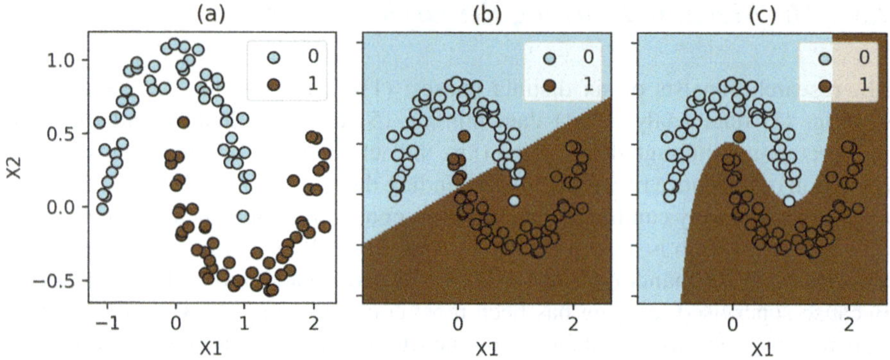

Fig. 3 Binary classification example with 100 observations, feature values on the *x*- and *y*-axis and colored targets

Fig. 2b where a linear regression is used for approximation. An ML algorithm that is able to learn non-linearities within the data, such as SVR, is thus eminently superior in this case, as depicted in Fig. 2c.

In the case of a classification task, the algorithm needs to find a decision boundary that separates the classes from each other. Figure 3a represents a binary classification example, again with 100 observations. In this example, there are two features, one on the *x*-axis and one on the *y*-axis. The corresponding class is visualized by the color of the dots. Similar to the regression task, one can see that a linear class separation is not optimal. Figure 3b, in which a logistic regression is used, confirms this. The background color corresponds to the class prediction of each dot in the graph. However, an ML algorithm with non-linear learning abilities, such as the SVM, separates the two classes almost perfectly (cf., Fig. 3c).

3 Machine Learning in Accounting Research

As discussed above, ML techniques with non-linear learning abilities extend ML techniques with linear learning abilities by increasing the models' ability to detect non-linearities and interdependent patterns that may uncover otherwise hidden dependencies between given feature and target variables. Therefore, ML opens new research opportunities which also benefit accounting research. We structure our review of the literature along the main lines of ML applications in accounting research, being (1) financial accounting and auditing and (2) management accounting.

3.1 Financial Accounting and Auditing

Financial accounting refers to the preparation of financial statements, whereas auditing is concerned with the verification of (annual) financial statements. The objective of an audit is to confirm with reasonable assurance that a financial statement complies with generally accepted accounting principles (GAAP). As this section demonstrates, comparatively more work has been done with respect to ML in audit research-related topics than in financial accounting.

As an example, Baldwin et al. (2006) discuss some major audit tasks suitable for AI based on an earlier classification of these tasks by Abdolmohammadi (1991). They show that many of the 332 audit tasks (e.g., computation of various inventory ratios; comparative studies of sales, bad debts, cash receipts, warranties, and returns) which Abdolmohammadi (1991) deemed suitable for employing decision aid systems are also amenable to automation through ML. More specifically, Baldwin et al. (2006) identify classification tasks like differentiating between collectible and bad debts or legitimate and questionable transactions and risk-assessment tasks like misstatement detection or going-concern predictions. Following Baldwin et al. (2006), there have been renewed calls for more research on the possibilities of AI in auditing (e.g., Brandas et al., 2018; Cao et al., 2015; Earley, 2015; Gepp et al., 2018). Besides the studies already mentioned, many more provide an overview on the application of AI in the field of auditing (e.g., IAASB, 2016; Kokina & Davenport, 2017; T. Sun, 2019; T. Sun & Vasarhelyi, 2017). The main takeaway is that ML makes auditing more efficient and effective because it enables auditors to deal with large amounts of structured and unstructured data which would otherwise be impossible to process.

The literature often suggests ML for specific audit tasks like going-concern prediction or misstatement detection instead of regarding the entire audit process as a potential ML application. As an example for the latter, No et al. (2019) present a potential integration of ML into a larger part of the entire audit process in the form of an ML-based sampling technique. Auditors commonly resort to sampling a (small) percentage of the population of auditable items (e.g., assets, transactions). As a second step, audit findings from the sample items are extrapolated onto the full population. One can imagine that this procedure is not always fail-safe for achieving reasonable assurance for the overall financial statement. Therefore, the authors present a framework called Multidimensional Audit Data Selection (MADS) which is based on ML. First, an auditor trains the AI by filtering items that have higher risks of being misstated out of the entire population. Then, based on these items, an ML outlier detection technique is used to identify further outliers. Afterwards, the outliers are prioritized by a weighting scheme to narrow down the auditor's examination set. MADS improves the efficiency and effectiveness of an auditor by highlighting the transactions with a higher risk of material misstatement (No et al., 2019). Such an approach remains rather rare in the audit research literature; in the following sections, we turn to ML-supported audit tasks that have gained much more traction recently—namely, the detection of fraud and the prediction of going-concern or bankruptcy.

3.2 *Fraud Detection*

Accounting fraud is a global problem, as seen in the many high-profile cases such as Enron in the US, Sino-Forest in China, Vivendi Universal in France and, more recently, Wirecard in Germany. There are estimates that fraud causes global financial losses of US$4.5 trillion each year (Association of Certified Fraud Examiners, 2020). Auditors are responsible for ensuring that financial statements are free from material misstatements originating from either (unintentional) error or (intentional) fraud. However, Fanning and Cogger (1998) state that most auditors possess a lack of knowledge when it comes to the characteristics of accounting fraud and that they are not experienced enough to detect it. Additionally, they point out that managers involved in accounting fraud try to deceive auditors. Besides being the result of intentional misstatements, fraud can be further divided into fraudulent financial reporting (i.e., management fraud) and misappropriation of assets (i.e., employee theft/fraud). Examples of fraudulent financial reporting would be the "manipulation, falsification or alteration of accounting records or supporting documents from which financial statements are prepared or misrepresentation in or intentional omission from the financial statements of events, transactions, or other significant information" (SAS No. 99 Par. 6). Misappropriation of assets involves "the theft of an entity's assets where the effect of the theft causes the financial statements not to be presented, in all material respects, in conformity with GAAP" (SAS No. 99 Par. 6). There is evidence that misappropriation of assets occurs eight times more often than financial statement fraud, but financial statement fraud results in far greater financial losses (Association of Certified Fraud Examiners, 2020). This could be one reason for the greater academic attention to financial statement fraud detection, as discussed below. A commonly used target dataset for financial statement fraud detection in the US is the SEC's Accounting and Auditing Enforcement Releases (AAERs).[2]

The use of ML to detect financial statement fraud can be justified by the associated improvements in auditor decisions and regulators' abilities to identify potentially fraudulent firms by having (more accurate) fraud detection systems (e.g., Hooda et al., 2018; SEC, 2015). By construction, fraud detection is a supervised classification task. Before the application of ML, most research in this area thus relied on logistic regression (e.g., Dechow et al., 2011), which still acts as a popular benchmark in contemporaneous studies (e.g., Bao et al., 2020). The related literature relies heavily on publicly available financial data in structured form (i.e., financial

[2] AAERs contain financial statements with fraudulent account balances identified within two years after the audited financial statement was released (e.g., Green & Choi, 1997).

statement numbers; e.g., Cecchini et al., 2010a; Dechow et al., 2011; Green & Choi, 1997). Nevertheless, unstructured data are used as well, mostly in textual form extracted from the MD&A sections of the financial reports (e.g., Cecchini et al., 2010b; Humpherys et al., 2011; Purda & Skillicorn, 2015). Other unstructured data source examples are social media for textual data or earnings conference calls for auditive data (Dong et al., 2018; Hobson et al., 2012). Methods of processing textual data include counting words that are predictive of fraudulent behavior or analyzing sentiments contained in social media data.[3] This information is then used as features for the classification task. Along with the general challenges of ML (e.g., finding general patterns within the data without overfitting), fraud detection comes with its own challenges. Fraud, in general, is rare and conducted adversarially, meaning fraudsters try their hardest to prevent learning from past events (Bao et al., 2020). The (relative) scarcity of fraud compared to non-fraud cases results in an uneven ratio between fraud and non-fraud cases in any dataset. This issue is also known as the "imbalance problem." Fraud is not only rare, but it is often not detected, and if so, only years later (Bao et al., 2020). Additionally, fraud is rarely a single event but often preceded by a time-series of violations or a slippery slope beginning with minor infractions, despite most research handling fraud as single one-off events. Lastly, misclassification of fraudulent firms is more costly than misclassification of non-fraudulent firms. In line with the respective literature (Bao et al., 2020; Perols, 2011), we refer to this as the "cost problem."

Initial studies linking fraud detection and ML employ neural networks (e.g., Fanning & Cogger, 1998; Green & Choi, 1997). For example, Green and Choi (1997) constructed a sample with an even number of fraud and non-fraud cases extracted from the AAER dataset. They report an improvement of fifty percent by using the neural network instead of random choice.[4] Fanning and Cogger (1998) use a much bigger target and feature set. They consider twenty potential predictors, including some related to the firms' governance structure, such as board size, percentage of outside directors and the duality of roles between chairperson of the board and CEO. With the increased popularity of ML, many more classification methods are used and compared. Kotsiantis et al. (2006) use financial ratios to predict fraud within manufacturing firms listed on the Athens Stock Exchange. Instead of just using individual classification methods and comparing their results, they build a classification ensemble. More specifically, they train individual classification models and combine their predictions according to a voting scheme.[5] Among others, they use classification models based on decision trees, neural networks, logistic regressions, and SVMs. With this approach, they outperform the prediction of each individual ML algorithm.

[3] For more information about social media analytics, see Kinra et al. (2022).

[4] Of course, random choice would result in a fifty percent chance of making the correct prediction due to the balanced dataset.

[5] For example, counting the classification predictions of each model and selecting the majority class.

Perols (2011) criticizes the prior literature for not appropriately considering the challenges of fraud detection. He uses undersampling[6] to solve the imbalance and cost problem. In an experimental setting, the author determines the best undersampling ratio (i.e., ratio between fraud and non-fraud cases) in the training and test dataset. Perols (2011) uses similar algorithms as Kotsiantis et al. (2006). A subsequent study by Perols et al. (2017) employs two more methods to address the imbalance problem: (1) the abundance of already identified features in the literature, which can result in the "curse of dimensionality,"[7] and (2) the common handling of fraud as homogeneous events, although one could differentiate between, for example, revenue and expense fraud. Besides undersampling the observations, they use two variations of undersampling on the feature level: randomly selecting features and selecting features based on a priori knowledge to group them into specific types of fraud, e.g., revenue versus expense fraud (Perols et al., 2017). Observation undersampling and feature undersampling with *a priori* knowledge work best under the out-of-sample (OOS) approach[8] and result in an accuracy improvement of about ten percent compared to the benchmarks (Perols et al., 2017). Rather than changing the sample composition, Kondo et al. (2019) use an ensemble model that still performs well on imbalanced data. They incorporate a weighted random forest that penalizes misclassifications of fraudulent cases more than of non-fraudulent cases (Chen et al., 2004).

Li et al. (2016) are the first who used raw accounting variables (i.e., publicly available financial data) instead of financial ratios (e.g., modified Jones model discretionary accruals) or non-financial ratios (e.g., abnormal change in employees, Dechow et al., 2011). While raw accounting variables form the basis for financial and non-financial ratios, they argue that raw accounting variables contain more information because ratios lose information when they get constructed. They use SVMs with different kernel functions for the prediction and ensemble methods. It is worth noting that they specifically use an OOS procedure instead of an in-sample (IS) approach that is commonly used for causal inferences (Li et al., 2016). IS results in very optimistic predictions and is not recommended because predictions are made on data already seen by the model; hence, the more the model overfits, the better the predictions. They show superior performance for all methods using raw accounting variables to the benchmarks with financial and non-financial ratios (Li et al., 2016). Bao et al. (2020) conduct a similar study, but they compare more ML methods and use different evaluation metrices. The predictive power of unstructured, textual data from the MD&A section in combination with financial

[6] Undersampling means randomly deleting cases from the majority class (i.e., non-fraudulent cases in the context of fraud detection). In contrast, oversampling results in the duplication of cases in the minority class (i.e., fraudulent cases in the context of fraud detection). Undersampling, as compared to oversampling, is more effective against class and cost imbalances (Drummond & Holte, 2003).

[7] The curse of dimensionality describes that a complete search for an optimal solution on the entire feature space is becoming computationally harder with every additional feature (Bellman, 1961).

[8] Target prediction on novel data, i.e., data not used in the training process.

ratios is studied by Craja et al. (2020). They present a deep learning model to benefit from unstructured and structured data at the same time. The authors report a substantial predictive improvement compared to commonly used ML techniques such as random forests or SVMs. Furthermore, the deep learning architecture allows them to look into the "black-box" and to identify early warning indicators on the word- and sentence-level. On the word-level, they report early warning indicators like "cost" or "acquisition" and on the sentence-level sentences like "If we are unable to fully integrate acquired products, technologies or businesses, or train, retain and motivate personnel from the acquired businesses, we may not receive the intended benefits of those acquisitions, which could seriously harm our business, operating results and financial condition."

Many studies try to detect fraudulent financial statements, but only a few also take errors (i.e., unintentional misstatements) under consideration. Dutta et al. (2017) fill this research gap by forecasting erroneous as well as fraudulent financial statements. They incorporate a two-step approach consisting of feature selection (i.e., removal of less significant and redundant features) and restatement prediction based on algorithms like decision trees, neural networks, and SVMs. Bertomeu et al. (2020) extend this research by replacing the two-step approach with a regression tree ensemble model, referred to as gradient-boosted regression trees, and the incorporation of additional features.

3.3 Bankruptcy Prediction

Bankruptcy prediction, sometimes also referred to as financial distress prediction, has a long history in accounting and finance research, beginning with the works of Altman (1968) and Beaver (1966). This is quite unsurprising as corporate failures are relevant to a wide array of stakeholders, including but not limited to employees, creditors, shareholders, and even customers and suppliers. In audit research, the same topic is referred to as going-concern prediction, since auditors need to attest whether they believe that a firm will continue to operate in the following fiscal year. For simplicity, this chapter uses bankruptcy prediction as a general term. Similar to fraud detection, bankruptcy prediction is a binary classification problem of whether a company will declare bankruptcy. This line of research started with Beaver (1966), who was the first to employ financial statement variables to predict bankruptcy via logistic regression, and was advanced through the introduction of ML in the 1990s.

The early use of ML within bankruptcy prediction examined structured financial data such as profitability ratios, growth ratios and debt ratios (e.g., Boritz & Kennedy, 1995; Kumar & Ravi, 2007; J. Sun & Li, 2008). In addition to established and well-understood statistical learning methods such as logistic regression, many researchers now favor the supervised learning approach with neural networks, followed by SVMs (Lin et al., 2012). Hybrid models (i.e., the combination of different

ML techniques), unsupervised learning techniques, and genetic algorithms[9] are also applied (Lin et al., 2012). In general, financial data significantly improves bankruptcy prediction accuracy; however, backward-looking financial statement data hardly contains all the relevant information to predict future bankruptcies. As a remedy, recent literature has introduced non-financial, unstructured textual data from annual reports (e.g., Hajek et al., 2014; Shirata et al., 2011), specifically from the MD&A section (e.g., Cecchini et al., 2010b). Features are constructed from this data, for example, by counting words, extracting key phrases, or assigning textual sentiments. Although financial data still dominates the research on bankruptcy prediction, there is convincing evidence that the combination of financial and non-financial data results in superior predictive power (e.g., Cecchini et al., 2010b; du Jardin, 2016; Hajek et al., 2014). Similar to fraud detection research, deep learning is used to extract more meaningful information from unstructured and structured data to further improve predictive performance (e.g., Mai et al., 2019).

3.4 *Other Fields*

Thus far, all studies presented in this review use ML in a predictive sense. This does not always have to be the case, as shown by Bertomeu et al. (2021). The authors study conditional conservatism, which is an asymmetric stock market reaction to good versus bad news, whereby good news is associated with positive returns and bad news with negative returns. Traditionally, this has been done by reverse regression (i.e., regressing earnings on returns) with an interaction term between a negative return indicator and returns (Basu, 1997). It is shown that the coefficient of the interaction term is positive and significant, meaning that earnings react asymmetrically to good and bad news. Instead of simply identifying linearities in the identification of conservatism with a linear regression, the authors study the richness of non-linearities. Specifically, they treat the coefficients not as constants but as a functional form of other explanatory variables, such as book-to-market, size, and leverage. These coefficients are fitted by a neural network and studied afterwards. The main objective is thus to understand the non-linear behavior of conservatism. They report three novel insights on conservatism: (1) conservatism has been decreasing since the 1980s and is now at an all-time low; (2) the relation between conservatism and size or book-to-market equity is convex, while it is concave between conservatism and leverage or volatility; (3) the relation between conservatism, investment, and cost of capital has a greater economic magnitude when using ML and less measurement noise.

[9] Genetic algorithms are inspired by natural selection, meaning a model evolves through generations and the allowance for random mutations, which will be kept if they serve the model objective.

4 Management Accounting

Management accounting, also referred to as managerial accounting, is distinct from financial accounting and reporting in that it refers to internal reporting systems. The Institute of Management Accountants defines management accounting more specifically as "a profession that involves partnering in management decision making, devising planning and performance management systems, and providing expertise in financial reporting and control to assist management in the formulation and implementation of an organization's strategy" (Institute of Management Accountants, 2008). Accordingly, as compared to financial accounting, management accounting focuses more on value-creation, decision-making, planning, and forecasting, as well as risk management (e.g., Wang & Wang, 2016). In practice, tasks of management accountants include cost management to achieve long-term goals and objectives, management and operational control through performance measurement, and internal (cost) activity planning (e.g., budgeting). The use of companies' big data thus gives management accountants the perfect tools to answer questions about what has happened, what likely will happen, and what is the optimized solution. For these tasks, they can employ descriptive statistics, predictive analytics (i.e., extrapolating the status quo into the future), and prescriptive analytics (i.e., prescribing the optimal solution or suggesting changes to operational practices) within each of these tasks (e.g., Appelbaum et al., 2017). ML is ideal for predictive analytics, which arguably is becoming more important than descriptive statistics because of the intensified competition triggered by globalization and technological advances (see Cokins, 2013). This section considers exemplary studies of performance management, cost management and risk control.

Performance management can be subdivided into employee performance evaluation and project performance evaluation. With employee performance evaluation, ML is used to support decision-making in the human resource management functions of hiring and monitoring processes (Hagemann and Klug, 2022). In terms of methodology, variants of decision trees are most often used due to their interpretability. For example, Al-Radaideh and Al Nagi (2012) study features that may affect employees' performance in IT companies with the help of two decision tree variations. The target (i.e., employee performance) consists of three classes: *accomplish*, *exceed*, and *far exceed*. They report that the job title and the type of university from which the employee graduated have the strongest predictive power. Based on the same classification techniques, Kirimi and Moturi (2016) conduct a similar study with data from the Kenyan School of Government. Here, the employees' experience has the strongest predictive power. With respect to project performance evaluation, ML is used to analyze large amounts of data to extract hidden knowledge which helps decision-makers to manage workforces, cash flows and other resources. For more general purposes of company performance evaluation, Cheriyan et al. (2018) predict sales of e-commerce companies. They compare different models with gradient-boosted regression trees exhibiting the best predictive performance. Another means to evaluate companies' performance is by analyzing costumer satisfaction. As an example, Katarya et al. (2020) train a model on Yelp[10] online reviews, with the text of reviews representing features and the star ratings assigned by customers representing sentiment. Every review with three or more stars is coded as one, and every other review as zero, i.e., it is a binary classification task. The trained model can then be applied to reviews without stars in order to automatically evaluate these costumers' sentiment towards the firm.

Cost management follows the cycle of resource planning, cost estimation, cost budgeting and cost control (Bhimani et al., 2019). An important task of management accountants is to correctly estimate costs of upcoming projects to support the firms' strategic decision-makers efficiently (Lum et al., 2008). It mainly takes place in the pre-project planning phase, as the vast majority of costs are only influenceable early on. Estimating construction projects is a prominent area in which ML is already integrated into cost management (Hashemi et al., 2020). Here, the aim of ML is to increase predictive power by taking advantage of non-linearities while using more features and simultaneously being able to handle multicollinearities. Son et al. (2012), for example, incorporate a hybrid model consisting of a PCA to deal with multicollinearities and an SVR to predict the cost performance of commercial building projects. They report higher predictive performance compared to other commonly used data mining techniques such as neural networks, decision trees and stand-alone SVRs. A more adapted neural network, with various regularization techniques for better generalization and less overfitting, is used by Chandanshive and Kambekar (2019), who also report successful predictive abilities. While the aforementioned studies only use structured data as features, Williams and Gong (2014) combine structured (financial) data with unstructured textual data. The authors predict construction cost overruns and show that certain words and phrases contained in tender (i.e., bidding) documents are associated with unplanned cost increases for construction projects. Other industries in which the use of ML to estimate costs is documented in the scientific literature are software development and healthcare (e.g., Al Asheeri & Hammad, 2019; Koh & Tan, 2011).

In the area of risk control, ML is used to detect early warning signs of financial distress that could potentially result in bankruptcy. This makes this line of research comparable to the going-concern-related research in the audit literature. Koyuncugil and Ozgulbas (2012) present such a system for small and medium-sized enterprises. Their focus is on building a system that is understandable for managers and decision-makers who do not have financial or data mining expertise. For that reason, they use a variation of the highly interpretable decision trees. With financial features (categorized into liquidity ratios, ratios of financial position, turnover ratios and profitability ratios) and binary targets (e.g., poor versus strong financial performance), the authors identify two meaningful early warning signs, namely profit before tax to own funds and return on equity. Credit scoring is another area in which ML supports the risk control function. Better decisions about whether loan applicants are eventually accepted result in reduced creditor risks and, most

[10] Yelp is a crowd-sourced platform for business reviews.

importantly, costs (Huang et al., 2007). In their study, Huang et al. (2007) use the combination of a genetic algorithm for feature selection and an SVM for prediction purposes, i.e., a hybrid model. The SVM is used due to the high performance with relatively few features compared to neural network or decision tree classifiers. Since even small accuracy improvements are effective in terms of future cost savings, it does not come as a great surprise that the use of data mining in this field is studied quite rigorously (M. R. Kumar & Gunjan, 2020). A recent trend in the credit scoring literature is the use of deep learning (e.g., Dastile & Celik, 2021; Gunnarsson et al., 2021; Wu et al., 2021).

In summary, ML in management accounting allows hidden relations and tendencies to be uncovered while using different data types, such as semi-structured and unstructured data, or by using more data overall (Wang & Wang, 2016). We find that the use of ML is comparatively well established in the financial accounting and audit literature. In management accounting, ML is still a niche topic, apart from the literature on credit scoring, which shows extensive similarities to, for instance, the research on predicting bankruptcies.

5 State of the Art and Future Opportunities

In most fields, the application of ML has followed a similar path. Suitable research areas for ML initially evolved by using simple, structured data sets that were mostly processed using classical statistical models, such as logistic regressions for classification and linear regression for regression tasks. With the rise of ML, such tasks have been applied more often across many fields, but to similar research questions as before. With generally greater acceptance of ML, researchers in the field turn to methodological improvements, such as the comparison of individual ML techniques and model ensemble creations. As the usefulness of unstructured data becomes recognized, combined applications of structured and unstructured data follow suit. Deep learning is then introduced to extract information most efficiently from structured and unstructured data alike. A simultaneous phase focuses on interpretability with, for example, explainable ML, although its application nevertheless remains rare.

As can be seen in the fraud detection literature, structured and unstructured data are already studied, but deep learning is applied only partially. Future research could further concentrate on deep learning or on explainable ML to gain a better understanding of the relations between features and targets (Psychoula et al., 2021). More specifically, the time-series dependence of accounting fraud with various features could be studied. This could then be used to uncover still hidden fraud cases, providing auditors, regulators, and investors with an early warning system for fraudulent behavior. Unsupervised learning or semi-supervised learning can be used for this purpose. Although the imbalance problem is solved by changing the sample composition through random sampling, it is also possible to apply classification models which are well suited for imbalanced datasets (see Kondo et al., 2019). Such models use a weighted random forest instead of a simple random forest. Another model warranting consideration would be the extreme gradient-boosting algorithm, which is insensitive to imbalances (Zięba et al., 2016).

Similar to accounting fraud detection, the bankruptcy prediction literature already exploits the use of structured and unstructured data as well as the application of deep learning techniques. Despite extensive research using various data types and classification techniques, the predictive performance has not improved much in recent years, and the investigation of predictive features is still called for (Lin et al., 2012; Tang et al., 2020). A possible solution would be a greater focus on model interpretability. Researchers could thereby answer hypotheses more efficiently, and practitioners' acceptance of ML-based bankruptcy prediction models would increase (H. Son et al., 2019). To our knowledge, there are not many studies with a focus on interpretability. The work of Tang et al. (2020) is among the rare exceptions. They compare different prediction horizons and many ML techniques, from simple logistic regression over SVMs to deep neural networks, with a focus on interpretability—not necessarily model interpretability, but rather the interplay between feature (data) types, prediction horizons and predictive performance. Methodically, they see great potential in the use of deep learning, which could be especially valuable given its capabilities in processing structured and unstructured data simultaneously.

Another improvement might entail the implicit handling of imbalances. Bankruptcies, much like accounting fraud, are rare events in real-world data, rarely exceeding one percent of the population (Kuger, 2019). Therefore, it is necessary to deal with the imbalance problem, which is typically ignored or bypassed by drawing evenly distributed samples. There are only some studies that deal with this imbalance problem implicitly, by, for example, modifying the sample distribution through random sampling or using ML algorithms that are suitable under an imbalanced dataset, e.g., extreme gradient-boosting tree (e.g., Gruszczyński, 2019; Le et al., 2018; Le et al., 2018; Zięba et al., 2016).

For management accounting research, specifically cost estimation and decision-making support, ML is particularly suited to processing external data, such as data from suppliers, partners, and competitors (Wang & Wang, 2016). So far, mainly cost figures estimated on internal business operations have been used (Lanen et al., 2013). The application of deep learning would also be feasible since most external data are available in unstructured form. Lastly, for risk control, there is great potential for predicting such outcomes as sales, cash flows and earnings to detect discontinuities early on, in the manner of an early warning system.

References

Abdolmohammadi, M. J. (1991). Factors affecting auditors' perceptions of applicable decision aids for various audit tasks. *Contemporary Accounting Research, 7*(2), 535–548.

Al Asheeri, M. M., & Hammad, M. (2019). Machine learning models for software cost estimation. *International Conference on Innovation and Intelligence for Informatics, Computing, and Technologies, 3ICT 2019* (pp. 1–6). IEEE.

Al-Radaideh, Q. A., & Al Nagi, E. (2012). Using data mining techniques to build a classification model for predicting employees performance. *International Journal of Advanced Computer Science and Applications, 3*(2), 144–151.

Altman, E. I. (1968). Financial ratios, discriminant analysis and the prediction of corporate bankruptcy. *Journal of Finance, 4*, 589–609.

Appelbaum, D., Kogan, A., Vasarhelyi, M. A., & Yan, Z. (2017). Impact of business analytics and enterprise systems on managerial accounting. *International Journal of Accounting Information Systems, 25*, 29–44.

Association of Certified Fraud Examiners. (2020). *Report to the Nations: 2020 Global Study on Occupational Fraud and Abuse.*

Baldwin, A. A., Brown, C. E., & Trinkle, B. S. (2006). Opportunities for artificial intelligence development in the accounting domain: The case for auditing. *Intelligent Systems in Accounting, Finance and Management, 14*(3), 77–86.

Bao, Y., Hilary, G., & Ke, B. (2020). Artificial intelligence and fraud detection. In *Innovative technology at the interface of finance and operations* (working paper).

Bao, Y., Ke, B., Li, B., Yu, J., & Zhang, J. (2020). Detecting accounting fraud in publicly traded U.S. firms using a machine learning approach. *Journal of Accounting Research, 58*(1), 199–235.

Basu, S. (1997). The conservatism principle and the asymmetric timeliness of earnings. *Journal of Accounting and Economics, 24*(1), 3–37.

Beaver, W. H. (1966). Financial ratios as predictors of failure. *Journal of Accounting Research, 4*, 71–111.

Bellman, R. E. (1961). *Adaptive control processes*. Princeton University Press.

Bertomeu, J., Cheynel, E., Floyd, E., & Pan, W. (2020). Using machine learning to detect misstatements. *Review of Accounting Studies, 26*, 468–519.

Bertomeu, J., Cheynel, E., Liao, Y., & Milone, M. (2021). Using machine learning to measure conservatism. Working Paper Washington University in St. Louis, available under: https://papers.ssrn.com/sol3/papers.cfm?abstract_id=3924961

Bhimani, A., Datar, S. M., Horngren, C. T., & Rajan, M. V. (2019). *Management and cost accounting* (7th ed.). Pearson Education, Limited.

Boritz, E. J., & Kennedy, D. B. (1995). Effectiveness of neural network types for prediction of business failure. *Expert Systems with Applications, 9*(4), 503–512.

Brandas, C., Muntean, M., & Didraga, O. (2018). Intelligent decision support in auditing: Big data and machine learning approach. In *17th International Conference on Informatics in economy, IE 2018*, Education, Research & Business Technologies, The Bucharest University of Economic Studies, Bucharest, Romania, pp. 425–430.

Brown, N. C., Crowley, R. M., & Elliott, W. B. (2020). What are you saying? Using topic to detect financial misreporting. *Journal of Accounting Research, 58*(1), 237–291.

Cao, M., Chychyla, R., & Stewart, T. (2015). Big data analytics in financial statement audits. *Accounting Horizons, 29*(2), 423–429.

Cecchini, M., Aytug, H., Koehler, G. J., & Pathak, P. (2010a). Detecting management fraud in public companies. *Management Science, 56*(7), 1146–1160.

Cecchini, M., Aytug, H., Koehler, G. J., & Pathak, P. (2010b). Making words work: Using financial text as a predictor of financial events. *Decision Support Systems, 50*(1), 164–175.

Chandanshive, V. B., & Kambekar, A. R. (2019). Estimation of building construction cost using artificial neural networks. *Journal of Soft Computing in Civil Engineering, 3*(1), 91–107.

Chen, C., Liaw, An., & Breiman, L. (2004). Using random forest to learn imbalanced data. In *Technical report 666,* Statistics Department of University of California at Berkley.

Cheriyan, S., Ibrahim, S., Mohanan, S., & Treesa, S. (2018). Intelligent sales prediction using machine learning techniques. In *International Conference on Computing, Electronics & Communications Engineering (ICCECE).*

Cokins, G. (2013). Top 7 trends in management accounting. *Strategic Finance, 95*(6), 21–30.

Craja, P., Kim, A., & Lessmann, S. (2020). Deep learning for detecting financial statement fraud. *Decision Support Systems, 139*, 113421.

Dastile, X., & Celik, T. (2021). Making deep learning-based predictions for credit scoring explainable. *IEEE Access, 9*, 50426–50440.
Dechow, P. M., Ge, W., Larson, C. R., & Sloan, R. G. (2011). Predicting material accounting misstatements. *Contemporary Accounting Research, 28*(1), 17–82.
Dong, W., Liao, S., & Zhang, Z. (2018). Leveraging financial social media data for corporate fraud detection. *Journal of Management Information Systems, 35*(2), 461–487.
Drummond, C., & Holte, R. C. (2003). C4.5, class imbalance, and cost sensitivity: Why undersampling beats oversampling. In *Proceedings of the Twentieth International Conference on Machine Learning: Workshop – Learning from imbalanced data sets II*, pp. 1–8.
du Jardin, P. (2016). A two-stage classification technique for bankruptcy prediction. *European Journal of Operational Research, 254*(1), 236–252.
Dutta, I., Dutta, S., & Raahemi, B. (2017). Detecting financial restatements using data mining techniques. *Expert Systems with Applications, 90*(30), 374–393.
Earley, C. E. (2015). Data analytics in auditing: Opportunities and challenges. *Business Horizons, 58*(5), 493–500.
Fanning, K. M., & Cogger, K. O. (1998). Neural network detection of management fraud using published financial data. *Intelligent Systems in Accounting, Finance and Management, 7*(1), 21–41.
Gepp, A., Linnenluecke, M. K., O'Neill, T. J., & Smith, T. (2018). Big data techniques in auditing research and practice: Current trends and future opportunities. *Journal of Accounting Literature, 40*, 102–115.
Géron, A. (2017). *Hands-on machine learning with Scikit-learn and TensorFlow*. O'Reilly Media, Inc.
Goodfellow, I., Bengio, Y., & Courville, A. (2016). *Deep learning*. MIT Press.
Green, B. P., & Choi, J. H. (1997). Assessing the risk of management fraud through neural network technology. *Auditing: A Journal of Practice & Theory, 16*(1), 14–28.
Gruszczyński, M. (2019). On unbalanced sampling in bankruptcy prediction. *International Journal of Financial Studies, 7*(2), 28.
Gunnarsson, B. R., vanden Broucke, S., Baesens, B., Óskarsdóttir, M., & Lemahieu, W. (2021). Deep learning for credit scoring: Do or don't? *European Journal of Operational Research, 295*(1), 292–305.
Hagemann, V., & Klug, K. (2022). Human resource management in a digital environment. In L. Hornuf, *Diginomics research perspectives: The role of digitalization in business and society*, (pp. @@@). Springer international publishing.
Hajek, P., Olej, V., & Myskova, R. (2014). Forecasting corporate financial performance using sentiment in annual reports for stakeholders' decision-making. *Technological and Economical Development of Economy, 20*(4), 721–738.
Hashemi, S. T., Ebadati, O. M., & Kaur, H. (2020). Cost estimation and prediction in construction projects: A systematic review on machine learning techniques. *SN Applied Science, 2*, 1703.
Hobson, J. L., Mayew, W. J., & Venkatachalam, M. (2012). Analyzing speech to detect financial misreporting. *Journal of Accounting Research, 50*(2), 349–392.
Hoitash, R., & Hoitash, U. (2018). Measuring accounting reporting complexity with XBRL. *The Accounting Review, 93*(1), 259–287. https://doi.org/10.2308/ACCR-51762
Hooda, N., Bawa, S., & Rana, P. S. (2018). Fraudulent firm classification: A case study of an external audit. *Applied Artificial Intelligence, 32*(1), 48–64.
Huang, C.-L., Chen, M.-C., & Wang, C.-J. (2007). Credit scoring with a data mining approach based on support vector machines. *Expert Systems with Applications, 33*(4), 847–856.
Humpherys, S. L., Moffitt, K. C., Burns, M. B., Burgoon, J. K., & Felix, W. F. (2011). Identification of fraudulent financial statements using linguistic credibility analysis. *Decision Support Systems, 50*(3), 585–594.
Institute of Management Accountants. (2008). *Statements on management accounting: Definition of management accounting*. www.imanet.org
International Auditing and Assurance Standards Board. (2016). *Exploring the growing use of technology in the audit, with a focus on data analytics*. IFAC.

James, G., Witten, D., Hastie, T., & Tibshirani, R. (2013). *An introduction to statistical learning*. Springer. https://doi.org/10.1007/978-1-4614-7138-7

Kashyap, P. (2017). *Machine learning for decision makers*. Apress.

Katarya, R., Gautam, A., Bandgar, S. P., & Koli, D. (2020). Analyzing customer sentiments using machine learning techniques to improve business performance. In *International Conference on Advances in Computing, Communication Control and Networking (ICACCCN)*.

Kinra, A., Kotzab, H., & Siekmann, F. (2022). Social media analytics in operations and supply chain management: Opportunities, challenges and paradoxes. In L. Hornuf (Ed.), *Diginomics research perspectives: The role of digitalization in business and society*, (pp. @@@). Springer international publishing.

Kirimi, J. M., & Moturi, C. A. (2016). Application of data mining classification in employee performance prediction. *International Journal of Computer Applications, 146*(7), 28–35.

Koh, H. C., & Tan, G. (2011). Data mining applications in healthcare. *Journal of Healthcare Information Management, 19*(2), 64–72.

Kokina, J., & Davenport, T. H. (2017). The emergence of artificial intelligence: How automation is changing auditing. *Journal of Emerging Technologies in Accounting, 14*(1), 115–122.

Kondo, S., Miyakawa, D., Shiraki, K., Suga, M., & Usuki, M. (2019). Using machine learning to detect and forecast accounting fraud. *RIETI*.

Kotsiantis, S., Koumanakos, E., Tzelepis, D., & Tampakas, V. (2006). Forecasting fraudulent financial statements using data mining. *International Journal of Computational Intelligence, 3*(2), 104–110.

Koyuncugil, A. S., & Ozgulbas, N. (2012). Financial early warning system model and data mining application for risk detection. *Expert Systems with Applications, 39*(6), 6238–6253.

Kuger, M. (2019). *Global bankruptcy report 2019*. Dun & Bradstreet Worldwide Network.

Kumar, M. R., & Gunjan, V. K. (2020). Review of machine learning models for credit scoring analysis. *Ingeniería Solidaria, 16*(1), 1–16.

Kumar, P. R., & Ravi, V. (2007). Bankruptcy prediction in banks and firms via statistical and intelligent techniques: A review. *European Journal of Operational Research, 180*(1), 1–28.

Lanen, W., Anderson, S., & Maher, M. (2013). *Fundamentals of cost accounting* (4th ed.) McGraw-Hill Education.

Le, T., Lee, M. Y., Park, J. R., & Baik, S. W. (2018). Oversampling techniques for bankruptcy prediction: Novel features from a transaction dataset. *Symmetry, 10*(4), 79.

Le, T., Son, L. H., Vo, M. T., Lee, M. Y., & Baoik, S. W. (2018). A cluster-based boosting algorithm for bankruptcy prediction in a highly imbalanced dataset. *Symmetry, 10*(7), 250.

Lee, I. (2017). Big data: Dimensions, evolution, impacts, and challenges. *Business Horizons, 60*(3), 293–303.

Li, B., Yu, J., Zhang, J., & Ke, B. (2016). Detecting accounting frauds in publicly traded U.S. firms: A machine learning approach. *Asian Conference on Machine Learning, PMLR, 45*, 173–188.

Lin, W.-Y., Hu, Y.-H., & Tsai, C.-F. (2012). Machine learning in financial crisis prediction: A survey. *IEEE Transactions on Systems, Man, and Cybernetics, 42*(4), 421–436.

Lum, K. T., Baker, D. R., & Hihn, J. M. (2008). The effects of data mining techniques on software cost estimation. *IEEE international conference on engineering management (EMC)*.

Mai, F., Tian, S., Lee, C., & Ma, L. (2019). Deep learning models for bankruptcy prediction using textual disclosures. *European Journal of Operational Research, 274*(2), 743–758.

Melo-Acosta, G. E., Duitama-Munoz, F., & Arias-Londono, J. D. (2017). Fraud detection in big data using supervised and semi-supervised learning techniques. *Proceedings of the 2017 IEEE Colombian conference on communications and computing, COLCOM 2017*. https://doi.org/10.1109/COLCOMCON.2017.8088206.

Mishra, B. K., Hazra, D., Tarannum, K., & Kumar, M. (2016). Business intelligence using data mining techniques and business analytics. *International conference on System Modeling & Advancement in research trends (SMART)*.

No, W. G., Lee, K. K., Huang, F., & Li, Q. (2019). Multidimensional audit data selection (MADS): A framework for using data analytics in the audit data selection process. *Accounting Horizons, 33*(3), 127–140.

Office of Compliance Inspections and Examinations of the Securities and Exchange Commission (2015). Examination priorities for 2015. http://www.sec.gov/about/offices/ocie/national-examination-program-priorities-2015.pdf

Perols, J. L. (2011). Financial statement fraud detection: An analysis of statistical and machine learning algorithms. *Auditing: A Journal of Practice & Theory, 30*(2), 19–50.

Perols, J. L., Bowen, R. M., Zimmermann, C., & Samba, B. (2017). Finding needles in a haystack: Using data analytics to improve fraud prediction. *The Accounting Review, 92*(2), 221–245.

Psychoula, I., Gutmann, A., Mainali, P., Lee, S. H., Dunphy, P., & Petitcolas, F. A. P. (2021). Explainable machine learning for fraud detection. *IEEE Computer Special Issue on Explainable AI and Machine Learning*, forthcoming.

Purda, L., & Skillicorn, D. (2015). Accounting variables, deception, and a bag of words: Assessing the tools of fraud detection. *Contemporary Accounting Research, 32*(3), 1193–1223.

Shirata, C. Y., Takeuchi, H., Ogino, S., & Watanabe, H. (2011). Extracting key phrases as predictors of corporate bankruptcy: Empirical analysis of annual reports by text mining. *Journal of Emerging Technologies in Accounting, 8*(1), 31–44.

Son, H., Hyun, C., Phan, D., & Hwang, H. J. (2019). Data analytic approach for bankruptcy prediction. *Expert Systems with Applications, 138*(30), 112816.

Son, H., Kim, C., & Kim, C. (2012). Hybrid principal component analysis and support vector machine model for predicting the cost performance of commercial building projects using pre-project planning variables. *Automation in Construction, 27*, 60–66.

Sun, T. (2019). Applying deep learning to audit procedures: An illustrative framework. *Accounting Horizons, 33*(3), 89–109.

Sun, J., & Li, H. (2008). Data mining method for listed companies' financial distress prediction. *Knowledge-Based Systems, 21*(1), 1–5.

Sun, T., & Vasarhelyi, M. A. (2017). Detailed record title: Deep learning and the future of auditing: How an evolving technology could transform analysis and improve judgment. *CPA Journal, 87*(6), 25–29.

Tang, X., Li, S., Tan, M., & Shi, W. (2020). Incorporating textual and management factors into financial distress prediction: A comparative study of machine learning methods. *Journal of Forecasting, 39*(5), 769–787.

Wang, Y., & Wang, Z. (2016). Integrating data mining into managerial accounting system: Challenges and opportunities. *Chinese Business Review, 15*(1), 33–41.

Williams, T. P., & Gong, J. (2014). Predicting construction cost overruns using text mining, numerical data and ensemble classifiers. *Automation in Construction, 43*, 23–29.

Wu, C.-F., Huang, S.-C., Chiou, C.-C., & Wang, Y.-M. (2021). A predictive intelligence system of credit scoring based on deep multiple kernel learning. *Applied Soft Computing, 111*, 107668.

Zięba, M., Tomczak, S. K., & Tomczak, J. M. (2016). Ensemble boosted trees with synthetic features generation in application to bankruptcy prediction. *Expert Systems with Applications, 58*, 93–101.

Asset Pricing in Digital Assets

Steffen Günther, Tobias Glas, and Thorsten Poddig

1 Digital Assets on the Rise

With the rise of "meme" stocks in Q1 of 2021, the power of large internet communities became apparent once again. Retail investors frequently meet to discuss investment strategies on social media platforms like Reddit. In the latest and most prominent examples of GameStop or AMC Entertainment, this has led to rectified actions even against large institutional investors. Thus, private investors again proved to have a significant impact on the market when synchronizing their behavior, which can result in subsequent returns of several hundred percent. Such sharp rises in the value of these stocks are not connected to the fundamentals of the firm, but only driven by the online community itself.

While a similar phenomenon could be observed for digital assets in their infancy, large virtual coins depend less and less on internet communities today. Small digital assets nevertheless remain dependent on retail investor sentiment, which leads to large swings in their prices. Large digital assets are more mature than small ones, which results in a very heterogeneous digital asset universe. Bitcoin, for instance, which was created in 2009, was one of the first digital assets as we know them today. However, the idea of a means of anonymous and digital payments dates back to Chaum (1983), who also founded the company DigiCash, which used private and public keys to make payments untraceable. His idea turned out to be too revolutionary for its time, leading to a default of his company (see Pitta, 1999). After that venture, other web-based forms of payments emerged, including such companies as PayPal, WebMoney, and e-gold (see Griffith, 2014). It took some years before the idea of bitcoin was formulated.

S. Günther · T. Glas · T. Poddig (✉)
Faculty of Business Studies and Economics, University of Bremen, Bremen, Germany
e-mail: steffen.guenther@uni-bremen.de; glas@uni-bremen.de; poddig@uni-bremen.de

L. Hornuf (ed.), *Diginomics Research Perspectives*, Advanced Studies in Diginomics and Digitalization, https://doi.org/10.1007/978-3-031-04063-4_7

Bitcoin is also currently the largest cryptocurrency[1] by market capitalization, trading at prices above US$40,000 per coin as of September 2021. The tradable universe of digital assets grew from only a handful in 2009 to almost 10,000 in 2021.[2] Hedge funds, banks, treasury departments of big firms, and institutional investors began adopting digital assets in 2020 and 2021, leading to investments in bitcoin of US$1.5 billion by Tesla and over US$1 billion by MicroStrategy, with many others following that trend. Hence, the importance and value of bitcoin and other digital assets are no longer determined by small internet communities, but by many private and professional investors around the world.

This chapter focuses on digital assets as a new asset class from a financial perspective and investigates whether traditional financial theory is applicable to them. This chapter is divided into two major parts. Section 2 provides a general introduction to digital assets from a technical and institutional perspective. The aim is to provide a basic understanding of the cryptocurrency universe for every reader, not necessarily those in the finance community. It is also demonstrated how the cryptocurrency universe relates to other asset classes such as the stock market, pointing to similarities and differences from an economic perspective.

Section 3 focuses on asset pricing, which was traditionally developed with respect to stocks, but is now also applicable to different types of assets such as bonds, currencies, and even commodities. We revisit important topics in asset pricing theories and examine whether these findings may be applicable to digital assets, providing results from the academic literature and the authors' own research. The power of an internet community, for example, could be used to determine the "fair" value of virtual coins. The internet community could be seen as the network of a specific digital asset. According to Metcalfe's law, the value of a network is proportional to the square of the number of users, which can be easily determined for bitcoin and other digital assets. This could be a first step in arriving at a fair value for assets that only exist in virtual form. Other questions related to asset pricing are: Is there a common source of variation in digital assets (e.g., risk factors) that explains the cross-section of cryptocurrency returns? If so, can the returns be predicted? Are the risk factors priced significantly? Is there a market beta, as proclaimed by the capital asset pricing model? These are only some of the questions the academic community faced decades ago with respect to stocks and are highly relevant today, especially with respect to digital assets.

Section 3 takes a more practical orientation by concretely addressing how well-known investment strategies in stocks may or may not apply to digital assets. Perhaps the most prominent and most intuitive example is momentum. Momentum strategies in stocks rely on the empirically observed phenomenon that winners (stocks showing a high price increase) tend to outperform losers in the future and vice-versa. This allows for simple and successful investment strategies in stocks. Does this also apply to the digital asset universe? No! This section draws from past

[1] The terms "digital asset" and "cryptocurrency" are used interchangeably in this chapter.

[2] See https://coingecko.com/, last visited September 30, 2021.

and present research to demonstrate a very strong reversal effect in digital assets—simply speaking, the extreme opposite of momentum. This shows that we cannot simply transfer knowledge from stocks to this young asset class; digital assets are thus emerging as a compelling subject for asset pricing studies of their own.

2 Digital Assets and their Role in the Global Financial System

2.1 How Does a Blockchain Work?

While the term "cryptocurrency" is very common nowadays, it does not apply to every digital asset. The term rather describes digital assets with their own blockchain, such as bitcoin, litecoin, and forks thereof. A fork in this context is a cryptocurrency based on the same underlying code but with slight adjustments. An example would be bitcoin cash, which is a fork of bitcoin. A cryptocurrency is thus a sort of virtual coin that is connected to its own blockchain and which can be mined (i.e., created) and sent to other users connected to the same blockchain. It can also be used as a general means of payment.

A blockchain is the basis of every cryptocurrency and is also known as the "digital ledger." The digital ledger stores information in the form of "blocks" and adds one block to another with each transaction that occurs. This concatenation is the "chain" of blocks storing transaction information until a predefined block size is reached. The process of adding blocks to the blockchain is essentially as follows:

1. Users of the blockchain send virtual coins to each other.
2. These transactions are stored in the "mempool".
3. Miners draw transactions from the mempool and store them in a block until the maximum block size is reached.
4. In order to add the block to the blockchain, miners complete a mathematical calculation using trial-and-error.
5. The miner who first finds the solution to the problem—i.e., the "nonce" (number used once)—adds the block to the blockchain.
6. Other miners in the network acknowledge the newly mined block by confirming the transactions inside the block.

After the newly mined block has been confirmed by other miners, the transactions actually take place. That process can range from a few seconds to several minutes and depends on various factors such as network hash rate or difficulty. This whole process serves two main purposes: first, it makes the transactions made by users actually happen; second, it ensures that the whole system works properly, that there are no transactions processed twice, and that there is a record of all the processed transactions.

2.2 Digital Asset Classification

Although cryptocurrencies were the first digital assets and dominated the digital asset universe in the first years starting in 2009,[3] other digital assets evolved, especially starting around 2016. Cryptocurrencies, despite what the name might suggest differently, are overwhelmingly not currencies in the sense of being a common basis for storing value and exchanging goods and services. In fact, a distinction in digital assets is made between "cryptocurrencies" and "tokens," with the main difference being that the former have their own blockchains while the latter are built upon existing blockchains. Digital assets include any form of virtual asset, such as ERC-20 tokens, stablecoins, and NFTs. The Ethereum blockchain, for example, allows its users to create various virtual coins (i.e., ERC-20 tokens) that do not have their own blockchain, but instead use the Ethereum blockchain for transactions and other tasks. Digital assets are also distinguished in a financial context, namely as currencies, utility tokens, and security tokens.[4] Stablecoins, in contrast, are said to be backed by some other asset, such as the US dollar or gold. A relatively new phenomenon is NFTs (non-fungible tokens), which essentially track the ownership of digital files like artworks, videos, and images. They can be compared to traditional (fungible) artworks or prints, with the sole difference being their virtual character.

The term digital asset thus carries a variety of technological and financial connotations that coalesced rather quickly from 2009 to 2021—a very short time when compared to other asset classes. Perhaps the oldest form of asset class as we know it today are bonds or, in broader terms, debt. People in ancient times were accustomed to borrowing and lending money and repaying their debts. That debt market evolved into a highly regulated tradeable market with different kinds of debt, which can still be traded today, both on exchanges and over-the-counter. Another very common asset class is equities or stocks. A stock is a part of the equity of a firm or company. Hence, stockholders are also the owners of a specific company, unlike bond holders. Other asset classes like FX (foreign exchange) or commodities are not necessarily tied to a specific firm and might be comparable to digital assets. With an overall market capitalization of US$1.56 trillion,[5] digital assets are rather small compared to the market capitalization of global equity markets, which amounts to approximately US$44 trillion.[6]

---

[3] See https://www.blockchain.com/btc/block/0, last visited May 24, 2021.

[4] A digital (crypto-) currency serves the purpose of transferring value from one user to another. Utility tokens can be used to access different services or information on a web platform connected to that specific utility token. Security tokens, on the other hand, are able to track or mimic the price behavior of any other asset, such as the S&P 500 stock index or even the temperatures in northern California.

[5] See https://coinmarketcap.com/, last visited May 24, 2021.

[6] See https://www.nasdaq.com/articles/us-stock-market-biggest-most-expensive-world-us-economy-not-most -productive-2018-04-02, last visited June 6, 2021.

Digital assets thus differ clearly from other traditional asset classes. Investors own a claim against the assets of a specific company through stocks and debt, and FX is a claim against a currency-issuing central bank; however, digital assets, in terms of "economic" value, are more comparable to commodities such as oil, gold, or silver. Gold, for example, has no "intrinsic" value and its industrial use cases are limited. Gold (and thus ostensibly bitcoin) is often seen as a store of value or even a safe haven asset, which performs well if financial markets crash. This proposition is rejected by Smales (2019), who finds that bitcoin cannot be seen as a (safe) haven asset even during normal market states due to its high volatility and other factors. Klein et al. (2018) even argue that the opposite behavior is true of bitcoin when compared to gold. Haven properties are also rejected by Wang et al. (2019) when comparing to international financial indices, although they do find some hedging effectiveness[7] for larger and more liquid virtual coins. Such a hedging ability is also documented by Fang et al. (2019), depending on global economic uncertainty and the asset class under consideration. Baur and Hoang (2021) propose that stablecoins such as tether (which is said to be backed by one US dollar per unit)[8], however, do exhibit haven properties.

Since digital assets do not inherently have such properties, finance research has debated whether this new financial product comprises its own asset class. Following the original definition by Sharpe (1992), desirable attributes of asset classes are to be "mutually exclusive," "exhaustive," and to "have returns that 'differ'" (Sharpe, 1992, p. 8). This means that digital assets would need to be distinct from other asset classes (in the sense of purpose or regulatory categorization), that they should include a variety of different "coins," and that their return/risk behavior needs to differentiate itself from other asset classes. To investigate these propositions, researchers often measure the dependence between asset classes. The most common and "easiest" statistical tool to do so is correlation analysis. If there are no clear links (i.e., significant correlations) to other asset classes, a certain group of digital assets can be termed an "independent" asset class. Sifat (2021) finds that the cryptocurrency market is not connected to global investor sentiment and therefore supports the idea of virtual assets being an independent class. Charfeddine et al. (2020) also find only weak and changing correlations of crypto assets to traditional assets, which are sensitive to external events. However, they also find no hedging abilities. Such a relationship is documented by Khelifa et al. (2021), who find interactions between digital assets and some hedge fund strategies, especially hedge funds investing in virtual assets. Glas (2019), on the other hand, finds virtually no connection to more established asset classes like equities, commodities or FX.

---

[7] In this context, the term "hedge" can be interpreted as a protection against a loss in market value.

[8] See https://tether.to/faqs/, last visited June 6, 2021.

2.3 The Global Digital Asset Market

The digital asset market has developed rapidly since its inception. While there were only about a dozen digital assets at the early stages (see Glas & Poddig, 2018), the digital asset market now consists of 9456 actively tradable virtual coins[9] and 1673 "dead" (i.e., inactive) coins.[10] Dead coins can constitute failed projects, scam coins, and those with low or even no trading volume or an inactive developer community. That also means that about one-fifth of the whole digital asset universe is made up of dead coins, with probably more to follow.

Another interesting point about the digital asset market is its concentration. Just a few digital assets account for most of the US$1.92 trillion total market capitalization of all coins.[11] The top three coins (as of September 30, 2021) are valued at a combined US$1.242 trillion (bitcoin accounts for approximately $819 billion, Ethereum accounts for $355 billion, and tether is valued at about $68 billion).[12]

Hence, only three coins account for about two-thirds of the total market value of digital assets (approximately 42% market share for bitcoin, 19% for Ethereum, and 4% for tether). Within this group of three, bitcoin's clear dominance in terms of market value points to its importance for the whole digital asset space, as illustrated in Fig. 1, which plots the relative market share of bitcoin, Ethereum, litecoin, and ripple over time. Table 1 provides context for understanding the return behavior of large digital assets.

The most obvious key figure turns out to be the risk, with annualized volatilities up to 254%. The maximum drawdown (i.e., the percentage of invested capital an investor would have lost if investing at the peak and selling at the lowest price) shows high possible losses. Digital assets are thus highly risky assets for which a near total loss is highly plausible.

Another interesting effect can be observed in the trade volume on digital asset exchanges. The daily total spot crypto trading volume amounts to around US$95 billion on September 30, 2021.[13] The highest trading volume is handled by the exchange Binance, which accounts for approximately US$18 billion (19% market share). The second most volume is traded on the Mandala exchange (US$15 billion), followed by BKEX (US$9 billion) and OKEx (US$5 billion). The remaining volume is traded on more than 300 other crypto exchanges, which means trading is also dominated by few exchanges, but to a lesser extent than the largest three crypto assets dominating all other digital assets.[14]

---

[9] See https://www.coingecko.com/, last visited September 30, 2021.

[10] See https://99bitcoins.com/deadcoins/, last visited September 30, 2021.

[11] See https://coinmarketcap.com/charts/, "Total Cryptocurrency Market Cap," last visited September 30, 2021.

[12] See https://coinmarketcap.com/charts/, last visited September 30, 2021.

[13] See https://coinmarketcap.com/, "24 h Vol," last visited September 30, 2021.

[14] See https://coinmarketcap.com/rankings/exchanges/, last visited September 30, 2021.

Fig. 1 Relative market share of selected digital assets over time. Data is retrieved from www.coinpaprika.com

Table 1 Descriptive summary statistics of four of the leading cryptocurrencies and a value-weighted market index

Asset	Mean (%)	Median (%)	Std (%)	Start	Max Drawdown (%)
BTC	1.496	1.224	77.0	2014–01	−79.17
ETH	4.237	1.531	142.77	2015–08	−93.72
LTC	1.650	0.539	121.44	2014–01	−84.84
XRP	3.726	−0.617	253.99	2014–01	−94.91
Index	2.425	1.661	83.73	2014–01	−83.83
S&P500	0.245	0.377	16.40	2014–01	−33.93

"BTC" is bitcoin, "ETH" is Ethereum, "LTC" is litecoin, and "XRP" is the currency used on RippleNet. "S&P500" denotes the Standard & Poor's stock market index of the largest US companies. Mean (%) and Median (%) are from weekly discrete returns. Std (%) denotes the annualized standard deviation of weekly returns. Start indicates the year and month of the first observation in the data sample, with observation ranges ending in June 2021. Data is retrieved from www.coinpaprika.com

All these numbers refer to spot trading, which is buying or selling the digital asset under consideration "physically." It is also possible to trade derivatives[15] on digital coins on those exchanges. The total derivative trading volume on the same day is

[15] Derivatives are products referenced to an underlying, such as a stock. As such the value of a derivative product is *derived* from its underlying. Futures, forwards, options or swaps are all examples for derivatives which can have stocks, bonds, exchanges rates or even houses as an underlying. Derivatives tend to be more liquid than the underlying.

even higher (US$151 billion) than the spot trading volume and is dominated by the exchange Binance. On September 30, 2021, derivative trades on Binance amounted to US$58 billion, followed by Huobi Global with US$19 billion, OKEx with almost US$14 billion, FTX with US$10 billion, Bybit with US$9 billion, and CoinTiger with US$8 billion.[16]

Only 37 of the 312 crypto exchanges offer derivative trading, but the trade volume in derivatives clearly exceeds the spot trading volume, making the whole crypto space vulnerable to large derivative bets, which might need to be liquidated at large adverse price moves. In traditional asset classes, the derivative trading volume exceeds spot trading volume as well.[17] However, with clear regulations in place, the effect of derivative trading on spot market volatility is heavily debated in the academic literature. There are no clear indications for stabilizing or even destabilizing effects, which means derivative trading does not necessarily have an impact on spot market trading. The striking difference between derivatives in traditional asset classes and crypto derivatives is regulation and organization. Equity futures, for example, are based on a sound regulatory framework, and open positions on one exchange can be closed on another exchange. The same does not apply to digital assets. There remains no clear regulatory framework, and positions cannot be transferred, which makes the trader dependent on the crypto derivative's exchange of choice.

Spot trading volume, on the other hand, is not dominated by bitcoin, but by the stablecoin tether. Tether is said to be backed by US$1 per unit and therefore provides an easy way to convert crypto holdings into fiat money and vice-versa. It is also heavily relied on by crypto exchanges, which explains its high trade volume of US$67 billion. Tether is followed by bitcoin and Ethereum, with US$31 billion and US$18 billion trade volume, respectively.[18]

There is thus significant concentration in many parts of the digital asset market, which can have a large impact on any scientific study focusing on this young and emerging asset class. For example, when using market- or volume-weighted market indices, the results are driven by bitcoin or tether, respectively. Therefore, researchers need to account for these market structural implications in their studies. Asset pricing studies are especially prone to such dominance, since asset pricing often uses portfolio (sorts) and indices to arrive at conclusions. The next section thus discusses asset pricing methods and how to cope with skewed or missing data and details the results of some published studies and their implications for crypto

[16] See https://coinmarketcap.com/rankings/exchanges/derivatives/, last visited September 30, 2021.

[17] The daily derivatives trading volume for DAX index futures on July 19, 2021 amounted to 49,992,040,175 EUR on the EUREX exchange (see https://www.eurex.com/resource/blob/2721176/029c20796dfde46909b3de42ef061610/data/dailystat_20210719.xls, last visited July 20, 2021), whereas the spot trading volume was only 4,398,312,516 EUR at Börse Frankfurt at the same day (see https://www.boerse-frankfurt.de/indices/dax/price-history/historical-prices-and-volumes, last visited July 20, 2021).

[18] See https://coinmarketcap.com/, "Volume (24 h)," last visited September 30, 2021.

investment strategies. Section 3 also focuses on investments into digital assets and various investment strategies that can be used to harvest the high return potential of this emerging asset class.

First, we look at digital assets in combination with other asset classes. Especially for retail or institutional investors, the question arises of whether digital assets increase diversification when added to a portfolio of traditional asset classes. This is important for justifying investments into digital assets from a multi-asset perspective and digs deeper into the question of whether digital assets constitute a unique asset class with relevance for private and institutional investors.

3 Investments into Digital Assets

3.1 Can Digital Assets Be a Good Diversifier?

With the increasing importance of hedge funds in the 1990s and early 2000s, researchers confronted the question of whether hedge funds can add value to a portfolio consisting of traditional assets.[19] The same question applies to digital assets today. To conduct such an analysis, different methods can be used. One is the application of spanning tests, which investigate whether the addition of digital assets to a portfolio of reference (traditional) assets shifts the return/risk relationship significantly to the upside. Markowitz (1952, 1959) introduced efficient portfolios with optimal trade-off between risk and return. Efficiency in this context refers to a portfolio with minimal risk for a given level of desired return. For digital assets with low or almost no correlation to traditional asset classes, the addition of these assets to a portfolio of traditional assets might reduce standard deviations while simultaneously keeping the same return potential.

Chuen et al. (2018) find favourable results for the inclusion of the CRIX index,[20] while Glas and Poddig (2018) do not arrive at a significant upward shift of the efficient frontier (i.e., return/risk profile) when adding an index of digital assets. Schmitz and Hoffmann (2020) also find that digital assets do not shift the efficient frontier upwards in general, but only in some specific periods of time. Similar results are reported by Kajtazi and Moro (2019), who attribute their findings to the positive performance of bitcoin, especially in 2013. Symitsi and Chalvatzis (2019) also arrive at only limited benefits when adding bitcoin to various types of portfolios. They additionally find that commodities are a better way to increase diversification than by adding bitcoin.

---

[19] See for example Edwards and Liew (1999), Schneeweis and Martin (2001), and Karavas and Georgiev (2000).

[20] The CRIX index is an index that includes the largest digital assets by market capitalization and thus tracks the broader market movements. It can be retrieved here: https://thecrix.de/, last visited July 21, 2021.

There is thus no clear evidence of a positive contribution of digital assets to portfolios made up of traditional assets or asset classes. This comes as no surprise, due to the high volatility of digital assets. Most of the traditional portfolio construction approaches aim to reduce risk, which results in only a minimal inclusion of digital assets in such a portfolio. As such, the impact of digital assets is limited, and most of the studies above find no clear benefits for an addition of digital assets to a portfolio of reference assets. Right now, it does not seem to be reasonable for multi-asset investors to add digital assets to their portfolios. Nevertheless, even with these disappointing results, digital assets still provide interesting investment opportunities. It is only necessary to shift from an external view on digital assets to an internal perspective. That is, questions remain on how to structure a portfolio consisting of digital assets exclusively and which digital assets to invest in at which point in time. Some digital assets offer a low correlation to traditional assets such as stocks, bonds or commodities by having a large return potential and high standard deviations (i.e., "risk") at the same time. Therefore, it is even more important to search for drivers of digital asset returns and ways to structure a portfolio containing virtual coins only. In terms of traditional finance, digital asset management needs to follow a strict risk management approach to cope with the high risk and volatility of digital assets. Consequently, to be able to harvest the high-risk premiums in digital assets, digital asset investors need to be aware of the possible risks and get a sense of how to manage their portfolios without losing all of their invested capital (drawdowns of 90%, for example, are not uncommon for digital assets; see Table 1).

3.2 Asset Pricing and Investments

Switching to an "internal" perspective to investigate how digital assets can be priced efficiently, it is advisable to construct investment strategies based on asset characteristics. A characteristic in this context is a variable that describes the price action in the asset class under consideration. Examples of such characteristics are the momentum of all single digital assets, fundamental variables like network hash rate or number of transactions of a blockchain, or simply the nominal price of an asset. Such a characteristic might or might not predict future returns of (digital) assets. For instance, in the stock market, momentum predicts future stock returns – stocks with high momentum are likely to show high returns in the near future. Do we find this in digital assets, too?

To answer such questions, one must grasp the fundamentals of today's empirical asset pricing, which dates back over 300 years to the times when European explorers started exchanging goods with East India and Asia. The financial requirements for such journeys were huge, and while providing lucrative possible returns, the risk of not succeeding was tremendous. To fund such activity, companies began to publicly offer stocks to investors. Remarkably, little was understood about risk and return until the early 1950s with the emergence of modern portfolio theory (see Markowitz

1952, 1959).[21] Tobin's separation theorem (1958), which adds a risk-free investment to the Markowitz model in order to show the independence of investors' risk preference to a portfolio's risk composition itself, is the underlying concept of the well-known capital asset pricing model (CAPM). Sharpe (1964), Lintner (1965) and Mossin (1966) introduce this model proposing a linear relationship between risk and return, specifically between the expected return of an asset and its covariance with the market (portfolio). Thus, referring back to Tobin's separation theorem, it is not the composition of risky assets in the market portfolio that is of interest, but the sensitivity of an asset's return to the return of the market portfolio (the return of the market portfolio is also called market factor). Although this concept was revolutionary and worthy of the 1990 Nobel Memorial Prize in Economics, the single-factor model lacks empirical evidence. After decades of further research and dozens of new proposed risk factors, Fama and French (1993) augmented the CAPM, by adding a value and size factor, to form the Fama–French three-factor model. While the former novelty relies on accounting measurements and covers the effect of higher (lower) returns of firms with higher (lower) book-to-market ratios, size – originally introduced by Banz (1981) – refers to the observation of smaller firms (on average) outperforming larger capitalized companies over long horizons. However, the augmented model is insufficient to cover the full variation in the cross-section of stock returns, leaving possibilities for further research. Most prominently, Carhart (1997) added momentum, a factor originally introduced by Jegadeesh and Titman (1993), and even Fama and French proposed two more risk-factors (profitability and investment), to the Fama–French five-factor model (2015). Today, a proverbial "factor zoo" exists (Cochrane, 2011), counting several hundreds of factors being described in the empirical asset pricing literature (see Harvey et al., 2015). These factors shape the return behavior of various asset classes, but research on digital asset factors is still in its early stages. Therefore, all these prior studies in other asset classes serve as the methodological framework for studies looking at digital assets specifically.

The diversity of factors found in the empirical asset pricing literature raises questions about market efficiency. Are these factors an expression of the pricing mechanism of efficient markets or do they contradict the assumption of efficient markets? Without going into detail exceeding the scope of this chapter, it should be stated that there exist two strands of literature. First is the covariance story based on the efficient market hypothesis of Fama (1970), whose rationale is that factors represent systematic risk, which is priced by the markets. A certain factor model (e.g., the three-factor model) leaving significant intercepts (i.e., alphas) in the regression of returns on these risk factors is due to misspecification and simply calls for more complex models. However, another strand of literature (e.g., Daniel & Titman, 1997) rejects this assumption, arguing that the excess return results from the factor itself (often called a characteristic in this context), rather than the additional risk. The implications for investors nevertheless are tremendous. If the

[21] See Perold (2004).

covariance story is true, investors can do no better than holding a combination of risk factors. Deviations from this efficient portfolio would only increase its variance but not expected returns (Daniel & Titman, 1997). However, if differences in stock returns occur due to mispricing, investors should build hedge portfolios on characteristics by going long (buying) on firms with a high characteristic (e.g., high momentum) value and short-selling firms with low characteristic (e.g. momentum) values (or vice-versa, depending on the characteristic) (Fieberg et al., 2016). These so-called portfolio sorts are common practice in empirical asset pricing (for factor/characteristic exploration) and the investment literature (called investment styles). Applying the same methodology of risk factors and investment styles to digital assets is described in more etail below.

3.3 Investment Strategies Across Asset Classes

The heterogeneity of digital assets as discussed above might raise questions about the comparability of different virtual assets in asset pricing and investment studies. Intuitively, does it make sense to mix assets representing a currency, utility, or traditional security together? One would not mix stocks, bonds, currencies or commodities and treat them equally in traditional market studies. This topic may be addressed in two ways. First, from the authors' own (unreported) results, and in line with the findings of Nakavachara et al. (2019), we can not find statistical differences in returns between different groups of digital assets; however, this issue is still relatively unexplored and in need of further research. Additionally, the previous sub-section mainly focuses on the stock market for asset pricing studies. However, a large strand of literature has transferred portfolio sorts to other asset classes, such as currencies, bonds, and commodities. Asness et al. (2013, 2015) show that several characteristics (i.e., investment styles) are indeed present in and create significant spreads in returns across different asset classes, including stocks. In particular, the authors show that value, momentum, and defensive are robust across asset classes and the time periods under investigation and fulfil liquidity concerns. That being said, even if different digital assets are distinguishable with longer time-series availability, one can expect several characteristics to be asset-class-independent.

The rationale for using certain characteristics as investment styles is straightforward. For a large cross-section of (digital) assets and a predefined reallocation period (normally weeks, for stocks months), assets are sorted into portfolios depending on their characteristic (e.g., in ascending order into quantile or decile portfolios) in period $t = 0$, and the portfolio returns are then value-weighted or equally weighted asset returns in $t = 1$. The process is repeated for the entire sample period. As an example, and for the sake of simplicity, imagine the whole sample of cryptocurrencies contains ten different assets and only two portfolios (high and low). The high portfolio buys all its assets (i.e., going long), whereas the low portfolio short sells all its assets (i.e., going short). To form the momentum characteristic, which simply states that past winners will continue to outperform past losers, the five assets with returns above the 50th percentile (median) in $t = 0$ are sorted into the high portfolio, whereas the five assets below the median are sorted into the low portfolio. The portfolio returns of the next period $t = 1$ are then calculated before moving one period further in the dataset and repeating the same procedure again. Given that the theoretical background of a characteristic holds, the portfolio returns should differ significantly between the lowest and the highest portfolio—that is, past winners do continue to outperform past losers. This is commonly tested by subtracting the returns of the lowest (short) from the returns of the highest (long) portfolio (i.e., net-zero-investment-strategy or hedge-portfolio, as one would sell the short portfolio in order to finance the long position) and running a simple t-test on the average return of the hedge-portfolio against the null hypothesis of a zero-mean return. Of course, this approach can be applied to any other characteristic under consideration (e.g., nominal price, market capitalization, hash rate).

Characteristics used in recent studies, including our own, are so far only derived from price, turnover, and market capitalization data. The horizon under investigation does not normally start before the beginning of 2014, due to the lack of time-series data as well as cross-sectional availability of cryptocurrencies. Broadly speaking, characteristics in cryptocurrency research can be grouped into (1) momentum/reversal based, (2) size based, (3) volume based, and (4) volatility-based characteristics (e.g., Liu et al. 2019; Günther et al., 2020; Han et al., 2021). Fundamental characteristics such as hash rate are also applicable in principle, but have rarely been used.

3.4 *Investment Characteristics in Digital Assets*

Here, we present results from several peer-reviewed studies, including the authors' own, performing portfolio sorts on well-known and established characteristics, especially but not exclusively from the equity market. The reader may stumble over the high returns. After all, 3% weekly returns results in an astonishing 365% annualized.[22] For comparison, the mean annual return of the S&P 500 for the past 30 years lies around 10%. However, focusing on returns alone conceals that the digital asset market itself is extremely volatile. Risk-adjusted performance measures (e.g., the ratio of return to risk, also called the Sharpe ratio) produce far less impressive results. Furthermore, the reader may be confused at negative returns. This results from the direction of sorting. It is therefore noteworthy that only the absolute value of the returns really matters, whereas the sign just indicates the direction of effect. For example, as shown below, sorting digital assets in ascending order by the turnover volume in the week of the portfolio formation leads to negative

[22] Imagine you invest US$1000 today and earn 3% each week. Then your invested funds rise to US$4650 after 52 weeks. The formula for calculation is $4650 = 1000 \times (1 + 3\%)^{52}$. Your return after one year is therefore: $365\% = (4650-1000)/1000$.

hedge-portfolio returns (resulting from a long position in the high portfolio and a short position in the low portfolio). This means that digital assets with low previous turnover volume create higher returns in the future than assets with high previous turnover volume. Knowing the direction of effects, investors would sell the "high" portfolio and buy the "low" portfolio in real-world practice to make profit. However, in academic studies, it is common to sort in ascending order by the value of the characteristic (i.e., high characteristic value in the high portfolio and vice-versa). Thus, we follow this academic practice and leave the sign in order to report the direction in which the characteristic affects returns.

Among the first to investigate common risk characteristics in cryptocurrencies are Liu and colleagues (2019), with data ranging from January 2014 to December 2018. They find several momentum characteristics in particular that create significant hedge-portfolio returns (one-week, two-week, three-week and four-week momentum strategies with 2.5%, 3.3%, 4.1% and 2.5% average weekly returns, respectively), as well as the last week's (US) dollar quoted turnover volume (−3.2%) and the respective standard deviation of last week's dollar volume (−3.0%). Interestingly, last day's nominal price (−3.9%), last week's maximum dollar price (−4.1%) and last day's market capitalization (−3.4%) are highly significant, suggesting a size effect in cryptocurrency. This effect is in line with the usual stock market literature finding that small-cap stocks on average outperform large-cap ones. Therefore, the authors augment the cryptocurrency CAPM with momentum and size to form a three-factor cryptocurrency risk model, similar to the Fama–French three-factor model described above. Building upon these results and with data reaching until January 2020, Han et al. (2021) revisit most of these characteristics and find similar results. The momentum portfolios, ranging from one to four weeks, exhibit weekly (mean) excess hedge-portfolio returns of 3.4%, 3.7%, 3.3%, and 0.96%, respectively. Last day's dollar price (−3.3%), last week's maximum dollar price (−2.5%), and last day's market capitalization (−4.6%) share the same sign, although they differ slightly in magnitude. The turnover volume in notional value creates a spread of −7.4%, and sorting for the standard deviation of trading volume creates a spread of −7.1% for weekly excess returns.

Shen et al. (2020) also introduce a three-factor model; however, instead of a momentum factor, the authors find the exact opposite, a reversal. This is in line with Glas (2019) and Günther et al. (2020), who find a strong reversal effect in a large cross-section of cryptocurrencies, although in daily instead of weekly data. With some caution, one could interpret several signs of short-term reversal price movements in the characteristics results of the studies reported above. For example, last day's dollar price, or market capitalization, in the portfolio formation week leads to high negative spreads in expected returns the following period. This is in fact a reverse reaction to a former price appreciation. Next, we examine the reversal effect in cryptocurrency in greater detail.

An outstanding difference in the mentioned publications is the characteristic construction. While the stock market momentum is normally calculated as the past year's cumulative monthly returns, excluding the most recent month (Jegadeesh & Titman, 1993), researchers in cryptocurrency have tended to increase the data frequency to weekly observation, simply due to limited historical data feeds. Excluding Glas (2019), who is among the first to investigate characteristics in cryptocurrencies and use the classical momentum portfolios of Jegadeesh and Titman (1993), most researchers nowadays focus on the past week's (or weeks') performance of a digital asset, without excluding the most recent period. However, as already mentioned earlier, characteristics representing very short-term changes in price or market capitalization (i.e., previous day) predominantly create large negative hedge-portfolio returns. Liu and colleagues (2019) report −4.6% average weekly returns from last day's market capitalization, similar to Günther et al. (2020) (−2.79% daily) and Han et al. (2021) (−4.8%). The divergent results in magnitude, but not sign, may be explained by technical differences. Often value-weighted returns are calculated; however, as seen in Fig. 2, bitcoin has always had an overwhelming market share and subverts most influences of the large cross-section of digital assets. Figure 2 displays this effect. The interconnection of momentum and reversal is therefore examined in more detail. Specifically, Günther et al. (2020) investigate this phenomenon by calculating both equally- and value-weighted portfolios of several momentum/reversal strategies. The *y*-axis displays the periods excluded before portfolio formation.

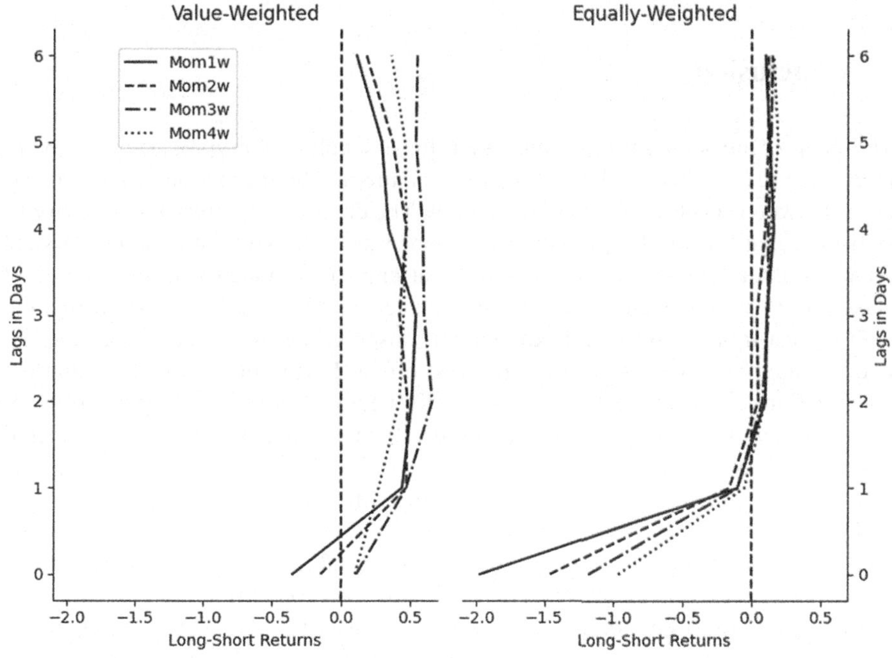

Fig. 2 Two weighting methods for momentum portfolios. The y-axis denotes the excluded periods prior to portfolio formation. The x-axis denotes the mean daily returns of the hedge-portfolio. Data is retrieved from www.coingecko.com

Consider the different (equally weighted) returns between lag zero and lag one on the y-axis. For all momentum strategies (one-week to four-week), the returns of the strategy are highly negative when taking all data into consideration (lag zero). However, if the last observation before forming the portfolios is omitted, the returns for all strategies are close to zero and even positive when omitting the last two observations. This shows that the last observation before forming the portfolios has a high negative impact and does not support the idea of momentum strategies (i.e., that past winners continue to outperform). In contrast, in the very short term, this dependency reverts and hence is called the reversal effect.

The two plots differ significantly, indicating large reversal movements in smaller cryptocurrencies and no momentum effect. Value-weighted portfolios, however, do have both a smaller reversal of around −0.5% daily returns in the very short term (equal to −3.5% weekly returns) and over 0.5% daily returns (3.5% weekly) if lags are included. The most powerful (momentum) predictor of future returns is the three-weeks' cumulative returns with exclusion of the last two days. These results show the differences occurring due to portfolio construction but coincide with the findings of the literature introduced earlier. Furthermore, the importance of details in implementing the investment strategy is highlighted, as the impact on returns is drastic and can even shift from a reversal to a momentum.

4 Conclusion

This chapter introduces the new and emerging asset class of cryptocurrencies. After presenting several technical details on blockchains and their functionality, the differences between cryptocurrencies are laid out. The chapter continues with descriptive statistics regarding market growth, performance and risk. After introducing classical financial asset pricing theory, we show that empirical evidence from other asset classes such as stocks cannot simply be transferred. Specifically, we show that the well-known momentum effect, known and observed across several asset classes, is dominated by a very short-term reversal effect. Furthermore, we show that the construction of the characteristic, especially heavy exposure to cryptocurrencies with large market share such as bitcoin, drastically changes the results compared to the equally weighted counterpart. Although investment strategies in digital assets can generate very high returns, it is co-moving with high-risk exposures.

Digital assets therefore offer high uncorrelated returns; however, they are connected to large price swings and the risk of a total loss of the initial investment. Investments into this asset class should thus rely on strict risk management principles and must be monitored carefully. The risk of hacks, fraud, or a changing regulatory framework still exists, and needs to be taken into account when investing into this asset class.

Research on this young asset class is still in its early stages. Since traditional finance theories cannot easily be transferred, there are many other (mostly) uncovered or emergent topics. One topic, the search for risk factors, needs to be taken on the same methodological basis as equities and other asset classes. The question nevertheless remains whether "fundamental" characteristics of digital assets (e.g., hash algorithms or data from the blockchain itself) shape return behavior. Other topics, including clusters in digital assets, have not yet been researched as intensively. Much work thus remains to be done to fully understand the behavior of digital assets and their impact on more traditional asset classes.

References

Asness, C. S., Ilmanen, A., Israel, R., & Moskowitz, T. J. (2015). Investing with style. *Journal of Investment Management, 13*(1), 27–63.

Asness, C. S., Moskowitz, T. F., & Pedersen, L. H. (2013). Value and momentum everywhere. *Journal of Finance, 68*(3), 929–985.

Banz, R. W. (1981). The relationship between return and market value of common stocks. *Journal of Financial Economics, 9*, 3–18.

Baur, D. G., & Hoang, L. T. (2021). A crypto safe haven against bitcoin. *Finance Research Letters, 38*(January), 101431. https://doi.org/10.1016/j.frl.2020.101431

Carhart, M. M. (1997). On persistence in mutual fund performance. *Journal of Finance, 52*(1), 57–82.

Charfeddine, L., Benlagha, N., & Maouchi, Y. (2020). Investigating the dynamic relationship between cryptocurrencies and conventional assets: Implications for financial investors. *Economic Modelling, 85*(February), 198–217. https://doi.org/10.1016/j.econmod.2019.05.016

Chaum, D. L. (1983). Blind signatures for untraceable payments. In *Advances in cryptology* (pp. 199–203). Springer.

Chuen, D. L., Guo, L., & Wang, Y. (2018). Cryptocurrency: A new investment opportunity? *Journal of Alternative Investments, 20*(3), 16–40. https://doi.org/10.3905/jai.2018.20.3.016

Cochrane, J. (2011). Presidential address: Discount rates. *Journal of Finance, 66*(4), 1047–1108.

Daniel, K., & Titman, S. (1997). Evidence on the characteristics of cross sectional variation in stock returns. *Journal of Finance, 52*(1), 1–33.

Edwards, F. R., & Liew, J. (1999). Managed commodity funds. *Journal of Futures Markets, 19*(4), 377–411.

Fama, E. F. (1970). Efficient capital markets: A review of theory and empirical work. *Journal of Finance, 25*(2), 383–417.

Fama, E. F., & French, K. R. (1993). Common risk factors in the returns on stocks and bonds. *Journal of Financial Economics, 33*(1), 3–56.

Fama, E. F., & French, K. R. (2015). A five-factor asset pricing model. *Journal of Financial Economics, 116*(1), 1–22.

Fang, L., Bouri, E., Gupta, R., & Roubaud, D. (2019). Does global economic uncertainty matter for the volatility and hedging effectiveness of bitcoin? *International Review of Financial Analysis, 61*(January), 29–36. https://doi.org/10.1016/j.irfa.2018.12.010

Fieberg, C., Varmaz, A., & Poddig, T. (2016). Covariances vs. characteristics: What does explain the cross-section of the German stock market returns? *Business Research, 9*, 27–50.

Glas, T. N. (2019). Investments in cryptocurrencies: Handle with care! *Journal of Alternative Investments, 22*(1), 96–113. https://doi.org/10.3905/jai.2019.22.1.096

Glas, T. N., & Poddig, T. (2018). Kryptowährungen in der Asset- Allokation: eine empirische Untersuchung auf Basis eines beispielhaften deutschen Multi-Asset-Portfolios. *Vierteljahrshefte zur Wirtschaftsforschung/Quarterly Journal of Economic Research, 87*(3), 107–128. https://doi.org/10.3790/vjh.87.3.107

Griffith, K. (2014). A quick history of cryptocurrencies BBTC: Before bitcoin. *Bitcoin Magazine*. https://bitcoinmagazine.com/articles/quick-history-cryptocurrencies-bbtc-bitcoin-1397682630/.

Günther, S., Fieberg, C., & Poddig, P. (2020). The cross-section of cryptocurrency risk and return. *Vierteljahrshefte zur Wirtschaftsforschung, 89*, 7–28.

Han, W., Newton, D., Platanakis, E., Sutcliffe, C., & Ye, X. (2021). Cryptocurrency factor portfolios: Performance, decomposition and pricing models. *Decomposition and Pricing Models* (May 31, 2021).

Harvey, C. R., Liu, Y., & Zhu, C. (2015). … and the cross-section of expected returns. Available at SSRN:https://papers.ssrn.com/sol3/papers.cfm?abstract_id=2249314.

Jegadeesh, N., & Titman, S. (1993). Returns to buying winners and selling losers: Implications for stock market efficiency. *Journal of Finance, 48*(1), 65–91.

Kajtazi, A., & Moro, A. (2019). The role of bitcoin in well diversified portfolios: A comparative global study. *International Review of Financial Analysis, 61*(January), 143–157. https://doi.org/10.1016/j.irfa.2018.10.003

Karavas, V. N., & Georgiev, G. (2000). Alternative investments in the institutional portfolio. *Journal of Alternative Investments, 3*(December), 11–25. https://doi.org/10.3905/jai.2000.318962

Khelifa, S. B., Guesmi, K., & Urom, C. (2021). Exploring the relationship between cryptocurrencies and hedge funds during COVID-19 crisis. *International Review of Financial Analysis, 76*(July), 101777. https://doi.org/10.1016/j.irfa.2021.101777

Klein, T., Thu, H. P., & Walther, T. (2018). Bitcoin is not the new gold: A comparison of volatility, correlation, and portfolio performance. *International Review of Financial Analysis, 59*(October), 105–116. https://doi.org/10.1016/j.irfa.2018.07.010

Lintner, J. (1965). Security prices, risk and maximal gains from diversification. *Journal of Finance, 20*(4), 587–615.

Liu, Y., Tsyvinski, A., & Wu, X. (2019). Common risk factors in cryptocurrency (No. w25882). National Bureau of Economic Research.

Markowitz, H. (1952). Portfolio selection. *Journal of Finance, 7*, 77–91.

Markowitz, H. (1959). *Portfolio selection: Efficient diversification of investments*. John Wiley.

Mossin, J. (1966). Equilibrium in a capital asset market. *Econometrica, 34*(4), 768–783.

Nakavachara, V., Potipiti, T., & Lertmongkolnam, T. (2019). Should all blockchain-based digital assets be classified under the same asset class? Available at SSRN:https://ssrn.com/abstract=3437279.

Perold, A. F. (2004). The Capital Asset Pricing Model. *Journal of Economic Perspectives, 18*(3), 3–24. https://doi.org/10.1257/0895330042162340

Pitta, J. (1999). Requiem for a bright idea. Forbes https://www.forbes.com/forbes/1999/1101/6411390a.html#5fa0a2de715f.

Schmitz, T., & Hoffmann, I. (2020). Re-evaluating cryptocurrencies' contribution to portfolio diversification: A portfolio analysis with special focus on German investors. *SSRN working paper*, (July). https://papers.ssrn.com/sol3/papers.cfm?abstract_id=3625458.

Schneeweis, T., & Martin, G. A. (2001). The benefits of hedge funds: Asset allocation for the institutional investor. *Journal of Alternative Investments, 4*(3), 7–26. https://doi.org/10.3905/jai.2001.319017

Sharpe, W. (1964). Capital asset prices: A theory of market equilibrium under conditions of risk. *The Journal of Finance, 19*(3), 425–442.

Sharpe, W. (1992). Asset allocation: Management style and performance measurement. *Journal of Portfolio Management, 18*, 7–19.

Shen, D., Urquhart, A., & Wang, P. (2020). A three-factor pricing model for cryptocurrencies. *Finance Research Letters, 34*, 101248.

Sifat, I. (2021). On cryptocurrencies as an independent asset class: Long-horizon and COVID-19 pandemic era decoupling from global sentiments. *Finance Research Letters, 43*, 102013. https://doi.org/10.1016/j.frl.2021.102013

Smales, L. A. (2019). Bitcoin as a safe haven: Is it even worth considering? *Finance Research Letters, 30*(September), 385–393. https://doi.org/10.1016/j.frl.2018.11.002

Symitsi, E., & Chalvatzis, K. J. (2019). The economic value of bitcoin: A portfolio analysis of currencies, gold, oil and stocks. *Research in International Business and Finance, 48*(April), 97–110. https://doi.org/10.1016/j.ribaf.2018.12.001

Wang, P., Zhang, W., Li, X., & Shen, D. (2019). Is cryptocurrency a hedge or a safe haven for international indices? A comprehensive and dynamic perspective. *Finance Research Letters, 31*(December), 1–18. https://doi.org/10.1016/j.frl.2019.04.031

Artificial Intelligence, Surveillance, and Big Data

David Karpa, Torben Klarl, and Michael Rochlitz

1 Introduction

During the late 2000s and early 2010s, a number of publications on recursive learning in multi-layered neuronal networks led to a breakthrough in the field of artificial intelligence (Hinton and Salakhutdinov 2006; Hinton et al. 2006; Krizhevsky 2009; Krizhevsky et al. 2012). The studies laid the foundation for a new approach to machine learning: recursively self-improving algorithms are structured in layers to create programmable neural networks, which are then used to sort through large amounts of data in a process called "deep learning." Unlike traditional machine-learning methods, most deep learning algorithms no longer require labeled training data. Instead, they are able to autonomously reach a goal set at the beginning, with the speed and quality of learning increasing with the amount of raw data available.

In a short span of time, machine-learning techniques based on deep learning have led to a number of major breakthroughs in various fields such as image, speech and facial recognition, medicine, particle physics, neuroscience, and language translation (LeCun et al. 2015). More recent advances have also led to applications in accounting (Fieberg et al. 2022), human resource management (Hagemann and Klug 2022) or university education (Pijetlovic and Mueller-Christ 2022), as well as progress in many other fields.

The larger public became aware of the new technology when a team from Deep Mind, an AI firm now acquired by Google, managed to beat Lee Sedol, one of the highest ranking professional Go players, in a five-game match in March 2016 (Silver et al. 2016). While for the game of chess IMB's Deep Blue had already managed to beat world champion Garry Kasparov in 1997, Go is orders of magnitude more

D. Karpa · T. Klarl · M. Rochlitz (✉)
Faculty of Business Studies and Economics, University of Bremen, Bremen, Germany
e-mail: dkarpa@uni-bremen.de; tklarl@uni-bremen.de; michael.rochlitz@uni-bremen.de

L. Hornuf (ed.), *Diginomics Research Perspectives*, Advanced Studies in Diginomics and Digitalization, https://doi.org/10.1007/978-3-031-04063-4_8

difficult to solve than chess.[1] Winning the game against one of the world's leading players thus demonstrated the potential of the new technology (Bory 2019; Silver et al. 2017).

Deep Mind's win against Sedol had another important implication. Go was invented in China, is mostly played in China, Japan and Korea, and is still considered by many people in East Asia as a quintessentially Asian game (Moskowitz 2013). That a Western company managed to win the game with the help of a computer program against a leading Asian player led to a spike in interest in artificial intelligence research in China, triggering a large-scale government program to promote and support the already fast-developing sector.[2] Five years later, China has become—together with the USA—a world leader in the field of AI research, with both countries engaged in a tight race for dominance.

Figure 1 shows that while China has already overtaken the USA in terms of the overall quantity of AI-related research publications, it still lags behind with respect to the number of high-quality publications in applied AI research, where China today is at about the same level as Germany or the UK.[3] A similar picture—higher quantity but still lower quality, on average—also exists with respect to patents, for example in the case of the Internet of Things (Kshetri 2017) and when comparing research institutions. Here American and European universities are still ahead when looking at high-quality output, whereas Chinese institutions have recently overtaken all other countries in the world with respect to the overall number of AI-related publications per university (Savage (2020), see also Tables 1 and 2 in Sect. 4).

The present chapter examines whether China has the potential to overtake the USA in terms of research quality. To answer this question, we focus on one fundamental difference between both countries—their respective authoritarian and democratic institutions. While the USA is a competitive democracy, China is an authoritarian single-party state. Our objective is to study how this difference in political institutions can affect the quality of research and innovation in the field

[1] While Deep Blue beat Garry Kasparov in 1997 by using brute force computing, this approach does not work for Go, a game with 250 possible moves each turn, and a typical game depth of 150 moves, resulting in about 250^{150}, or 10^{360} possible moves—more than the number of atoms in the observable universe.

[2] Lee (2018, page 3) compares the effect of Deep Mind's win against Lee Sedol to America's Sputnik moment: "Overnight, China plunged into an artificial intelligence fever. The buzz did not quite rival America's reaction to Sputnik, but it lit a fire under the Chinese technology community that has been burning ever since".

[3] As a proxy for research quality in artificial intelligence, we use the Nature Index for the year 2020. The index counts publications in applied artificial intelligence published in Nature and its sub-journals, such as Science, the Proceedings of the National Academy of Sciences (PNAS), and others. The list can be accessed under https://www.natureindex.com/faq, and the source of our data can be found here: https://www.natureindex.com/supplements/nature-index-2020-ai/tables/countries. As a proxy for the overall quantity of publications in artificial intelligence, we use the Nature Index Dimensions database, which counts all publications in AI from a specific country between 2015 and 2019: https://www.natureindex.com/supplements/nature-index-2020-ai/tables/dimensions-countries.

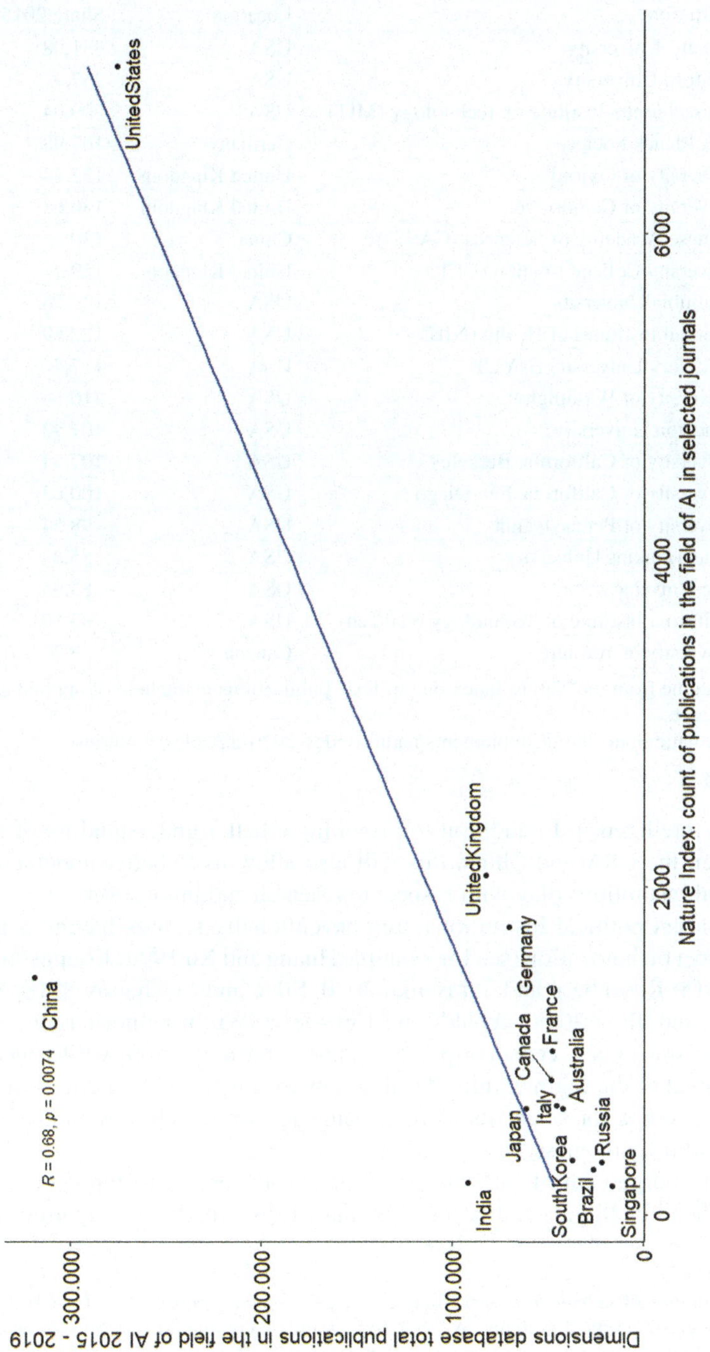

Fig. 1 Publications in selected journals (x-axis); publications total (y-axis)

Table 1 Top 20 research institutions in artificial intelligence (Nature Index)

Rank	Institution	Location	Share 2015–2019
1	Harvard University	USA	331,08
2	Stanford University	USA	257,9
3	Massachusetts Institute of Technology (MIT)	USA	209,04
4	Max Planck Society	Germany	167,98
5	University of Oxford	United Kingdom	132,34
6	University of Cambridge	United Kingdom	130,68
7	Chinese Academy of Sciences (CAS)	China	130
8	University College London (UCL)	United Kingdom	129,7
9	Columbia University	USA	127,56
10	National Institutes of Health (NIH)	USA	122,69
11	New York University (NYU)	USA	117,4
12	University of Washington	USA	110,68
13	Princeton University	USA	107,92
14	University of California, Berkeley	USA	107,54
15	University of California, San Diego	USA	100,63
16	University of Pennsylvania	USA	98,54
17	Johns Hopkins University	USA	85,8
18	Yale University	USA	83,95
19	California Institute of Technology (Caltech)	USA	83,59
20	University of Toronto	Canada	83,27

Note: Data come from the Nature Index on top-level publications in the field of applied artificial intelligence, see:
https://www.natureindex.com/supplements/nature-index-2020-ai/tables/countries.

of artificial intelligence. In addition to providing a better understanding of the AI race between the USA and China, this will also allow us to better understand the role political institutions play with respect to research and innovation.

Authoritarian political institutions are conventionally seen as having a mostly negative effect on innovation (see for example Huang and Xu 1999; Josephson 2005; Knutsen 2015; Rosenberg and Tarasenko 2020; Silve and Plekhanov 2018; Stokes 2000; Tang and Tang 2018; Tebaldi and Elmslie 2008). In authoritarian political systems, the story goes, censorship, surveillance and repression, while necessary for the survival of the regime, limit the free flow of information, and make it more difficult on average for scientists to freely engage in research, thus limiting their creativity and inventiveness.[4]

The central argument of this chapter is that, with respect to innovation in the field of artificial intelligence, this conventional wisdom might no longer hold, with

[4] A certain amount of censorship, surveillance and government control can of course also be found in democratic political systems. We therefore assume a continuum of repressiveness, from complete freedom to complete state control, with the negative effects on creativity increasing with growing government control.

Table 2 Top 20 research institutions in artificial intelligence (Dimensions Data)

Rank	Institution	Location	Publications in AI (2015–2019)
1	Tsinghua University	China	11, 867
2	University of Chinese Academy of Sciences	China	8, 835
3	Shanghai Jiao Tong University	China	8, 796
4	Beihang University	China	8, 605
5	Zhejiang University	China	8, 337
6	Harbin Institute of Technology	China	8, 315
7	Nanyang Technological University	Singapore	6, 985
8	University of Electronic Science and Technology of China	China	6, 954
9	Stanford University	USA	6, 609
10	Massachusetts Institute of Technology	USA	6, 314
11	Southeast University	China	6, 18
12	University of Tokyo	Japan	6, 058
13	Huazhong University of Science and Technology	China	6, 048
14	University College London	United Kingdom	5, 988
15	Wuhan University	China	5, 797
16	Beijing Institute of Technology	China	5, 641
17	Peking University	China	5, 612
18	Harvard University	USA	5, 553
19	University of Michigan	USA	5, 464
20	Xi'an Jiaotong University	China	5, 364

Note: Data come from the Nature Index Dimensions Database, which counts all publications in the field of artificial intelligence between 2015 and 2019, see https://www.natureindex.com/supplements/nature-index-2020-ai/tables/dimensions-countries.

the negative effects of authoritarian institutions potentially being offset by the opportunities offered through big data. As pointed out above, the most important input for deep learning algorithms to self-improve is large amounts of data (Beraja et al. 2021; Domingos 2015; Halevy et al. 2009; Hey 2009; Sun et al. 2017). With respect to the availability of large data sets, modern authoritarian states with sophisticated surveillance systems might have a significant advantage over democracies, where—on average—policies on government surveillance and data sharing are stricter than in autocracies (Chen and Cheung 2017; Kshetri 2014; Moreno and Pedreno 2021; Smuha 2021; Strittmatter 2020; Zeng 2020). Less-strict data-sharing laws permit authoritarian governments to allocate data gathered through surveillance as an input-subsidy to domestic IT firms, an industrial policy the Chinese government is already increasingly pursuing (Beraja et al. 2021; Lee 2018). A side-effect is that in this way, authoritarian states can use the data they have gathered through surveillance to further improve their AI-based surveillance capabilities, thus initiating a positive feedback loop. As a result of this process,

China has already become a leader in the field of surveillance technologies, and has started to export them to other authoritarian countries (Feldstein 2019).[5]

Our hypothesis is that whether China will manage to catch up to—and potentially overtake—the USA to become world leader with respect to cutting-edge innovation in AI will be determined by the trade-off between the negative effects of censorship, surveillance, and control on innovation and creativity, and the positive effects of having access to better and more data than countries that do not rely to the same extent on digital surveillance. As we argue in Sect. 3, for the foreseeable future China will remain at a disadvantage when it comes to conventional innovation, as its authoritarian institutions are hindering the free flow of information, as well as intrinsic motivation, creativity, and the possibility for scientists to freely determine their research agenda. On the other hand, China already has an advantage with respect to using big data as an input in AI research, as we document in Sect. 4. We argue that who will win the race in artificial intelligence ultimately depends on what type of research will be more important in the field during the next couple of years. If new and innovative ideas lead to another breakthrough after the deep learning revolution, the US might maintain its lead for the foreseeable future. If, however, large datasets to train and improve existing algorithms turn out to be most important during the next decade, China might well become the overall leader in the field.

This chapter is structured as follows. Section 2 introduces a simple theoretical framework, which will be used in the subsequent sections to guide our argument. The framework consists of three *actors* (the authoritarian regime, the public, and high-tech firms), a number of *strategies* used by the authoritarian regime to ensure its political survival (repression, censorship, surveillance and public spending), and a number of *outcomes* we are interested in, most importantly the amount of data available to research institutions, and the quality of research and innovation in AI. Section 3 discusses the negative effects of censorship and surveillance on research and creativity, thus reiterating and illustrating the conventional argument that, on average, authoritarian political institutions have a negative effect on innovation. Section 4 then introduces our argument, by showing how large amounts of data gained through government surveillance can potentially have a positive effect on innovation in AI. Section 5 summarizes our argument and concludes.

2 Theoretical framework

An extensive literature has examined the strategies used by authoritarian governments to remain in power, with Egorov and Sonin (2020) providing a recent overview. According to Svolik (2009), authoritarian regimes during the past 70 years

[5] See also "The Panopticon is Already Here", The Atlantic, September 2020, https://www.theatlantic.com/magazine/archive/2020/09/china-ai-surveillance/614197/.

have faced two principal challenges—revolution from below, and palace coups from within. Traditionally, most authoritarian regimes have reacted with either repression or co-optation to these challenges. While repression to get rid of regime opponents has taken the form of arrests, purges, deportation or worse (Blaydes 2018; Buckley et al. 2022; Gregory et al. 2011; Montagnes and Wolton 2019; Moore 1998), public spending has been used to either convince the general public that it is better off under the status quo than under an alternative regime (Acemoglu and Robinson 2006), or to co-opt a more narrowly defined elite, in order to prevent a coup (Bueno de Mesquita et al. 2003; Gallagher and Hanson 2015).

More recently, the growing importance of the internet and more sophisticated censorship, surveillance and propaganda techniques have led to the emergence of a new type of dictatorship. In these so-called "informational autocracies," the manipulation and targeted use of information has become the preferred strategy of the government, while repression is no longer as important as before (Guriev and Treisman 2019, 2020). Examples of modern informational autocracies include such diverse countries as Russia under Vladimir Putin, Hungary under Victor Orban, Turkey under Recep Tayyip Erdoğan, as well as contemporary China.[6] In this new type of informational autocracy, increasingly sophisticated surveillance technologies are used to keep the population in check, but can also permit the state to conduct a new kind of industrial policy by using data collected through surveillance as an input for research and innovation (Beraja et al. 2021).

Figure 2 illustrates our theoretical framework by presenting the different strategies used by authoritarian regimes in simplified form. Red arrows represent a negative relationship, whereas green arrows illustrate a positive effect. As can be seen, repression and censorship make it more difficult for the public to organize through collective action.[7] Surveillance plays a similar role by rendering censorship (Roberts 2020) as well as repression and co-optation (Xu 2021) more precise and cost-effective.[8] As a result, all four strategies reduce the propensity of the public to revolt, and strengthen the political control of the authoritarian state.

[6] As China does not have elections and is still using repression, it is sometimes not seen as a classic "informational autocracy" as invoked by Guriev and Treisman (2019, 2020). However, China has—more than any other country—perfected the strategic censorship of the internet (King et al. 2013, 2014; Roberts 2018), as well as modern authoritarian surveillance technologies (Kostka 2019; Kostka and Antoine 2020; Strittmatter 2020). Following Ringen (2016) and Minzner (2018), we maintain that it can therefore be argued that China has taken the idea of an "informational autocracy" to the next level, by combining sophisticated surveillance and censorship techniques with targeted repression.

[7] Whereas repression has a directly negative effect on the ability of the public to meet and protest, censorship limits the ability of the public to communicate, to access independent information, and to subsequently coordinate collective action.

[8] The red arrow from surveillance to public spending is motivated by Pan (2020) and Xu (2021), who show that with better surveillance, lower amounts of public spending have to be used to achieve the same reduction in the propensity to revolt.

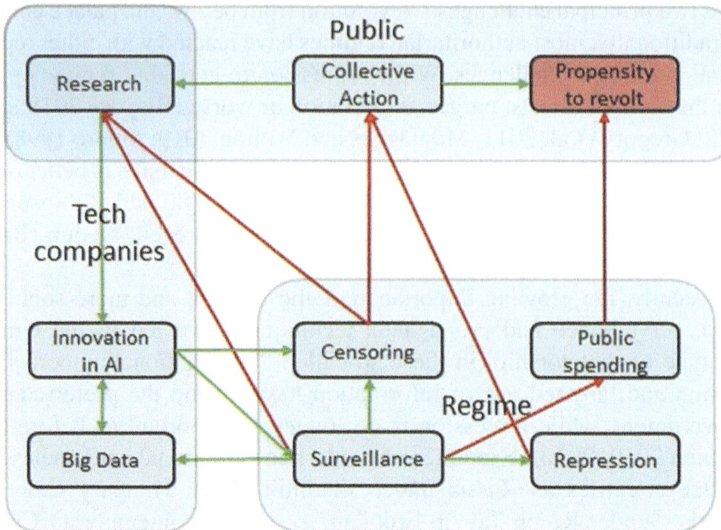

Fig. 2 Theoretical Framework

Repression, censoring, and surveillance, however, can also have direct negative effects on the ability of an economy to innovate. While the negative effects of repression on innovation are well documented,[9] we focus in particular on strategies used by informational autocracies, that is on how censorship and surveillance might hinder research and innovation. Section 3 will discuss these negative effects in detail.

Section 4 then turns to the effect of big data, and the potential positive interaction between authoritarian surveillance and innovation in AI. The green arrow from surveillance to big data, and from there to innovation in artificial intelligence, illustrates how data gathered by the authoritarian state can be used as an input to accelerate research in the field. The green arrows from innovation to censoring and surveillance in turn symbolize the positive feedback effect of innovation in AI helping to improve censoring and surveillance technologies, which can then be used to generate even more and better data. After outlining both the negative and positive effects of authoritarian control on innovation in Sects. 3 and 4, we discuss in Sect. 5 the circumstances under which the negative or positive effects might be more prominent.

[9] See for example Waldinger (2010, 2012) and Medawar and Pyke (2012) on how the expulsion of scientists from Nazi Germany in the 1930s affected the quality of research in Germany.

3 Authoritarian Control and Innovation: Negative Effects

3.1 Censorship

Censorship has been used as a control strategy by authoritarian regimes since ancient times. In this section, we first outline why and how censorship is used in modern autocracies, and then discuss how it affects innovation.

As outlined in Fig. 2, censorship can reduce the ability of the public to self-organize and revolt, both by making coordination more difficult and by reducing the amount of information critical of the government. Authoritarian governments, however, face a trade-off with respect to how much censorship to use. Particularly in large authoritarian states, some amount of uncensored information from institutions independent of the government might be necessary. Otherwise, the central government might become completely dependent on information provided by regional bureaucrats (Pan and Chen 2018) or the security services (Petrov and Rochlitz 2019; Soldatov and Rochlitz 2018), which can use this dependence to advance their own agendas.[10] As we will outline in more detail below, censorship also always imposes an economic cost, by rendering information more expensive.

Authoritarian governments have reacted to this dilemma using different strategies, which are classified by Roberts (2018) according to the mechanism through which they affect the user, namely *fear*, *friction*, and *flooding*. Fear-based censorship operates similarly to classic repression, with users being deterred from accessing or distributing certain types of information by threats of costly punishment. Many authoritarian regimes have adopted laws and regulations that set clear boundaries regarding information usage, with journalists and content creators having to fear the possibility of arrest or losing their jobs. Pan and Siegel (2020) show that fear-based strategies can work, by illustrating how repression of well-known online activists in Saudi Arabia in the form of imprisonment or torture makes them less likely to continue their criticism of the government after their release from custody.

If fear-based censorship is too overt, however, it can produce adverse effects. When the arrests of online activists became public knowledge in Saudi Arabia, Google search requests for their names increased significantly (an effect often referred to as the *Streisand effect*[11]), while anti-government sentiment and mobilization among the followers of the arrested activists also increased (Pan and Siegel 2020). In addition to the *Streisand effect*, Hobbs and Roberts (2018) also identify a *gateway effect* of censorship. When Instagram was blocked in China during the Hong Kong protests in 2014, users started to employ virtual private networks

---

[10] A detailed discussion of this trade-off for the case of Russia and China can be found in Libman and Rochlitz (2019), chapter 4.

[11] The Streisand effect occurs when an effort to conceal information increases its value or makes it more attractive (Hobbs and Roberts 2018). The effect is named for Barbra Streisand, who when trying to remove pictures of her home from the internet attracted even more attention to them.

(VPNs), and through this became familiar with additional politically sensitive content on other platforms that were blocked in China (Hobbs and Roberts 2018).

In order to avoid this kind of backlash, a more sophisticated form of censorship is to introduce some element of friction, which is often less easy to notice than outright repression. Instead of restricting information explicitly, selected content is made time- or resource-intensive to access, rendering it more costly than other information (Roberts 2018). Examples of friction include the use of firewalls that block specific websites (Qiang 2019), or the manipulation of results from search engines (Ruan et al. 2017). Here as well, China has been a pioneer, and is more advanced today than most other authoritarian countries. As shown by King et al. (2013, 2014), the Chinese state is not censoring all forms of government criticism from the Chinese internet. Instead, targeted censorship is used to get rid of posts that have the potential to result in collective action against the government. In this way, the Chinese state solves the authoritarian censorship dilemma described above, by permitting the internet to continue its role as a monitoring and information tool for the central government, while preventing it from playing the role of a "liberation technology", i.e. a tool that could be used by citizens to coordinate and organize public protests.

As illustrated by the green arrow from innovation to censorship in Fig. 2, these kinds of censorship technologies are fast evolving. While the censorship described by King et al. (2013, 2014) was still mostly a manual effort by thousands of Communist Party members and police officers, deep learning algorithms have since started to assist and sometimes already replace manual censorship, making censorship cheaper, more sophisticated, and less easy to recognize and evade (Dixon et al. 2016; Gao et al. 2021; Griffiths 2019; Roberts 2018; Strittmatter 2020; Tai and Fu 2020; Tiffert 2019).

Finally, flooding is a technique that in its results closely resembles the effect of introducing friction, i.e. access to certain types of information becomes more costly. It differs however in the way that it is implemented, with the cost of accessing independent information being increased by the widespread distribution of alternative information congruent with the agenda of the state. Flooding is particularly prevalent on social media, where government-affiliated actors systematically create information and distribute it. King et al. (2017) document how in the mid-2010s, the Chinese government was responsible for the fabrication of approximately 448 million social media posts per year. These posts were not used to argue with skeptics of the Communist party or the government, nor were they used to influence discussions of controversial issues, but rather to distract the public, change the subject, and altogether divert attention from discussions about politics or sensitive issues. In Russia, the government has been following a similar strategy, with troll factories flooding social media with pro-government messages, making it more difficult for users to identify information critical of the government within the vast mass of available content (Karpan 2019; Linvill and Warren 2020). As a result, while in the late 2000s social media was still described as a "liberation technology" and considered by many as constituting a danger to authoritarian regimes (Diamond 2010), modern informational autocracies have since reacted and seem now to be able to use social media as an additional tool to foster regime stability (Gunitsky 2015).

Censorship and Innovation While fear, friction, and flooding permit the authoritarian state to reduce the risk of collective action and public unrest, they also come at a cost. The present chapter focuses in particular on how these censorship technologies influence the ability of an economy to generate new ideas and innovate.

A classic example that has existed in traditional autocracies is the use of repression to get rid of scientists critical of the regime, or—inversely—the promotion of academics who refuse to criticize the government. In an excellent study of the Chinese university system, Perry (2020) shows that this still has a significant effect on scientific productivity in contemporary China, as the allocation of resources to individual researchers and projects is often based on political instead of scientific criteria. Similar problems were faced by the Soviet Union (Graham 1987, 1993), and most importantly Nazi Germany, which suffered from substantial brain drain as a result of the repressions of the 1930s (Waldinger 2010, 2012).

Less obvious and more sophisticated censorship techniques can nevertheless have a negative effect on innovation. One of the biggest problems faced by foreign companies in China is the way in which censorship and the "great firewall" are slowing down internet connections, especially to servers based abroad.[12] Similar problems are faced by scientists and researchers. While the domestic internet in China is easily accessible and fast, scientists who want to have unlimited access to the global web to participate in international scientific debates face significant technical hurdles and costs, as connections to the global net are slow and often many times more expensive than connections to the domestic internet.[13]

In addition to slow internet connections, problems with the accessibility of data also make research more difficult for scientists in China and other authoritarian countries. One problem is that data provided by the government might be strategically manipulated, if these data are also used as input for the performance evaluation of government officials (Kalgin 2016; Wallace 2016). Xiang (2019) maintains that, particularly with respect to research in the field of artificial intelligence, data quality for China-based researchers remains heterogeneous. While in surveillance and control technologies Chinese researchers enjoy a definite advantage over their peers in the West—as the security services have strong incentives to collaborate

[12] In a series of interviews with foreign investors carried out in Shanghai in May 2016 by one of the authors of this study, nearly all investors complained that internet censorship and slow connections are rendering their activities significantly more difficult. See also "China Internet Restrictions Hurting Business, Western Companies Say", *Wall Street Journal*, 12.02.2015, https://www.wsj.com/articles/BL-CJB-25952.

[13] According to an article published in *The Atlantic*, in 2013 Peking University charged $1.50 a month for unlimited domestic internet use, but $14.50 for unlimited access to the World Wide Web ("How Internet Censorship Is Curbing Innovation in China", *The Atlantic*, 22.04.2013, https://www.theatlantic.com/china/archive/2013/04/how-internet-censorship-is-curbing-innovation-in-china/275188/).

with IT firms with respect to the development of new surveillance infrastructure and the sharing of data (Xiang 2019, page 45)—this is not necessarily the case in other fields. With respect to research in autonomous driving, speech recognition and robotics, for example, the quality and amount of available data are mixed at best, and often lower than in the US or Europe, as local and regional governments have no incentives to make data available, but on the contrary fear that providing data as an input for scientific research can get them into trouble (Xiang 2019, p. 32).

A further issue is that, especially in the social sciences, Western publishers are facing increasing pressure by the authorities in Beijing to render articles critical of the Chinese government invisible in their academic journals. The articles are then not only not available for download, but Chinese researchers will never learn that they actually exist if they use only the domestic version of the Chinese internet to search for information (Wong and Kwong 2019). Similar problems exist with respect to the access to archives, to which researchers in China are only admitted if the historical information fits current political narratives (Roberts 2018). These developments are not limited to China, with for example the Russian State Duma continuously issuing new laws that make collaboration and the exchange of information between Russian and foreign researchers more difficult,[14] a problem also faced by scientists in Hungary (Enyedi 2018) and Turkey (Aydin 2021).

A common characteristic of all these censorship technologies is that they impose *taxes on information*, by making accessing or sharing information more costly. Although the primary aim of censorship is to limit anti-government activities and collective action, one externality is that research is becoming more costly. As shown in a seminal paper by Murray et al. (2016), who study a natural experiment in genetics research, a reduction in openness and available information can result in less innovation and a reduced diversity of research output. We argue that these results equate to the effect of censorship in authoritarian states, which—through imposing taxes on information—often has a significant negative effect on scientific research and innovation. In a study of China's higher education sector, Schulte (2019) makes precisely this point, by arguing that novel combinations—or innovations—need a diverse and open academic environment to emerge. Such an environment exists only to a limited extent in China, where attempts by the state to impose authoritarian stability may be in conflict with the objective of becoming an innovative knowledge economy (Cao et al. 2009; Schulte 2019).

3.2 Surveillance

While imposing taxes on information is one important channel through which authoritarian institutions can negatively affect innovation, another channel is

[14] "Russian academics decry law change that threatens scientific outreach", *Nature*, 12.02.2021, https://www.nature.com/articles/d41586-021-00385-5.

surveillance, although here the effect is less straightforward. On the one hand, surveillance can increase performance, when monitoring is inducing researchers to exert more effort. As we discuss in more detail in Sect. 4, surveillance can also generate data, which—under specific circumstances—can be used as input to accelerate research, especially in the field of deep learning.

However, surveillance can also have a negative effect on creativity. This trade-off is important for the AI race between China and the US (see Sect. 1), with the outcome of the race depending on the still-open question of which type of research will ultimately be more important in artificial intelligence. While some observers argue that big breakthroughs like the deep learning revolution are rare, and that for the foreseeable future it is the amount of available data and the resources invested in research that will determine who will win the race (Lee 2018; Spitz 2017; Sun et al. 2017), it is also conceivable that another breakthrough will once again change the fundamentals in the field, leading to a new paradigm. In Sect. 4, we argue that China has an advantage with respect to the amount of data and the ability to induce effort for average-quality researchers. In this section, we argue that with respect to creativity, however, China's authoritarian institutions impose a tax that is similar in its negative impact to the tax on information described in Sect. 3.1.

To illustrate what we mean by creativity, think of a maze that is characterized by having one entrance but many exits, and thus many different potential paths to take (Amabile 1996). When trying to find an exit, some solutions can be more elegant, or more *creative*, than others. In the face of extrinsic reward structures or surveillance, the narrowest and quickest path will be chosen to get out of the maze, and "all behavior is narrowly directed toward attaining that goal" (Hennessey 2003, page 262). In order to find a creative solution, however, immersion with the maze itself, experimentation with alternative paths, and focusing attention toward seemingly incidental aspects become important (Hennessey 2003). Without intrinsic motivation to do the task at hand, and with an external target goal in mind, individuals will most likely rush toward the end of the maze. As Reiss and Sushinsky (1975) have shown, evaluation competes with task enjoyment, and attention diffuses away from the task to the fact of being evaluated. Or as Hennessey (2003, page 262) puts it: "when individuals are distracted by their excitement about a soon-to-be delivered prize or their anxiety surrounding an impending evaluation, their intrinsic motivation and enjoyment of the task at hand are undermined and they rush through their work as quickly as possible." Surveillance can thus lead to faster results, but at the price of less creative solutions, and a lower probability that a new fundamental breakthrough is discovered.

Ecosystems of Surveillance The existence of so-called ecosystems of surveillance is one aspect in which authoritarian and democratic political systems do fundamentally differ. Although surveillance does also exist in democracies,[15] researchers in authoritarian systems face, on average, more surveillance both in their daily

[15] In Western democracies, digital surveillance technologies are being used for example to deliver targeted campaign ads during election campaigns in what (Tufekci 2014) calls "computational

lives and in their activity as researchers (Jiang 2020; Perry 2020; Schulte 2019; Strittmatter 2020; Xu 2021). The importance of surveillance in authoritarian states can be explained by the informational dilemma of the authoritarian government. As a result of censorship, media control and the absence or manipulation of elections, the regime does not know the true sentiments of its citizens (Edmond 2013; Egorov and Sonin 2020; Xu 2021). As a consequence, the efficient allocation of resources to co-opt regime opponents remains impossible, as the regime is uncertain which actors require co-optation, and which actors might be better controlled through repression. Such targeted co-optation or repression is however necessary, as large-scale mass repression is only rarely used in contemporary dictatorships (Guriev and Treisman 2019; Xu 2021), partially because of the disadvantages of international backlash in a globalized economy, but also because visible repression can signal that the regime is weak (Guriev and Treisman 2020).

New computational methods and the ability to infer new information from existing data through the application of AI technologies have now led to a dramatic increase in digital surveillance capabilities (Edmond 2013; Feldstein 2019; Tufekci 2014), which are increasingly being used by authoritarian regimes. Social credit systems are one such technology. While the best known system is currently being introduced in China, the technology is also exported by China to other authoritarian states (Feldstein 2019). The stated objective of China's social credit systems is to assess the "trustworthiness" of individuals by taking into account personal, financial, and behavioral data, in order to foster social control and pre-empt social instabilities (Kostka and Antoine 2020).

In combination with the largest video surveillance network in the world, and the collection of biometric information on individuals such as DNA samples and fingerprints, the Chinese social credit system is in the process of becoming a comprehensive database on hundreds of millions of individuals (Liang et al. 2018; Qiang 2019). The system is unprecedented in its scale and scope, with the scale at which data are collected and used being made possible by the lack of a legal system protecting personal data (Chen and Cheung 2017). Since March 2020, the development of the system has received an additional boost through the compulsory introduction of tracing apps during the Covid-19 pandemic (Knight and Creemers 2021).[16] The system thus far also seems to benefit from high levels of social approval, with various studies finding that Chinese citizens are indifferent to, or even in favor of this kind of digital surveillance (Kostka 2019; Kostka and Antoine 2020; Su et al. 2021; Xu et al. 2021).

As we will show in Sect. 4, this extensive reservoir of personalized data can play a substantial positive role in the further development of AI technologies, should the

politics", or when personal data is used for commercial purposes in what has become known as "surveillance capitalism" (Zuboff 2019).

[16] See also "China uses cover of Covid to expand Big Brother surveillance and coercion", *The Times*, 25.04.2021, https://www.thetimes.co.uk/article/china-uses-cover-of-covid-to-expand-big-brother-surveillance-and-coercion-ndpz3klmw.

Chinese government decide to make it systematically available to AI firms in the country. The Chinese social credit system is nevertheless also establishing a massive surveillance infrastructure, providing the Chinese state with the technical ability to tightly control every aspect of the lives of its citizens (Strittmatter 2020; Werbach 2022). It is in the interest of the Chinese government to make this surveillance infrastructure as visible and present as possible in everyday life. While censorship becomes more effective the less visible it is (see Sect. 3.1), surveillance relies on its ubiquitous nature to be effective (Feldstein 2019). Behavioral modifications, or "chilling effects," are created even in the absence of physical violence due to the omnipresence of surveillance and the potential subsequent assessment of behavior (Feldstein 2019; Kostka 2019; Kostka and Antoine 2020). In line with Foucault (1995), where the panopticon disciplines inmates of a prison through a state of constant potential observation, social credit systems can induce self-monitoring and adjustment of behavior in the interest of the government (Aho and Duffield 2020; Kostka 2019).

The social and societal implications of such a large-scale surveillance project remain unclear. The next section examines how the omnipresence of surveillance can negatively affect creativity and, through this, high-quality innovation.

Surveillance, Creativity and Innovation Creativity—that is the generation of novel and useful outcomes and ideas (Amabile and Pratt 2016)—is an important input for research and innovation (Acar et al. 2019; Anderson et al. 2014; Litchfield et al. 2015). At the macro level, it is sometimes described as a basic economic input shaping technological change (Attanasi et al. 2020; Mokyr 1992). Some scholars have even argued that creativity is more than just an input to innovation, with the boundary between both concepts remaining fluid (Anderson et al. 2014). Generally, however, creativity can be understood as the generation of new ideas, while innovation is their implementation (Acar et al. 2019).

Creative performance can suffer from a number of external constraints, such as tight deadlines and time pressure (Acar et al. 2019; Hennessey and Amabile 2010), evaluation and surveillance (Amabile et al. 1990), and other related factors (Acar et al. 2019). According to the *componential theory of creativity*,[17] in which domain-relevant skills, creativity-relevant skills, and intrinsic task-motivation are defined as the principal components of creative performance (Amabile 1983, 1988; Amabile and Pratt 2016), the main *external* influence on creativity is channeled through intrinsic task-motivation.[18] To understand how authoritarian surveillance affects creativity, one thus needs to understand how it affects intrinsic motivation.

[17] For an overview of other theoretical perspectives on creativity and innovation, see Anderson et al. (2014).

[18] A related focus is proposed by Cerasoli et al. (2014), who review 40 years of research on external incentives and intrinsic motivation. While we focus on external *constraints* and intrinsic motivation, Cerasoli et al. (2014, page 983) are in line with our argumentation when they show that intrinsic motivation is a strong predictor of performance, but suffers from "crowding-out" when external incentives are too directly tied to performance outcomes.

To better understand the psychological processes of intrinsic motivation, a useful framework is provided by self-determination theory (SDT) (Deci and Ryan 1985; Ryan and Deci 2019). According to SDT, humans have three innate needs that determine motivation: the need for interpersonal relatedness, the need for competence, and the need for autonomy (Ryan and Deci 2000).[19] Interpersonal relatedness refers to being affiliated with a group or team, competence is the feeling of mastering a task, and autonomy refers to having control over a situation. In the following we examine how the needs of competence and autonomy, and through them intrinsic motivation, are affected by government surveillance.

According to SDT, intrinsic motivation can either be supported or undermined by the context and external circumstances of a specific task (Ryan and Deci 2000). In this respect, perceived levels of competence and autonomy play a particularly important role (Deci 1975; Deci and Ryan 1985). Events such as positive feedback, awards or communications fostering feelings of competence can enhance intrinsic motivation. In an experiment involving university students, Deci (1975) for example finds that positive performance feedback led to higher levels of intrinsic motivation, whereas negative feedback decreased feelings of competence, and through this intrinsic motivation and creativity.

According to Ryan and Deci (2000, page 70), however, a sense of competence *alone* will not enhance intrinsic motivation, "unless accompanied by a sense of autonomy or [...] by an internal perceived locus of control".[20] In other words, in addition to a feeling of being competent, one also has to perceive the ability to independently determine one's actions in order for intrinsic motivation to play a role. In the literature, this is often paraphrased as an internal, as opposed to external, locus of control.[21]

In order to perceive the locus of control internally as opposed to externally, the *functional significance* of an event is highly relevant. According to Deci and Ryan (1985), the way a person perceives a specific context can have two functional aspects—either a controlling one, or an informational one. These two aspects can be of different salience, that is one of them can dominate the awareness of a person, and thus be more salient. A context is perceived as controlling in nature if a person experiences pressure from outside to reach a specific target or goal, resulting in an external locus of control (Koestner et al. 1984). On the other hand, so-called "effectance-relevant" feedback—feedback that is perceived as providing helpful information for the achievement of a particular task, without limiting the autonomous functioning of a person—is resulting in the locus of control being

[19] Beyond intrinsic motivation, these basic psychological needs appear to be essential for facilitating positive social development, personal well-being, and the avoidance of psychopathology (Ryan and Deci 2000, 2019).

[20] Other studies relying on different theoretical frameworks identify a similar importance of autonomy as catalyst to enable creative performance, see e.g. Li et al. (2018).

[21] An internal locus of control means that a person is autonomously able to control her or his actions, while an external locus of control signifies that the person's actions are determined by an outside actor or institution.

perceived as internal (Deci and Ryan 1985; Koestner et al. 1984). Here the effect on intrinsic motivation is positive.

Experiments testing this theory have shown that imposing limits with the intention to control has a negative effect on intrinsic motivation and creativity, in contrast to imposing informational limits that provide feedback but are not coercive in nature (Koestner et al. 1984).[22] Similar effects were found by Pittman et al. (1980), who look at verbal rewards that also reveal an intention to control, or Lepper and Greene (1975), Pittman et al. (1980) and Plant and Ryan (1985), who study the effects of video surveillance. Enzle and Anderson (1993) look at different forms of surveillance, and find that surveillance with the intention to evaluate,[23] or to check that rules are being followed, had a negative effect on motivation. Surveillance where these intentions were not openly stated or visible, but where the subjects suspected that either evaluation or distrust was motivating the surveillance, had an even stronger negative effect on intrinsic motivation. If, on the other hand, subjects were convinced that surveillance was in place not to control but to assist them in their tasks, the effect on intrinsic motivation was positive.

These results are highly relevant for our study. As Enzle and Anderson (1993, p. 261) put it, "it is not surveillance per se that is important, but the belief that the surveillant intends to exercise social control." For now, it seems that even though digital surveillance is becoming increasingly ubiquitous in China, it is not yet seen in a negative light by most Chinese citizens (Kostka 2019; Kostka and Antoine 2020; Xu et al. 2021)—possibly because gamification is diverting attention from the control aspects of digital surveillance (Ramadan 2018). Whether these sentiments will remain stable or change in the future remains an open question. It is possible that once the intention of the Chinese state to use surveillance for social control becomes more visible, the negative effects on intrinsic motivation described above will become more salient as well.

Surveillance and Innovation in Chinese Academia In Chinese research institutions and universities, this already seems to be the case. The Chinese education system is characterized by high levels of performance-oriented surveillance and control. Competition to pass the national college entry exam is extremely high, and can often have a traumatizing effect on students who participate (Howlett 2021). As students and academics are seen as a political "risk group", political surveillance is especially intense in Chinese universities (Shao 2020; Yan 2014), with the use of digital surveillance and social credit systems being combined with personal monitoring by senior researchers and students (Perry 2020). Materialistic incentives

---

[22] Here the difference between controlling and informational limits lies in how an external constraint of behavior is framed. When the activities of subjects were met with "shoulds" and "musts," their intrinsic motivation and creative performance were reduced. Conveying the same behavioral constraint with compassion and without external pressure had no negative effect on intrinsic motivation.

[23] A negative effect of evaluative surveillance has also been identified by Froming et al. (1982), who look at intrinsic motivation, and Amabile et al. (1990), who study creativity.

and career opportunities are offered with the specific intention to exercise political control (Perry 2020, page 14), while video surveillance in classrooms and the ability of students to report professors in real time via apps is used to monitor teaching activities. Reports can lead to warnings, salary reductions or dismissal (Perry 2020, p. 11).

This system of intense surveillance is used to tightly control potential political activities of researchers and students in Chinese academia, while also being used to incentivize researchers to follow research directions indicated by the state. As a result, academic and scientific interests are subordinated to social stability and the interests of the Communist Party (Liu 2017), with most university professors strictly following the party line in their activities and research (Hao and Guo 2016). This does not mean, however, that the system is not able to generate high levels of scientific output. On the contrary, during the last 10 years the overall number of scientific publications has increased significantly in China.[24]

Accordingly, our hypothesis—based on the discussion above—is that *ceteris paribus*, the Chinese university and research system will for some time continue to perform worse in terms of research quality than a university system in a competitive democracy, as a result of the negative effects of surveillance on intrinsic motivation and creativity. In terms of the overall quantity of produced research, tight surveillance might however offer an advantage, as surveillance allows to incentivize researchers to exert effort.

For now, this hypothesis has not been tested empirically in any comprehensive way.[25] It could, however, provide an explanation for why China is still lagging behind with respect to research quality in the field of artificial intelligence, while having overtaken all other countries in the world with respect to overall research output in the field (as illustrated by Fig. 1 in Sect. 1). Table 1 provides additional evidence on this point, showing how the top 20 research institutions in the world with respect to research quality in AI (as measured by the Nature Index of research output in applied artificial intelligence) are still mainly located in the USA. When looking at the overall number of publications in AI, however, 14 out of the world's top 20 institutions are already located in China (Table 2).

[24] "China declared world's largest producer of scientific articles", *Nature*, 18.01.2018, https://www.nature.com/articles/d41586-018-00927-4.

[25] During the last 30 years, the Chinese bureaucratic system has proven that it can very efficiently incentivize state officials to exert effort to reach pre-determined performance criteria, such as economic growth (Jia et al. 2015; Li and Zhou 2005; Libman and Rochlitz 2019; Rochlitz et al. 2015; Yao and Zhang 2015). Schedlinsky et al. (2020) however show experimentally that even for relatively simple tasks, surveillance can reduce the motivation and hence the effort exerted. Hence, more research is needed to better understand how surveillance can affect performance with respect to complex and less complex tasks in authoritarian environments, and if—for example—a difference exists between performance in academic and scientific environments, and performance in bureaucratic settings.

4 Authoritarian Surveillance and Big Data

The hypothesis of this study is that while the USA still has an advantage with respect to research quality and creativity, China has an advantage with respect to the number and motivation of average-quality researchers and internet entrepreneurs, as well as with respect to the quantity of data available for research. Accordingly, who can win the AI race will ultimately depend on what will be more important in future research in AI—big data or new ideas. This section provides an outline of the symbiotic relationship between the Chinese state and private companies with respect to the gathering of data, before looking at how this data can be used to promote innovation.

4.1 Cooperation Between the State and the Private Sector

While Sects. 3.1 and 3.2 examine the landscape of surveillance in China from a political perspective, this section takes the different stakeholders into account, and shows how their cooperation permits the collection of large amounts of data on Chinese citizens. In China, a handful of big tech companies shape the digital environment, with Baidu, Alibaba, and Tencent being the three biggest players (Jia et al. 2018). They offer a vast array of services, including online payment, e-commerce, social media, medical services and cloud services, as well as all kinds of additional convenience apps, enabling them to gather large amounts of data on their customers (Arenal et al. 2020). They have also developed their own social credit systems, which combine and bundle data gathered across different domains.

The government meanwhile is developing smart cities with surveillance technologies in the form of CCTV and a range of other sensors in metropolitan areas, with the number of surveillance cameras installed in China having increased almost exponentially in recent years.[26] The Chinese state also places a high priority on technologies like the Internet of Things that are relevant for smart cities, as they facilitate economic growth but also render censorship and surveillance more effective (Kshetri 2017).

Similar trends are observable for the AI sector as a whole, where the state takes a leading role in financing AI development, buying AI solutions and determining strategies for future development (Arenal et al. 2020; Ding 2018; Righi et al. 2020). Through this kind of symbiosis, data are shared between public and private domains, for example in the financial sector through Alibaba's social credit system Zhima Score. In addition to transaction data from more than half a billion Alipay users, Zhima Score also has access to external government data derived from

[26] According to a recent report by China File, central and local Chinese governments spent US$ 2.1 billion between 2016 and 2020 to buy surveillance cameras, "State of Surveillance: Government Documents Reveal New Evidence on China's Efforts to Monitor Its People", *China File*, 30.10.2020, https://www.chinafile.com/state-surveillance-china.

interactions between individuals and public services (Arenal et al. 2020). The use of facial recognition software to identify deception by potential borrowers is another example from the financial sector where the state-owned Bank of China and Tencent cooperate (Kshetri 2020). Other projects include the sharing of legal data on criminals between the government and private companies providing digital service solutions such as video identification systems or remote trials on social media (Arenal et al. 2020). In an attempt to automate legal decision-making, courts purchase AI-powered solutions from tech companies for gathering data on court decisions (Stern et al. 2021). This data is subsequently made public in markets where companies and courts trade raw and repackaged data for research and commercial purposes. Additional examples include the use of facial recognition technologies to identify jaywalkers, or smart glasses for the police, with the technology being developed by private companies that also benefit from shared data to further improve their systems (Arenal et al. 2020).

The sharing of large amounts of data between the state and the private sector is made possible by data privacy regulations that are much weaker than in Europe or the US (Kshetri 2014; Moreno and Pedreno 2021; Wu et al. 2011). Particularly with respect to data sharing, Chinese companies are allowed to operate with very few regulations (Jia and Kenney 2016). This is being facilitated by consumers being less concerned about data privacy in China than in many other countries (Kshetri 2017).

Although the Chinese government has recently started a crackdown on the country's big tech companies, this does not mean that the symbiotic relationship between the private sector and the state is about to end. Rather, it can be understood as a signal by the Communist Party to the country's leading tech companies, to show who ultimately remains in charge.[27]

4.2 Big Data and Innovation in AI

According to Lee (2018, p. 14), at the current stage of AI research, "successful AI algorithms need three things: big data, computing power, and the work of strong—but not necessarily elite—AI algorithm engineers. Bringing the power of deep learning to bear on new problems requires all three, but in this age of implementation, data is the core. That is because once computing power and engineering talent reach a certain threshold, the quantity of data becomes decisive."[28]

Beraja et al. (2021) show that data from the symbiotic relationship between private firms and the Chinese state is already having a measurable positive effect on

[27] "What China Expects from Businesses: Total Surrender", *The New York Times*, 19.07.2021, https://www.nytimes.com/2021/07/19/technology/what-china-expects-from-businesses-total-surrender.html.

[28] See also Halevy et al. (2009) and Sun et al. (2017) on the role of big data in deep learning, especially with respect to vision tasks and facial recognition.

the number of commercial AI innovations in China, with the positive effect being larger than the potential crowding-out effect resulting from state intervention. The provision of government data to fuel private-sector innovation can thus be seen as an industrial policy tool used by the Chinese state, with the data gathered through surveillance being used as subsidy.

For the moment, the positive effects of this symbiotic relationship are mostly concentrated in the field of surveillance technologies (Beraja et al. 2021; Xiang 2019), where China has already gained world leadership and is exporting its technological solutions to other countries (Feldstein 2019). In other sectors, China is not quite there yet, with various institutional and technological factors hindering the efficient sharing of data between government institutions and private companies (Xiang 2019). In the health sector, for example, millions of personalized dossiers have been created, but implementation and data use are still hampered by institutional deficiencies (Zhang et al. 2020). Similar problems exist with respect to automated court decisions, where insufficient analytical capabilities hinder the effective implementation of the system (Stern et al. 2021). Even facial recognition is still suffering from implementation problems, with the efficiency of AI-automated CCTV applications remaining limited by various hardware and software problems (Peterson 2020).

China is nevertheless a leader in combining datasets from different sources and making them available for research institutions and private companies, at a much larger scale than other countries. Once these massive datasets are available, their use as input for deep learning algorithms can have significant transformative potential for various sectors (Qiu et al. 2016). If one considers China's population size, its extensive and rapidly evolving surveillance infrastructure, and especially the fact that the country only seriously embarked on using deep learning technologies a couple of years ago, the potential for future development is vast. What remains to be seen is whether it can outweigh the negative effects of surveillance and control on creativity and innovation.

5 Conclusion

This chapter examines the implication of a new technology—deep learning—on the effect political institutions have on innovation. Traditionally, authoritarian political institutions have been seen as having a mostly detrimental effect on innovation, as they block the free flow of information and hinder researchers' creative exploration of new ideas. Section 3 shows that these negative effects are persistent today. In authoritarian or semi-authoritarian countries such as China, Russia, Turkey, or Hungary, the free flow of information is disrupted by various forms of censorship, and researchers face substantial pressure and control from the side of the state. This chapter reviews an extensive theoretical and empirical literature from the field of psychology—in particular works related to self-determination theory (Deci 1975; Deci and Ryan 1985, 1987, 1990)—to show how the attempts of a government to exercise social control can negatively affect intrinsic motivation and creativity. In view of the recent initiative by the Chinese state to introduce a large-scale system of digitized social surveillance, these studies hold particular relevance, showing that, although China and other authoritarian states often have ambitious strategies to foster innovation and build knowledge economies, their institutions can act as a significant obstacle and stumbling block in this regard.

We then introduce a novel hypothesis, arguing that with respect to research in artificial intelligence and in particular deep learning, the negative effects of censorship and surveillance might be attenuated—or even outweighed—by the positive effects of having large amounts of data available. As outlined in Sect. 4, due to extensive government surveillance, lax data privacy rules and the bundling and sharing of data between state and private actors, in some areas such as facial recognition, research institutions in China have access to much larger and better datasets than their competitors in democratic countries. As data are the most important input in this type of research (Halevy et al. 2009; Sun et al. 2017), the potential positive effects on future innovation might be substantial.

Empirical research on these questions remains scarce. Beraja et al. (2021) present one of the few studies examining in a rigorous empirical setting how the sharing of data between private and government institutions affects innovation in AI in China, with the authors finding a significant and positive effect for the sector of surveillance technologies. To understand how deep learning technologies as well as different institutional approaches with respect to data sharing and surveillance might affect the race for leadership in artificial intelligence, much more empirical and theoretical research is needed. Here two lines of research are of particular importance—how political institutions affect intrinsic motivation, creativity and innovation in contemporary academic institutions, and how the role played by big data is driving innovation in artificial intelligence. We hope that this study can provide a first building block for a new research agenda in this direction.

References

Acar, O. A., Tarakci, M., & van Knippenberg, D. (2019). Creativity and innovation under constraints: A cross-disciplinary integrative review. *Journal of Management, 45*(1):96–121.

Acemoglu, D. & Robinson, J. A. (2006). *Economic origins of dictatorship and democracy*. New York: Cambridge University Press.

Aho, B. & Duffield, R. (2020). Beyond surveillance capitalism: Privacy, regulation and big data in Europe and China. *Economy and Society, 49*(2):187–212.

Amabile, T. M. (1983). The social psychology of creativity: A componential conceptualization. *Journal of Personality and Social Psychology, 45*(2), 357–376.

Amabile, T. M. (1988). A model of creativity and innovation in organisations. *Research in Organisational Behaviour, 10*, 123–167.

Amabile, T. M. (1996). *Creativity in context: Update to the social psychology of creativity*. Boulder: Westview Press.

Amabile, T. M. & Pratt, M. G. (2016). The dynamic componential model of creativity and innovation in organizations: Making progress, making meaning. *Research in Organizational Behavior, 36*, 157–183.

Amabile, T., Goldfarb, P., & Brackfield, S. C. (1990). Social influences on creativity: Evaluation, coaction, and surveillance. *Creativity Research Journal, 3*, 6–21.

Anderson, N., Potočnik, K., & Zhou, J. (2014). Innovation and creativity in organizations. *Journal of Management, 40*(5), 1297–1333.

Arenal, A., Armuña, C., Feijoo, C., Ramos, S., Xu, Z., & Moreno, A. (2020). Innovation ecosystems theory revisited: The case of artificial intelligence in China. *Telecommunications Policy, 44*(6), 101960.

Attanasi, G., Chessa, M., Gallen, S. G., & Llerena, P. (2020). A survey on experimental elicitation of creativity in economics. *GREDEG Working Papers*, 20.

Aydin, B. (2021). Politically motivated precarization of academic and journalistic lives under authoritarian neoliberalism: The case of Turkey. *Globalizations, 19*(5), 677–695.

Beraja, M., Yang, D., & Yuchtman, N. (2021). Data-intensive innovation and the state: Evidence from AI firms in China. *NBER Working Paper No. 27723.*

Blaydes, L. (2018). *State of repression: Iraq under Saddam Hussein*. Princeton: Princeton University Press.

Bory, P. (2019). Deep new: The shifting narratives of artificial intelligence from Deep Blue to AlphaGo. *Convergence: The International Journal of Research into New Media Technologies, 25*(4), 627–642.

Buckley, N., Reuter, J., Rochlitz, M., & Aisin, A. (2022). Staying out of trouble: Criminal cases against Russian mayors. *Comparative Political Studies*. https://doi.org/10.1177/00104140211047399.

Bueno de Mesquita, B., Smith, A., Siverson, R. M., & Morrow, J. D. (2003). *The power of political survival*. Boston: MIT Press.

Cao, C., Fred Simon, D., and Suttmeier, R. P. (2009). China's innovation challenge. *Innovation, 11*(2), 253–259.

Cerasoli, C. P., Nicklin, J. M., & Ford, M. T. (2014). Intrinsic motivation and extrinsic incentives jointly predict performance: a 40-year meta-analysis. *Psychological Bulletin, 140*(4), 980–1008.

Chen, Y. & Cheung, A. S. Y. (2017). The transparent self under big data profiling: Privacy and Chinese legislation on the social credit system. *The Journal of Comparative Law, 12*(2), 356–378.

Deci, E. L. (1975). *Intrinsic motivation*. Boston: Springer.

Deci, E. L. & Ryan, R. M. (1985). *Intrinsic motivation and self-determination in human behavior*. Boston: Springer.

Deci, E. L. & Ryan, R. M. (1987). The support of autonomy and the control of behavior. *Journal of Personality and Social Psychology, 53*(6), 1024–1037.

Deci, E. L. & Ryan, R. M. (1990). A motivational approach to self: Integration in personality. *Nebraska Symposium on Motivation. Nebraska Symposium on Motivation, 38*, 237–288.

Diamond, L. (2010). Liberation technology. *Journal of Democracy, 21*(3), 69–83.

Ding, J. (2018). *Deciphering Chinas AI-dream*. Oxford: Centre for the Governance of AI, Future of Humanity Institute, University of Oxford.

Dixon, L., Ristenpart, T., & Shrimpton, T. (2016). Network traffic obfuscation and automated internet censorship. *IEEE Security & Privacy, 14*(6), 43–53.

Domingos, P. (2015). *The master algorithm: How the quest for the ultimate learning machine will remake our world*. London: Penguin Books.

Edmond, C. (2013). Information manipulation, coordination, and regime change. *The Review of Economic Studies, 80*(4), 1422–1458.

Egorov, G. & Sonin, K. (2020). The political economics of non-democracy. *CEPR Discussion Paper, 2020*, 1–55.

Enyedi, Z. (2018). Democratic backsliding and academic freedom in Hungary. *Perspectives on Politics, 16*(4), 1067–1074.

Enzle, M. E. & Anderson, S. C. (1993). Surveillant intentions and intrinsic motivation. *Journal of Personality and Social Psychology, 64*(2), 257–266.

Feldstein, S. (2019). The road to digital unfreedom: How artificial intelligence is reshaping repression. *Journal of Democracy, 30*(1), 40–52.

Fieberg, C., Hesse, M., Loy, T., & Metko, D. (2022). Machine learning in accounting research. In Hornuf, L. (Ed.). *Diginomics research perspectives: The role of digitalization in business and society*. Cham: Springer International Publishing.

Foucault, M. (1995). *Discipline and punish: The birth of the prison*. New York: Vintage Books.

Froming, W. J., Walker, G., & Lopyan, K. J. (1982). Public and private self-awareness: When personal attitudes conflict with societal expectations. *Journal of Experimental Social Psychology, 18*(5), 476–487.

Gallagher, M. & Hanson, J. K. (2015). Power tool or dull blade? Selectorate theory for autocracies. *Annual Review of Political Science, 18*, 367–385.

Gao, X., Qiu, M., & Liu, M. (2021). Network traffic obfuscation and automated internet censorship. *2021 8th IEEE International Conference on Cyber Security and Cloud Computing (CSCloud)*, pp. 149–154.

Graham, L. R. (1987). *Science, philosophy, and human behavior in the Soviet Union*. New York: Columbia University Press.

Graham, L. R. (1993). *Science in Russia and the Soviet Union: A short history*. New York: Cambridge University Press.

Gregory, P., Schröder, P., & Sonin, K. (2011). Rational dictators and the killing of innocents: Data from Stalin's archives. *Journal of Comparative Economics, 39*(1), 34–42.

Griffiths, J. (2019). *The great firewall of China: How to build and control an alternative version of the internet*. London: Zed Books.

Gunitsky, S. (2015). Corrupting the cyber-commons: Social media as a tool of autocratic stability. *Perspectives on Politics, 13*(1), 42–54.

Guriev, S. & Treisman, D. (2019). Informational autocrats. *Journal of Economic Perspectives, 33*(4), 100–127.

Guriev, S. & Treisman, D. (2020). A theory of informational autocracy. *Journal of Public Economics, 186*, 104158.

Hagemann, V. & Klug, K. (2022). Human resource management in a digital environment. In Hornuf, L. (Ed.). *Diginomics research perspectives: The role of digitalization in business and society*. Cham: Springer International Publishing.

Halevy, A., Norvig, P., & Pereira, F. (2009). The unreasonable effectiveness of data. *Intelligent Systems, IEEE, 24*, 8–12.

Hao, Z. & Guo, Z. (2016). Professors as intellectuals in China: Political identities and roles in a provincial university. *The China Quarterly, 228*, 1039–1060.

Hennessey, B. A. (2003). The social psychology of creativity. *Scandinavian Journal of Educational Research, 47*(3), 253–271.

Hennessey, B. A. & Amabile, T. M. (2010). Creativity. *Annual Review of Psychology, 61*(1), 569–598.

Hey, T. (2009). *The fourth paradigm: Data-intensive scientific discovery*. Redmond: Microsoft Research.

Hinton, G. E. & Salakhutdinov, R. R. (2006). Reducing the dimensionality of data with neural networks. *Science, 313*(5786), 504–507.

Hinton, G., Osindero, S., & Teh., Y. (2006). A fast learning algorithm for deep belief nets. *Neural Computation, 18*(7), 1527–1554.

Hobbs, W. R. & Roberts, M. E. (2018). How sudden censorship can increase access to information. *American Political Science Review, 112*(3), 621–636.

Howlett, Z. M. (2021). *Meritocracy and its discontents: Anxiety and the national college entrance exam in China*. Ithaca: Cornell University Press.

Huang, H. & Xu, C. (1999). Institutions, innovations, and growth. *Economics of Transition and Institutional Change, 26*(3), 335–362.

Jia, K. & Kenney, M. (2016). Mobile internet platform business models in China: Vertical hierarchies, horizontal conglomerates, or business groups? *Berkeley Roundtable on the International Economy, BRIE Working Paper No. 2016-6.*
Jia, R., Kudamatsu, M., & Seim, D. (2015). Political selection in China: The complementary roles of connections and performance. *Journal of the European Economic Association, 13*(4), 631–668.
Jia, K., Kenney, M., Mattila, J., & Seppälä, T. (2018). The application of artificial intelligence at Chinese digital platform giants: Baidu, Alibaba and Tencent. *Berkeley Roundtable on the International Economy, BRIE Working Paper No. 2018-2*, p. 81.
Jiang, J. (2020). The eyes and ears of the authoritarian regime: Mass reporting in China. *Journal of Contemporary Asia, 51*(5), 828–847.
Josephson, P. R. (2005). *Totalitarian science and technology*. Amherst: Humanity Books.
Kalgin, A. (2016). Implementation of performance management in regional government in Russia: Evidence of data manipulation. *Public Management Review, 18*(1), 110–138.
Karpan, A. (2019). *Troll factories: Russia's web brigades*. New York: Greenhaven Publishing.
King, G., Pan, J., & Roberts, M. E. (2013). How censorship in China allows government criticism but silences collective expression. *American Political Science Review, 107*(2), 326–343.
King, G., Pan, J., & Roberts, M. E. (2014). Reverse-engineering censorship in China: Randomized experimentation and participant observation. *Science, 345*(6199), 1251722.
King, G., Pan, J., & Roberts, M. E. (2017). How the Chinese government fabricates social media posts for strategic distraction, not engaged argument. *American Political Science Review, 111*(3), 484–501.
Knight, A. & Creemers, R. (2021). Going viral: The social credit system and COVID-19. *Working Paper, available at SSRN*. https://ssrn.com/abstract=3770208.
Knutsen, C. H. (2015). Why democracies outgrow autocracies in the long run: Civil liberties, information flows and technological change. *Kyklos, 68*(3), 357–384.
Koestner, R., Ryan, R. M., Bernieri, F., & Holt, K. (1984). Setting limits on children's behavior: The differential effects of controlling vs. informational styles on intrinsic motivation and creativity. *Journal of Personality, 52*(3), 233–248.
Kostka, G. (2019). China's social credit systems and public opinion: Explaining high levels of approval. *New Media & Society, 21*(7), 1565–1593.
Kostka, G. & Antoine, L. (2020). Fostering model citizenship: Behavioral responses to China's emerging social credit systems. *Policy & Internet, 12*(3), 256–289.
Krizhevsky, A. (2009). Learning multiple layers of features from tiny images. *Working Paper, University of Toronto.*
Krizhevsky, A., Sutskever, I., & Hinton, G. (2012). ImageNet classification with deep convolutional neural networks. *Advances in Neural Information Processing Systems, 25*, 1097–1105.
Kshetri, N. (2014). China's data privacy regulations: A tricky tradeoff between ICT's productive utilization and cybercontrol. *IEEE Security & Privacy, 12*(4), 38–45.
Kshetri, N. (2017). The evolution of the internet of things industry and market in China: An interplay of institutions, demands and supply. *Telecommunications Policy, 41*(1), 49–67.
Kshetri, N. (2020). China's emergence as the global FinTech capital and implications for Southeast Asia. *Asia Policy, 27*(1), 61–81.
LeCun, Y., Bengio, Y., & Hinton, G. (2015). Deep learning. *Nature, 521*, 436–444.
Lee, K.-F. (2018). *AI superpowers: China, silicon valley, and the new world order*. Boston: Houghton Mifflin Harcourt.
Lepper, M. R. & Greene, D. (1975). Turning play into work: Effects of adult surveillance and extrinsic rewards on children's intrinsic motivation. *Journal of Personality and Social Psychology, 31*(3), 479–486.
Li, H. & Zhou, L.-A. (2005). Political turnover and economic performance: The incentive role of personnel control in China. *Journal of Public Economics, 89*(9–10), 1743–1762.
Li, H., Li, F., & Chen, T. (2018). A motivational–cognitive model of creativity and the role of autonomy. *Journal of Business Research, 92*, 179–188.

Liang, F., Das, V., Kostyuk, N., & Hussain, M. M. (2018). Constructing a data-driven society: China's social credit system as a state surveillance infrastructure. *Policy & Internet, 10*(4), 415–453.

Libman, A. & Rochlitz, M. (2019). *Federalism in China and Russia: Story of success and story of failure?* Cheltenham: Edward Elgar.

Linvill, D. L. & Warren, P. L. (2020). Troll factories: Manufacturing specialized disinformation on Twitter. *Political Communication, 37*(4), 447–467.

Litchfield, R. C., Ford, C. M., & Gentry, R. J. (2015). Linking individual creativity to organizational innovation. *The Journal of Creative Behavior, 49*(4), 279–294.

Liu, X. (2017). The governance in the development of public universities in China. *Journal of Higher Education Policy and Management, 39*(3), 266–281.

Medawar, J. & Pyke, D. (2012). *Hitler's gift: The true story of the scientists expelled by the Nazi regime*. New York: Arcade Publishing.

Minzner, C. (2018). *End of an era: How China's authoritarian revival is undermining its rise*. New York: Oxford University Press.

Mokyr, J. (1992). *Lever of riches: Technological creativity and economic progress*. Oxford: Oxford University Press.

Montagnes, P. & Wolton, S. (2019). Mass purges: Top-down accountability in autocracy. *American Political Science Review, 113*(4), 1045–1059.

Moore, W. H. (1998). Repression and dissent: Substitution, context, and timing. *American Journal of Political Science, 42*(3), 851–873.

Moreno, L. & Pedreno, A. (2021). *Europe vs USA and China: How to reverse decline in the age of artificial intelligence*. Seattle: Kindle Direct Publishing.

Moskowitz, M. L. (2013). *Go nation - Chinese masculinities and the game of Weiqi in China*. Berkeley: University of California Press.

Murray, F., Aghion, P., Dewatripont, M., Kolev, J., & Stern, S. (2016). Of mice and academics: Examining the effect of openness on innovation. *American Economic Journal: Economic Policy, 8*(1), 212–252.

Pan, J. (2020). *Welfare for autocrats: How social assistance in China cares for its rulers*. Oxford: Oxford University Press.

Pan, J. & Chen, K. (2018). Concealing corruption: How Chinese officials distort upward reporting of online grievances. *American Political Science Review, 112*(3), 602–620.

Pan, J. & Siegel, A. A. (2020). How Saudi crackdowns fail to silence online dissent. *American Political Science Review, 114*(1), 109–125.

Perry, E. J. (2020). Educated acquiescence: How academia sustains authoritarianism in China. *Theory and Society, 49*(1), 1–22.

Peterson, D. (2020). *Designing alternatives to China's repressive surveillance state*. Georgetown: Center for Security and Emerging Technology, Georgetown University.

Petrov, N. & Rochlitz, M. (2019). Control over the security services in periods of political uncertainty: A comparative study of China and Russia. *Russian Politics, 4*(4), 546–573.

Pijetlovic, D. & Mueller-Christ, G. (2022). HumanRoboLab: Experiments with chatbots in management education at universities. In Hornuf, L. (Ed.). *Diginomics research perspectives: The role of digitalization in business and society*. Cham: Springer International Publishing.

Pittman, T. S., Davey, M. E., Alafat, K. A., Wetherill, K. V., & Kramer, N. A. (1980). Informational versus controlling verbal rewards. *Personality and Social Psychology Bulletin, 6*(2), 228–233.

Plant, R. W. & Ryan, R. M. (1985). Intrinsic motivation and the effects of self-consciousness, self-awareness, and ego-involvement: An investigation of internally controlling styles. *Journal of Personality, 53*(3), 435–449.

Qiang, X. (2019), The road to digital unfreedom: President Xi's surveillance state. *Journal of Democracy, 30*(1), 53–67.

Qiu, J., Wu, Q., Ding, G., Xu, Y., & Feng, S. (2016). A survey of machine learning for big data processing. *EURASIP Journal on Advances in Signal Processing, 67*, 1–16.

Ramadan, Z. (2018). The gamification of trust: The case of China's "social credit". *Marketing Intelligence & Planning, 36*(1), 93–107.

Reiss, S. & Sushinsky, L. W. (1975). Overjustification, competing responses, and the acquisition of intrinsic interest. *Journal of Personality and Social Psychology, 31*(6), 1116–1125.

Righi, R., Samoili, S., López Cobo, M., Vázquez-Prada Baillet, M., Cardona, M., & De Prato, G. (2020). The AI techno-economic complex system: Worldwide landscape, thematic subdomains and technological collaborations. *Telecommunications Policy, 44*(6), 101943.

Ringen, S. (2016). *The perfect dictatorship: China in the 21st century*. Hong Kong: Hong Kong University Press.

Roberts, M. E. (2018). *Censored: Distraction and diversion inside China's great firewall*. Princeton: Princeton University Press.

Roberts, M. E. (2020). Resilience to online censorship. *Annual Review of Political Science, 23*(1), 401–419.

Rochlitz, M., Kulpina, V., Remington, T., & Yakovlev, A. (2015). Performance incentives and economic growth: Regional officials in Russia and China. *Eurasian Geography and Economics, 56*(4), 421–445.

Rosenberg, D. & Tarasenko, G. (2020). Innovation for despots? How dictators and democratic leaders differ in stifling innovation and misusing natural resources across 114 countries. *Energy Research & Social Science, 68*, 101543.

Ruan, L., Knockel, J., & Crete-Nishihate, M. (2017). We (can't) chat: "709 Crackdown" discussions blocked on Weibo and WeChat. *Citizen Lab Research Report No. 91*. Toronto: University of Toronto.

Ryan, R. M. & Deci, E. L. (2000). Self-determination theory and the facilitation of intrinsic motivation, social development, and well-being. *American Psychologist, 55*(1), 68–78.

Ryan, R. M. & Deci, E. L. (2019). Brick by brick: The origins, development, and future of self-determination theory. *Advances in Motivation Science, 6*, 111–156.

Savage, N. (2020). The race to the top among the world's leaders in artificial intelligence. *Nature, 588*(7837), 102–104.

Schedlinsky, I., Schmidt, M., & Wöhrmann, A. (2020). Interaction of information and control systems: How the perception of behavior control affects the motivational effect of relative performance information. *Accounting, Organizations and Society, 86*, 101171.

Schulte, B. (2019). Innovation and control: Universities, the knowledge economy and the authoritarian state in China. *Nordic Journal of Studies in Educational Policy, 5*(1), 30–42.

Shao, C. (2020). The surveillance experience of Chinese university students and the value of privacy in the surveillance society. PhD Dissertation, Chapel Hill: University of North Carolina.

Silve, F. & Plekhanov, A. (2018). Institutions, innovation and growth: Evidence from industry data. *Economics of Transition and Institutional Change, 26*(3), 335–362.

Silver, D., Huang, A., Maddison, C. J., Guez, A., Sifre, L., Van Den Driessche, G., Schrittwieser, J., Antonoglou, I., Panneershelvam, V., Lanctot, M., Dieleman, S., Grewe, D., Nham, J., Kalchbrenner, N., Sutskever, I., Lillicrap, T., Leach, M., Kavukcuoglu, K., Graepel, T., and Hassabis, D. (2016). Mastering the game of Go with deep neural networks and tree search. *Nature, 529*, 484–489.

Silver, D., Schrittwieser, J., Simonyan, K., Antonoglou, I., Huang, A., Guez, A., Hubert, T., Baker, L., Lai, M., Bolton, A., Chen, Y., Lillicrap, T., Hui, F., Sifre, L., van den Driessche, G., & Graepel, Thore Hassabis, D. (2017). Mastering the game of Go without human knowledge. *Nature, 550*, 354–359.

Smuha, N. A. (2021). From a 'race to AI' to a 'race to AI regulation': Regulatory competition for artificial intelligence. *Law, Innovation and Technology, 13*(1), 57–84.

Soldatov, A. and Rochlitz, M. (2018). The siloviki in Russian politics. In Treisman, D. (Ed.). *The new autocracy: Information, politics, and policy in Putin's Russia*, pp. 83–108. Washington, DC: Brookings Institution Press.

Spitz, M. (2017). *Daten - das Öl des 21. Jahrhunderts? Nachhaltigkeit im digitalen Zeitalter*. Hamburg: Hoffman und Campe.

Stern, R. E., Liebman, B. L., Roberts, M. E., & Wang, A. Z. (2021). Automating fairness? Artificial intelligence in the Chinese courts. *Columbia Journal of Transnational Law, 59*(515), 515–553.

Stokes, R. G. (2000). *Constructing socialism: Technology and change in East Germany, 1945-1990*. Baltimore: John Hopkins University Press.

Strittmatter, K. (2020). *We have been harmonized: Life in China's surveillance state*. New York: Custom House.

Su, Z., Xu, X., & Cao, X. (2021). What explains popular support for government surveillance in China? *Journal of Information Technology & Politics*, forthcoming.

Sun, C., Shrivastava, A., Singh, S., & Gupta, A. (2017). Revisiting unreasonable effectiveness of data in deep learning era. *CoRR*, abs/1707.02968.

Svolik, M. (2009). Power sharing and leadership dynamics in authoritarian regimes. *American Journal of Political Science, 53*(2), 477–494.

Tai, Y. & Fu, K.-w. (2020). Specificity, conflict, and focal point: A systematic investigation into social media censorship in China. *Journal of Communication, 70*(6), 842–867.

Tang, R. & Tang, S. (2018). Democracy's unique advantage in promoting economic growth: Quantitative evidence for a new institutional theory. *Kyklos, 71*(4), 642–666.

Tebaldi, E. & Elmslie, B. (2008). Institutions, innovation and economic growth. *MPRA Working Paper*, No. 9683.

Tiffert, G. D. (2019). Peering down the memory hole: Censorship, digitization, and the fragility of our knowledge base. *The American Historical Review, 124*(2), 550–568.

Tufekci, Z. (2014). Engineering the public: Big data, surveillance and computational politics. *First Monday, 19*(7).

Waldinger, F. (2010). Quality matters: The expulsion of professors and the consequences for PhD student outcomes in Nazi Germany. *Review of Economic Studies, 79*(2), 2455–2503.

Waldinger, F. (2012). Peer effects in science: Evidence from the dismissal of scientists in Nazi Germany. *Journal of Political Economy, 129*(99), 838–861.

Wallace, J. L. (2016). Juking the stats? Authoritarian information problems in China. *British Journal of Political Science, 46*(1), 11–29.

Werbach, K. (2022). Panopticon reborn: Social credit as regulation for the algorithmic age. Champaign:University of Illinois Law Review.

Wong, M. Y. & Kwong, Y.-h. (2019). Academic censorship in China: The case of The China Quarterly. *PS: Political Science & Politics, 52*(2), 287–292.

Wu, Y., Lau, T., Atkin, D., & Lin, C. (2011). A comparative study of online privacy regulations in the U.S. and China. *Telecommunications Policy, 35*(7), 603–616.

Xiang, N. (2019). *Red AI: Victories and warnings from China's rise in artificial intelligence*. Amazon Digital Services.

Xu, X. (2021). To repress or to co-opt? Authoritarian control in the age of digital surveillance. *American Journal of Political Science, 65*(2), 309–325.

Xu, X., Kostka, G., & Cao, X. (2021). Information control and public support for social credit systems in China. *Working Paper*.

Yan, X. (2014). Engineering stability: Authoritarian political control over university students in post-Deng China. *The China Quarterly, 218*, 493–513.

Yao, Y. & Zhang, M. (2015). Subnational leaders and economic growth: Evidence from Chinese cities. *Journal of Economic Growth, 20*, 405–436.

Zeng, J. (2020). Artificial intelligence and China's authoritarian governance. *International Affairs, 96*(6), 1441–1459.

Zhang, H., Ni, W., Li, J., & Zhang, J. (2020). Artificial intelligence-based traditional Chinese medicine assistive diagnostic system: validation study. *JMIR Med Inform, 8*(6), e17608.

Zuboff, S. (2019). *The age of surveillance capitalism: The fight for a human future at the new frontier of power*. New York: PublicAffairs.

Digital Transformation of Maritime Supply Chains Focusing on Ocean Shipping, Port Management, and Hinterland Connection

Hans-Dietrich Haasis and Hapsatou

1 Innovation in Maritime Business and Transportation

The maritime economy and the transport industry have always been an innovative economic sector. For over half a century, shipping companies, terminal operators, port industry actors, and logistics service providers have been successfully engaged in innovating their assets, processes, and business activities. The industry has thus shown its innovative potential for change and adaptation and its ability to react to new market and technological conditions (Buer et al., 2019; Heilig et al., 2020).

Here, innovations are understood, as usual, to be innovations and changes in the company through the application of new ideas and techniques. In business consulting, innovations are generally understood to mean the introduction of new or significantly improved techniques, products, services, processes, or organizational principles.

Well-known innovations in logistics and transport include the pull principle and just-in-time delivery (both introduced by Taiichi Ohno as core aspects of the Toyota Production System) and the concept of anticipatory shipping (developed by Amazon) which uses data to predict the shopping behavior of customers and to automatically send them the corresponding products. The best-known and probably the most visible innovation has been the introduction of the standardized container by Malcolm McLean, considered the "father of containerization." It is

H.-D. Haasis (✉)
Universität Bremen, Chair in Maritime Business and Logistics, Bremen, Germany
e-mail: haasis@uni-bremen.de

Hapsatou
Universität Bremen, Chair in Maritime Business and Logistics, Bremen, Germany

Université de Ngaoundéré, Ngaoundéré, Cameroon
e-mail: hapsatou@uni-bremen.de

L. Hornuf (ed.), *Diginomics Research Perspectives*, Advanced Studies in Diginomics and Digitalization, https://doi.org/10.1007/978-3-031-04063-4_9

thanks to his personal commitment and capital that the container established itself worldwide as a standardized transport container in the middle of the twentieth century. The container is becoming the engine of globalization and revolutionizing the world economy (Tran et al., 2017; Tran & Haasis, 2015). In 2004, McLean was inducted into the Logistics Hall of Fame. This innovation can be credited for further innovations such as supply chain management, just-in-time delivery, port integration, ship size development, and linked hinterland connections.

There has been increasing discussion about automation, self-control, cloud logistics, electrification, decarbonization, zero-emission processes, and dematerialization. Despite the importance of all these innovations, digitalization and digital transformation of business activities and processes are considered the most significant since the introduction of the container. This has consequences for all business activities and business developments, presenting a wealth of challenges and opportunities for strategic and operational change management (Board of Academic Advisers to the Federal Minister of Transport and Digital Infrastructure, 2018; DHL Trend Research, 2018; Dujak & Sajiter, 2019; Federal Ministry of Transport and Digital Infrastructure, 2019; Lind et al., 2021).

Austrian economist Joseph Schumpeter, the author of *Theory of Economic Development*, published in 1912, spoke of "creative destruction" and the replacement of an existing one by something better. This characterization can and should even be transferred to the current activities in companies in connection with digitalization and digital transformation.

As is known, digital transformation is the process of implementing digital technologies and supporting capabilities to create digital business models. While digitization can be defined as the action to convert analog information into digital information, digitalization concerns the changing of tasks and processes in an organization with the objective of reconfiguration assets to develop new business models. Digital transformation goes one step further, and can be understood as a process of adoption and implementation of emerging technologies in all aspects of operations, with far-reaching implications for systems, from companies to entire supply chains (Haasis et al., 2015; Heilig et al., 2020; Heilig & Voß, 2017; Jahn & Saxe, 2017; Lind et al., 2021). Changes through digital transformation include digital connectivity, cross-company collaboration, changes to business ecosystems, digital service innovations, and the use of platforms as enablers. In this context, a rethinking of previous approaches to communication, coordination, and cooperation is appropriate and necessary.

With regard to process control management and information management between partners in maritime supply chains, there is substantial potential for improving efficiencies. Such improvements can be obtained through better coordination along the maritime-driven supply chain, by region-comprehensive cluster-orientated cooperation between seaports and port industry actors, and by an innovative shifting of control mechanisms into the cloud. To date, the options of modern information and communication technologies have been considerably underutilized. The reasons are related to high transaction costs and the necessary change management, as well as to unforeseeable consequences of the transfer of business data (Board of Academic Advisers to the Federal Minister of Transport and Digital Infrastructure, 2018; Haasis et al., 2021).

This shows that considering the design and operation of supply chains along international or intercontinental freight transport routes will be essential not only for spatial planning and construction industries. More than ever, it is important to invest in the provision and use of information, and in the development and assessment of innovative and trustworthy cooperation and business models (Haasis et al., 2021; Lind et al., 2021).

2 Present Developments and Trends

A visionary description of the future of the logistics and transport industry is provided by the Logistics 2030 Innovation Programme of the German Federal Ministry of Transport and Digital Infrastructure (2019). Today, the industry and its actors are on a visible path there.

Economic, reliable, and secure maritime supply chains are essential for a functioning national and global economy. Those involved in ocean shipping, port management, and hinterland connection therefore have an essential role in the sustainable development of the economy and society, highlighting the importance for them to seize the opportunities of digitalization and digital transformation of processes and business models.

Efficient and well-developed maritime supply chains are also important for the international networking of essential production sites with procurement and sales markets. Their design and expansion aim to ensure economic accessibility for supply chains, to increase the attractiveness and visibility of the regions along transport corridors, to increase the reliability, cost-effectiveness, and safety of freight transportation, and to ensure a future-oriented sustainable development of economic regions (Jahn et al., 2020; Jahn & Saxe, 2017; Kersten et al., 2020).

To support, test, and develop innovative solutions for the digitalization of the maritime supply chain, digital test fields have been established for the German seaports in the German Bight for some time by the Federal Ministry of Transport and Digital Infrastructure. Within Europe, such developments can also be found in the port of Antwerp and the port of Rotterdam, and outside Europe in the port of Singapore and in the port of Dubai. Capabilities of test fields should be developed to demonstrate, for example, how port processes can be carried out partially or fully automatically, how their control can be shifted to the cloud, how traffic and handling processes can be self-controlled, and how waiting times and congestion can be avoided.

Platform solutions are also currently being developed and even made available to make the transfer of data along the maritime supply chains as easy as possible in the sense of a sharing economy. Examples include the collaboration between Maersk Line and IBM (see: www.tradelens.com) as well as between CMA CGM and Alibaba (see: www.lloydsloadinglist.com) for the development of platform-oriented digital supply chain management. For several years now, the funding programs IHATEC (see: www.innovativehafentechnologien.de) of the German Federal Ministry of Transport and Digital Infrastructure have made a significant contribution to this development.

Various information and communication systems have been in use in German seaports for several years. These include systems for the automatic identification of ships, controlling traffic processes and port telematics; port community systems; access control systems for security-relevant areas of the port in accordance with the International Ship and Port Facility Security Code; and systems for shipment tracking using tracking and tracing for containers (Buer et al., 2019; Heilig et al., 2020; Heilig & Voß, 2017; Wan, 2021).

However, it is now time to undertake the process of implementing digital technologies and supporting capabilities to create digital business models. Thus, digitalization should focus both on digital infrastructure and on digital services. This entails more than the introduction of paperless procedures and extends to port community systems, terminal operating systems, and automated procedures, for example implemented in combination with automated guided vehicles. The time is ripe for the implementation of "smart" procedures enabled by the Internet of Things, big data, business analytics, cloud computing, and cyber-physical systems. These smart procedures allow object-to-object communication and decentralized control of processes.

By the way, this topic is also a high priority goal in China in connection with the Belt and Road Initiative. The prioritization of digital connectivity through the integration of the Internet of Things and e-commerce was already put forward in a white paper prepared by the National Development and Reform Commission in 2015. This policy of Digital Silk Roads was outlined by Lu Wei, the director of the Cyberspace Administration, at the China–EU Roundtable for Digital Cooperation in 2015, where he announced, "We can build a digital silk road, a silk road in cyberspace" (Brown, 2017).

In realizing smart procedures and object-to-object communication, it is interesting to note that many of the associated decision-making processes involve assignment problems. For these problems, existing operations research solutions can be applied, for example for the allocation of containers to ports according to conditions, for the assignment and shifting of services to selected ports, for the assignment of terminal operations to vessels, for the assignment of hinterland connections to containers, and for a multi-port and multi-terminal profit allocation based on transfer payments.

Smart procedures and new digital service innovations relevant to a smart service port include the re-direction and re-assignment of vessels to terminals and/or seaports, berth allocation and quay crane scheduling, container storage and handling in the yard, truck appointment and ramp management, interterminal transportation and empty container management, ship announcement and terminal preparation, and gate drive-through management (Buer et al., 2019; Fibrianto et al., 2020; Jahn & Saxe, 2017; Kersten et al., 2020; Lind et al., 2021; Philipp, 2021).

In view of bottleneck situations caused by port operations and hinterland transports and the associated focus on investments in port development and infrastructure provision, cooperation between seaports from time to time may already be an option today, but it will certainly be an option in the future. This may lead to such advantages as shorter wait times in front of gates and terminals, better usage of straddle carriers and container yard capacities, and more time-efficient transshipment processes. Such competitive cooperation (or "coopetition") can be supported by the installation of a web-based digital service and data platform covering the data exchange between all cooperating seaports (Haasis & Elbert, 2018; Hoshino, 2010; Lind et al., 2021; Notteboom et al., 2009; Philipp, 2021; Stamatovic et al., 2018). In general, the ports are competitors; however, for providing efficient and economic digital solutions, the ports could cooperate on a digital level. Areas with potential for digital service innovations based on collaborative decision-making include yard and container lot management, ship announcement after re-direction and terminal preparation, gate drive-through management, and flexible and conditional supply chain management. It should be kept in mind, however, that problems could arise in combination with dedicated terminals, loading plans, customs processes, container fumigation, or the assignment of trucks (Board of Academic Advisers to the Federal Minister of Transport and Digital Infrastructure, 2018).

Artificial intelligence will also play an important role in transforming processes related to ocean shipping and port management. The development of a "smart ship" (a fully digitized, autonomous ship without a crew) is one of the major goals, with a prominent example being the container ship Yara Birkeland, with a capacity of 120 TEU, launched in 2020 (see: www.yara.com).

3 Future Studies and Vision on Digital Maritime Supply Chains

One vision for digital maritime supply chains, ports, and hinterland connections is the Silicon Economy Logistics Ecosystem proposed and headed by the Fraunhofer Institute IML in Dortmund (see: www.iml.fraunhofer.de). According to the managing director of the IML, Michael ten Hompel, the philosophy behind this ecosystem and the related logistics and industrial value creation is characterized by the following issues: orchestrate instead of producing; together instead of alone: collaboration and coopetition; share instead of controlling: sharing economy; agile instead of pipeline: platform economy; ecosystems instead of hierarchy: crowds and communities; and open instead of proprietary: open source, open innovation.

However, the question remains how the individual parts of the ecosystem might fit together. Examples of parts or services of this ecosystem include automated ETA forecast with artificial intelligence, digitized pallet exchange, electronic bill of lading, e-navigation and emulation control, digital customs clearance using blockchain, and smart contracting for import and export processes (Chaising &

Haasis, 2021; Heilig et al., 2020; Jahn et al., 2020; Jahn & Saxe, 2017; Kreeb & Haasis, 2017; Lind et al., 2021).

Potential solutions might include a container ship deciding autonomously the best terminal and berth for container transshipment, or a vessel moored at a quay independently controlling the terminal operations for its containers. Or a retailer might control the transshipment of requested containers through hinterland transportation to the demanding shop based on the specified demand of customer products. The container itself might even self-control some of its operations on the container yard.

Future cloud-based applications may be operated on a digital web-based service platform across locations, upgraded on the basis of port community systems and terminal operating systems. The platform could have the characteristics of an essential facility. The related process model could be developed further toward a port-as-a-service model and the port that can be called a smart service port (Board of Academic Advisers to the Federal Minister of Transport and Digital Infrastructure, 2018; General Assembly of Terminal Industry Committee 4.0, 2021). For example, GAIA-X can be seen as a platform for the use case of supply chain collaboration, mainly for the automobile industry and for mobility (see: www.data-infrastructure.eu). It represents the next generation of data infrastructure for Europe.

Automation is already a current development, for example in selected terminals in the seaports of Hamburg, Busan, and Dubai. Visions of a future "seaport 4.0" can be seen in the Next Generation Port 2030 in Singapore or the well-known TradeLens initiative of Maersk and IBM based on a blockchain-enabled digital shipping platform. Based on the familiar principle of the landlord model, the digital platform could be provided as standardized public infrastructure, and the service applications could reflect that of customer-orientated private suprastructures. Then, algorithms and new data-driven applications for berth allocation, container yard operations, storage management, and crane scheduling policies can be shifted toward cloud solutions. Of course, similar considerations can be made for freight villages and, in general, for logistics hubs. In the future, services could be offered by new Internet enterprises powered by data sources (Haasis et al., 2015; Haasis et al., 2021; Jahn & Saxe, 2017; Lind et al., 2021).

To understand what is likely to continue and what could plausibly change is the topic of the scientific research field of future studies. In this context, considerations can be made as to how digital service innovations, new business models, and cooperation arrangements can be identified and deliberated.

Such considerations have been made for the aforementioned seaport of Singapore, which will feature a maritime single window, automated terminal, automated quay and yard cranes, automated guided vehicles, automated truck pilots, autonomous ships, e-navigation, a vessel traffic management system, unmanned aerial vehicle, and just-in-time planning and coordination systems. The port, located in Tuas in Singapore and operated by PSA International, is expected to be completed by 2040, with a total capacity of 65 million TEU. Construction commenced in 2019.

Blockchain technology is emerging from its first applications in cryptocurrency and is now likely to have a significant impact across almost all industries (DHL

Trend Research, 2018; Dujak & Sajter, 2019; Lind et al., 2021; Wan, 2021). In the context of logistics and ocean shipping, many projects are in progress applying blockchain technology to supply chain efficiency, security, and transparency, as well as the handling of administrative processes. For data transfer along the maritime supply chain as well, scientists and business experts are increasingly focusing on developing blockchain solutions.

For example, in 2020 Alibaba joined the International Port Community Systems Association's blockchain bill of lading initiative (see: www.ipcsa.int). This project aims to standardize blockchain applications in logistics and e-commerce. Alibaba, LOGINK, and IPCSA have created a working group to elaborate innovative digital logistics solutions. LOGINK is China's information network for sharing logistics data. COSCO shipping has signed a deal with Ant Group and Alibaba Group to examine applications of the Ant blockchain technology within the global shipping industry.

Of course, these developments will have consequences for the employment situation in maritime business, in seaports and terminal operators, as well as in logistics companies. Frey and Osborne (2013) have found that most workers in transportation and logistics occupations, together with quite a number of office and administrative support workers, are likely to be displaced by automation and digital solutions. In line with technological developments, more and more transportation and logistics processes are becoming automated and self-controlled. Algorithms for big data analytics are also rapidly entering domains reliant upon storing or accessing information (Frey & Osborne, 2013). However, this can also be a great opportunity to counteract the shortage of skilled workers in certain areas of activity.

Whatever the future may hold, there is no doubt that there will be an impact on both employment prospects and employment requirements—and impact for which not just companies in the shipping and logistics sector but also chambers of commerce should be prepared.

4 Digital Divide and Decision Culture

The development in the economy toward more digitalization and more digital transformation is encountering at least two issues worldwide: the digital divide and decision culture. Whether these factors are taken into account will determine the extent to which the gap between industrialized and developing countries continues to grow or can be closed. The ICT Development Index of the International Telecommunication Union clearly shows the differences between countries in terms of the availability, utilization, and further development of modern information and communication technologies (see: www.itu.int). The question remains how to handle the digital divide between companies and between regions. Therefore, related market consequences for international maritime supply chains and logistics hubs such as seaports and freight villages must be observed, analyzed, and challenged (Haasis et al., 2021). We must also decide about the extent of external web-based control. This is a thrilling and challenging topic that should be addressed in the context of the ethics of logistics.

The decision-making behavior of the actors involved in supply chains is largely shaped by their social, political, and cultural dispositions (Baumann et al., 2013; Hofstede et al., 2010). This has an impact on the willingness and scope of a digital transformation of processes, as well as the success of digitalization measures. Different cultural practices can have an impact on the design and control of logistics chains and their impacts on trade and social coexistence. The implementation and operation of maritime supply chains must therefore consider decision-makers and logistics service people with different cultural backgrounds. By the way, the indicators used for determining the Logistics Performance Index, a benchmarking tool published by the World Bank (Arvis et al., 2018), are largely dependent on people's decisions. This is exemplified in the widely recognized and accepted consideration of public holidays. But it should also be noted that in some regions, contracts are just a general commitment to do business together and are less meaningful than personal relationships between individuals. Or if you think there is a standard service contract with a warehouse service provider, which however contains a "change in circumstances" clause, this essentially means that the contract is not legally binding (Fawcett et al., 2004; Smyrlis, 2004).

The barriers to ensuring time-efficient and reliable processes are not limited to different languages, time zones, and measurement units, but also include behavior patterns and contextual interpretations. In the implementation of logistics information systems and decision support tools, it is not uncommon, mainly in developing countries, to hear something like: "We were used to work without pressure and postponing some tasks for later because the system was not synchronized. Everyone was working for themselves without pressure. However, with this synchronized system, work must be always done instantaneously so that operations can take place on time. As a result, we feel that we are under pressure from the system and that we are no longer acting according to our own free will, but that we are subject to the system." This statement highlights that cultural aspects must be considered as part of maritime supply chain decisions to avoid misunderstanding and miscommunication, which is known to increase uncertainty and risk and therefore costs, and can lead to miscalculation in supply chain decisions (Baumann et al., 2013; Haasis et al., 2021).

Heterogeneity in cultural backgrounds may thus influence the efficient and reliable execution of logistics processes, as well as decisions on how these processes may be digitalized. On the other hand, these backgrounds may result in the transfer of ideas, experiences, and knowledge between the regions and people along the international maritime supply chains, as has happened in the past. Thus, in addition to focusing on the supply chains of freight and goods and the corresponding digitalization and digital transformation, it is also enhancing and worthwhile to consider the cultural chain of ideas and knowledge to increase the understanding and appreciation among decision-makers and others who are communicating, cooperating, and working together (Haasis et al., 2021).

5 Power of Data and Consequences for Business Models

As discussed above, in future, maritime and logistics services could be offered by new Internet enterprises powered by data sources and by digital control of processes. Data and process owners of today may be substituted by tomorrow's unknown owners. Thus, it is not only a question for a member of the maritime blockchain community of whether to be or not to be. The questions are who will provide the digital business models on demand in the future, who has the data and process power, and how to handle the unevenly distributed access to data and thus the unevenly distributed power in competition between companies and between regions. From a conventional point of view, this could be the communications provider, the data provider, the automobile industry, the energy supply company, the city administration, the logistics infrastructure provider, the ocean shipping company, or the logistics service provider (Brinker & Haasis, 2020; Jahn et al., 2020). However, it could also be that logistics service providers and terminal operators will be downgraded to puppet figures in the future. Therefore, in terms of an early warning system, digitalization-related market consequences for seaports and the other actors in the maritime supply chains must be analyzed and challenged in good time.

As early as 1976 Joseph Weizenbaum, who has been awarded an honorary doctorate from the University of Bremen in 1998 in recognition of his services to computer science and the social responsibility of computer scientists, published his famous book *Computer Power and Human Reason: From Judgement to Calculation*, in which he criticized the power of computers and the "impotence of reason" (Weizenbaum, 1976). Weizenbaum warned against the wrong use of information and communication technology. It may be prudent to extend this wisdom to the power of digital processes and the power of data.

The consequences for business models are clear. Due to the power of digital processes and data, the conventional differentiation—1PL for cargo owners focusing on manufacturing or retailing, 2PL for carriers and forwarders providing transportation as a service, 3PL for logistics service providers providing logistics (mainly contract logistics) as a service, and 4PL for lead logistics providers and consultants focusing on supply chain management—must be extended to 5PL for big data-driven logistics providers focusing on demand chain management, and 6PL for digital Internet logistics providers realized by cloud logistics. Ultimately, the control and decision-making power can and will be shifted toward software on the Internet that is available 24 hours a day, every day, regardless of weekends and holidays.

As discussed above, this is an essential development because many decisions in ocean shipping, port management, and hinterland transportation are assignment problems for which easy-to-use and powerful algorithms have been available for years. Used with the right data, these algorithms can be used within software systems provided on demand on the Internet. This also highlights the need for and importance of digital data sharing. Such transformation will create opportunities for data analytics, digital innovations to support transport processes, and learning systems that enable better decision-making. This will give rise to new startups within the market of shared logistics, as seen in the case of Cargonexx or Sennder.

On a global scale, interoperability between the software and decision systems is necessary. It is therefore important to develop, test, and shape frameworks, for example the Silicon Economy Logistics Ecosystem designed by Fraunhofer IML. Platform technologies characterized by sharing principles, interoperability, data protection, and innovative digital services will play an important role in such ecosystems. For example, the platform DataPorts may provide a trusted and secure environment for all actors operating in the diverse maritime supply chains involved in European seaports (see: dataports-project.eu). Using this data platform across connected digital ports would support the transition to cognitive ports, which will open the way to new capabilities: real-time control of operations, streamlined decision-making, accurate prediction of events and situations, and prescriptive analytics. Examples include the aforementioned blockchain-enabled digital shipping platform TradeLens, jointly developed by A. P. Moller–Maersk and IBM, and a similar development realized by COSCO Shipping, Alibaba, and the Ant Group.

Of course, this implies increased shifting of power in maritime-driven supply chains. Needless to say, monopolistic platforms put competing market players and business models at risk, with such consequences as loss of data sovereignty and loss of direct customer relationships, as well as unequal distribution of process and market power. For this reason, the European Commission is currently discussing the adoption of the Digital Markets Act, a legislative proposal aimed at ensuring competition in digital markets.

6 Synopsis and Conclusions

The maritime industry and the logistics community have shown their innovative potential for change and adaptation and an ability to react to new market and technological conditions. Now and in the near future, digitalization and digital transformation of maritime supply chains will be the most powerful and challenging forces of innovation. The purpose of this chapter has been to reflect the opportunities and challenges related to this digital transformation, with a focus on ocean shipping, port management, and hinterland connectivity.

Knowing that world trade flows are interconnected and changeable, the logistics industry must ensure distributed production and supply in a dynamic environment. The aim here has been to identify and characterize expectations, opportunities, and peculiarities, as well as to sketch a picture of the future. Particular attention has been given to the influence of digital gaps, cultural differences, and the power of data.

Access to digital processes, innovations, and communication platforms is essential to increase the efficiency and reliability of logistics processes and supply chains worldwide, so now is the time to act with foresight. It is necessary to make innovation and development visible and transparent, to learn from each other, and to take people and employees with them on this journey. In this context, major changes are to be considered and established norms to be questioned. It will also be important to maintain vigilance toward monopolistic tendencies.

As this chapter points out, access to digital processes varies from company to company and from country to country, and it remains to be seen who will provide the digital business models and who possesses the data power. A stronger focus on the people and their cultural differences is thus essential to supporting the improvement of the logistics performance of companies and regions and their corresponding successful digitalization and digital transformation.

In the context of maritime supply chains, a robust discussion of digitalization and digital transformation may motivate not only investment in infrastructure and technology but also investment in knowledge, education, training, communication, and understanding. As Hajo Schumacher implores in the column *Netzentdecker*, it is essential that we expand the social market economy to include the ecological and the digital, and that we interlink modern technology and educational ideals. The focus could be on the Bhutan strategy. From now on, every political decision should be appraised by asking: Is the well-being of the individual and the community being promoted? (Schumacher, 2020). Perhaps now is the time to think more deeply about an ethics of logistics.

References

Arvis, J.-F., Ojala, L., et al. (2018). *Connecting to compete. Trade logistics in the global economy*. World Bank.

Baumann, T., Haasis, H.-D., & Nehlsen-Pein, T. (2013). Human decision making in business. Implications and application operations of neurosciences for business decisions. *Business Systems Review, 2*(1), 1–14.

Board of Academic Advisers to the Federal Minister of Transport and Digital Infrastructure. (2018). *Statement on "Chancen der Digitalisierung für die deutschen Seehäfen nutzen und Investitionen in die Infrastrukturen optimieren"*. Federal Ministry of Transport and Digital Infrastructur.

Brinker, J., & Haasis, H.-D. (2020). The impact of an asymmetric allocation of power on the digitalization strategy of port logistics. In C. Jahn, W. Kersten, & C. M. Ringle (Eds.), *Data science in maritime and city logistics* (pp. 457–484). ePubli.

Brown, R. (2017). *Beijing's silk road goes digital*. https://www.cfr.org/blog/beijings-silk-road-goes-digital.

Buer, T., Haasis, H.-D., Kinra, A., & Kotzab, H. (2019). An overview to contemporary maritime logistics and supply chain management decision areas. In P. M. Panayides (Ed.), *The Routledge handbook of maritime management* (pp. 113–123). Routledge.

Chaising, S., & Haasis, H.-D. (2021). Cloud computing for logistics and procurement services for SMEs and raw material supplier. *International Journal of Logistics Systems and Management, 38*(4), 459–474.

DHL Trend Research. (2018). *Blockchain in logistics*. Troisdorf.

Dujak, D., & Sajter, D. (2019). Blockchain applications in supply chain. In A. Kawa & A. Maryniak (Eds.), *Smart supply network* (pp. 21–46). Springer.

Fawcett, S. E., Magnan, G. M., & Williams, A. J. (2004). Supply chain trust is within your grasp. *Supply Chain Management Review, 8*(2), 20–26.

Federal Ministry of Transport and Digital Infrastructure. (2019). *Logistics 2030*. Innovation Programme.

Fibrianto, H. Y., Kang, B., Kim, B., Marbach, A., Buer, T., Haasis, H.-D., Hong, S., & Kim, K.-W. (2020). A simulation study of a storage policy for a container terminal. In M. Freitag, H.-D. Haasis, H. Kotzab, & J. Pannek (Eds.), *Dynamics in logistics* (pp. 62–69). Springer.

Frey, C. B., & Osborne, M. A. (2013). *The future of employment: How susceptible are jobs to computerization?* Oxford Martin School, University of Oxford, Working Paper.

General Assembly of Terminal Industry Committee 4.0. (2021). An introduction to the Terminal Industry Committee 4.0 (TIC4.0). White paper.

Haasis, H.-D., Du, J., & Sun, X. (2021). Logistics challenges along the new silk roads. In M. Freitag, H. Kotzab, & N. Megow (Eds.), *Dynamics in logistics: Twenty-five years of interdisciplinary logistics research in Bremen*. Springer.

Haasis, H.-D., & Elbert, R. (2018). Bringing regional networks back into global supply chains: Strategies for logistics service providers as integrators of logistics clusters. In W. Kersten, T. Blecker, & H. Flämig (Eds.), *Global logistics management* (pp. 21–31). Erich Schmidt Verlag.

Haasis, H.-D., Landwehr, T., Kille, G., & Obsadny, M. (2015). Cloud-based ebusiness standardization in the maritime supply chain. In J. Dethloff, H.-D. Haasis, H. Kopfer, H. Kotzab, & J. Schönberger (Eds.), *Logistics management: Products, actors, technologies* (pp. 265–276). Springer.

Heilig, L., Stahlbock, R., & Voß, S. (2020). From digitalization to data-driven decision making in container terminals. In J. W. Böse (Ed.), *Handbook of terminal planning* (pp. 125–154). Springer.

Heilig, L., & Voß, S. (2017). Information systems in seaports: A categorization and overview. *Information Technology Management, 18*, 179–201.

Hofstede, G., Hofstede, G. J., & Minkov, M. (2010). *Cultures and organisations: Software of the mind* (3rd ed.). New York.

Hoshino, H. (2010). Competition and collaboration among container ports. *The Asian Journal of Shipping and Logistics, 26*(1), 31–47.

Jahn, C., Kersten, W., & Ringle, C. M. (2020). *Data science in maritime and city logistics*. ePubli.

Jahn, C., & Saxe, S. (2017). *Digitalization of seaports: Visions of the future*. Fraunhofer.

Kersten, W., Blecker, T., & Ringle, C. M. (2020). *Digitalization in supply chain management and logistics*. ePubli.

Kreeb, M., & Haasis, H.-D. (2017). Sustainable cooperate information portals: Digital knowledge communities for SME. In T. Osburg & C. Lohrmann (Eds.), *Sustainability in a digital world: New opportunities through new technologies* (pp. 145–158). Springer.

Lind, M., Michaelides, M., Ward, R., & Watson, R. T. (2021). *Maritime informatics*. Springer.

Notteboom, T., Ducruet, C., & de Langen, P. W. (2009). *Ports in proximity: Competition and coordination among adjacent seaports*. Ashgate Publishing.

Philipp, R. (2021). *Smart seaports as innovation drivers for blue growth*. PhD thesis, Tallinn University of Technology.

Schumacher, H. (2020). *Kein Netz!: Geld, Zeit, Laune, Liebe – Wie wir unser wirkliches Leben zurückerobern*. Eichborn-Verlag.

Smyrlis, L. (2004). Cultural differences can trump the most logical of supply chain planning. *Canadian Transportation & Logistics, 107*(9), 4–5.

Stamatovic, K., de Langen, P. W., & Groznik, A. (2018). Port cooperation in the north Adriatic ports. *Research in Transportation Business & Management, 26*, 109–121.

Tran, N. K., & Haasis, H.-D. (2015). Literature survey of network optimization in container liner shipping. *Flexible Services and Manufacturing Journal, 27*(2), 139–179.

Tran, N. K., Haasis, H.-D., & Buer, T. (2017). Container shipping route design incorporating the costs of shipping, inland/feeder transport, inventory and CO_2 emission. *Maritime Economics & Logistics, 19*(4), 667–694.

Wan, Y. (2021). *Improving the information flows and business process in global maritime logistics chains considering digitization and digitalization aspects*. PhD thesis, University of Bremen.

Weizenbaum, J. (1976). *Computer power and human reason: From judgement to calculation*. W. F. Freeman and Company.

Social Media Analytics in Operations and Supply Chain Management: Opportunities, Challenges, and Paradoxes

Aseem Kinra, Fabian Siekmann, and Herbert Kotzab

Industrial and academic communities in the field of operations and supply chain management (OSCM) have been paying increasing attention to social media analytics (SMA). However, the disparity of social media has inspired new ways of thinking about how data are produced, organized, and analyzed. This chapter addresses how OSCM is affected by this disparity and provides an overview of SMA use, applications, and challenges in the domain. A directed content analysis of current application-oriented research is carried out to review SMA in OSCM from a signaling theory perspective. In particular, we shed light on data sources, opportunities, challenges, paradoxes, and current managerial issues and seek to inform research practices and policy in order to advance operations and supply chain management research. The chapter contributes to the understanding of SMA in OSCM by identifying a set of paradoxes and challenges that have not previously been identified in OSCM research. By relating SMA to social media data sources and OSCM activities, it sheds light on preferred sources and application scenarios and discusses the imponderables of social media signal processing in OSCM.

1 Introduction

Operations and supply chain management (OSCM) is the management of processes by which products and services are designed, procured, produced, and delivered. It includes transformational activities to create products and services, as well as the management of materials, money, people, and information (Seyedghorban et al., 2021). Spearman and Hopp (2020) define operations as "an act that utilizes

---

A. Kinra (✉) · F. Siekmann · H. Kotzab
University of Bremen, Faculty of Business Studies and Economics, Bremen, Germany
e-mail: kinra@uni-bremen.de; fab.siekmann@uni-bremen.de; kotzab@uni-bremen.de

L. Hornuf (ed.), *Diginomics Research Perspectives*, Advanced Studies in Diginomics and Digitalization, https://doi.org/10.1007/978-3-031-04063-4_10

resources to transform one or more attributes of an entity or set of entities into some good or service that is required to satisfy some external demand," encompassing a wide range of human activities. Mentzer et al. (2008) portray the logistics, marketing, and production function of the firm as the domain for operations management, while the supply chain management domain crosses organizational boundaries. Considering the operations area as part of the supply chain, the enormous complexity of operations and supply chain management becomes apparent. The decision scope of managers changes as it expands across functional and organizational boundaries, and suitable decision-making tools and frameworks are ultimately needed to enhance organizational performance.

Through advancements in digital technologies and data analysis techniques, big data analytics provides the possibility to positively affect the operation and supply chain design process and operational decision-making (Waller and Fawcett, 2013). Today, only 5% of all existing data is in such structured forms as spreadsheets or relational databases. Unstructured data, such as text, images, audio, and video, sometimes lack the structural organization required by machines for analysis, but constitute 95% of big data (Gandomi and Haider, 2015). In practice, 80% of all data possessed by organizations are in the form of unstructured textual data (Wenzel and Van Quaquebeke, 2018) and the expected increase in the use of image and video media will proliferate unstructured data yet more in the future. This abundance of unstructured big data holds enormous potential for OSCM.

Organizations, and all the operations within them, are part of the social world (Spearman & Hopp, 2020). Since operations and supply chain activities are ultimately run by people for people, they can benefit from the exchange of textual information publicly available in the form of user-generated content on social media (Kinra et al., 2019). These vast, largely untapped textual datasets have the potential to help address the management of goods and information flows under uncertainty and the dynamics of the environment (Hsuan et al., 2015; Seyedghorban et al., 2021) to advance decision support through SMA. Wamba et al. (2016) state that, when different types of analyses are properly applied, SMA can deliver business value to firms. However, despite the euphoria with which big data technology finds its way into organizations, research is still needed to address the many challenges and paradoxes in its adoption and use. As an example, Gupta and George (2016) describe the big data productivity paradox, referring to a failure in establishing a positive relationship between social media analytics investments and firm productivity. Similarly, George et al. (2014) emphasize the lack of clarity about how products, services, and data can be mixed into sustainable and economical models.

The purpose of this chapter is to depict current and future perspectives on the use of textual social media analytics in OSCM. It aims to provide an up-to-date assessment of the current state of social media analytics in operations and supply chain management, and to identify the problems that can arise from SMA-based decision-making in OSCM. Signaling theory as well as related organizational theories are adopted as a lens to understand the applications, problems, and paradoxes related to the usage of SMA in OSCM. A directed content analysis (Krippendorff, 2004) of SMA in OSCM research is carried out to describe the current developments in the growing field of SMA, highlighting its opportunities and challenges. Rather than a thorough analysis, this chapter seeks to provide a representative overview of the evolving research domain.

The chapter is structured as follows. First, a basic understanding of the terminology in the domain is established, and an overview of the current research on unstructured social media data and its big data characteristics is provided. Signaling theory is then applied to shed light on the process of social media communication between consumers and the organization. Various data sources for SMA are classified and presented along with exemplary text analytics techniques and application scenarios to illustrate the current state of research. This is followed by a detailed exploration of the problems, challenges, and a sampling of the paradoxes that organizations may be faced with in their future adoption and use of SMA. Examples are provided of the pressing issues that are necessitated by the use of big data and SMA in practice. The chapter concludes with a summary of the main findings.

2 Defining Big Data and SMA in OSCM

Big data is an umbrella term often used to describe data that is massive, complex, and generated in real time, therefore requiring sophisticated management and analytical and processing techniques to extract management insights (Waller & Fawcett, 2013; Dubey et al., 2019). According to Wenzel and van Quaquebeke (2018, p. 3), "Big Data can be defined as observational records that may be exceptionally numerous, highly heterogeneous, and/or generated at high rate and systematically captured, aggregated, and analyzed to useful ends."

In recent years, BDA has increasingly found its way into the research field of OSCM (Rahimi et al., 2020).The analysis of big data is known as big data analytics (BDA), also referred to as advanced analytics, which describes the collection of data, analytical tools, computer algorithms, and techniques to derive meaningful insights and patterns from the collected large datasets (Kamble & Gunasekaran, 2020) using pattern recognition techniques, statistics, machine learning, artificial intelligence, and data mining (Abbott, 2014; Kinra et al., 2019; Fieberg et al., 2022). One of the most important categories of big data is social media, which, taking a broad understanding of the term, refers to various communication technology platforms that allow people to share information and opinions connecting both existing and potential customers. Social media data falls under the definition of big data as it is generated in large quantities and in real time, can take the form of network graphs, text, image, and video data and the associated metadata, and often has a high degree of uncertainty due to the low level of traceability. The analysis of the data generated on social media is referred to as SMA. As a comprehensive concept, SMA encompasses BDA, social network analysis, topic modeling, and sentiment analysis (Kamble & Gunasekaran, 2020). The SMA process is conceptualized along three categories: aggregation, analysis, and interpretation of social media data (Wang et al., 2020). Accordingly, companies that successfully apply SMA have the ability to collect, store, and monitor social media data relevant to OSCM, analyze the collected data, and interpret and utilize the results to support OSCM decision-making (Huang et al., 2019). Although significant overlaps in the use of the different concepts may exist, Table 1 presents some selected definitions about the concepts and aids in differentiating these from each other as far as possible.

Another commonly accepted definition for big data is proposed by Gartner, defining big data according to its 3Vs: "high-volume, high-velocity and high-variety information assets that demand cost-effective, innovative forms of information processing for enhanced insight and decision making" (Pettey, 2017). Veracity is mentioned in the literature as a fourth V, reflecting the (un)certainty of the available data (Fosso Wamba et al., 2015). Together these also represent the different characteristics of big data and need to be addressed within all forms and categories, including SMA. However, before we perform a more in-depth analysis, we turn our attention to the main reasons and the dominant theoretical rationale for SMA in OSCM, namely signals and signaling theory. This will aid us in the overall analysis of the state of the art in the field, and the main challenges and paradoxes in the use of SMA.

3 Some Theoretical Perspectives on Textual Social Media Data for OSCM

3.1 User-Generated Content as Signals for OSCM

The markets in which the organizations operate are increasingly influenced by competition, technological change, shorter product life cycles, and increasingly demanding customers, who expect responsiveness to a dynamic set of requirements, which challenges firms in most industries (Bernardes & Hanna, 2009). The organization's responsibility is therefore to understand external stakeholders such as customers and suppliers and adjust its objectives accordingly (Slack et al., 2010). Since OSCM is concerned with producing goods and services and meeting the requirements of customers, their perceptions are of great interest to operations management (Slack et al., 2010), whose goal is to serve demand as effectively and efficiently as possible. Social media generates huge amounts of information on companies and customers in real time. This is because social media enables customers to share their experiences of products and services with a broad public, which not only consists of potential consumers, but also the manufacturers or distributors of these products. These publicly expressed customer experiences possess the properties of *signals*, which are "activities or attributes of individuals in a market which, by design or accident, alter the beliefs of, or convey information to, other individuals in the market" (Spence, 1974).

Table 1 Conceptual orientation

Concept	Source	Definition
Big data	Wenzel and van Quaquebeke (2018)	Big data can be defined as observational records that may be exceptionally numerous, highly heterogeneous, and/or generated at a high rate and systematically captured, aggregated, and analyzed to useful ends
	Gartner (2022)	Big data is high-volume, high-velocity and high-variety information assets that demand cost-effective, innovative forms of information processing for enhanced insight and decision-making
	Jeble et al. (2018)	Big data is defined as datasets that are too large for traditional data processing systems and therefore require new technologies to handle them
	Dubey et al. (2019)	The term "big data" is often used to describe massive, complex and real-time data that requires sophisticated management, analytical and processing techniques to extract management insights
Big data analytics (BDA)	Abbott (2014)	BDA is defined as the process of discovering meaningful patterns of data using pattern recognition techniques, statistics, machine learning, artificial intelligence and data mining
	Gandomi and Heider (2015)	Big data analytics can be viewed as a sub-process in the overall process of "insight extraction" from big data
	Kamble and Gunasekaran (2020)	Big data analytics (BDA) defined as collection of data, analytical tools, computer algorithms and techniques to derive meaningful insights and patterns from the collected large data sets
Social media analytics (SMA)	Chen et al. (2012)	A method to uncover what customers think and feel by analyzing structured and unstructured online data dispersed across a vast array of online sources
	Zeng et al. (2010)	Informatics tools and frameworks to collect, monitor, analyze, summarize and visualize social media data to facilitate conversations and interactions to extract useful patterns and intelligence
	Fan and Gordon (2014)	SMA as an interdisciplinary modelling and analytical paradigm consisting of three steps: (1) capturing data from various sources; (2) understanding data using various analytics and models; and (3) summarizing and presenting the findings for decision-making
	Wamba et al. (2016)	SMA is a more comprehensive analysis tool than BDA or social network or sentiment analysis, as SMA can encompass BDA, social network analysis and sentiment analysis to understand consumers

3.2 Signaling Theory and the Social Media Environment

Signaling theory is essentially concerned with reducing information asymmetry between two parties (Spence, 1974, 2002). Originating in the overcoming of information asymmetries in labor markets, signaling theory has been applied in numerous management research fields, expanding the range of potential signals and the contexts in which signaling occurs (Connelly et al., 2011; Wallenburg et al., 2017; Banerjee et al., 2020). The key components of signaling theory are signalers, signals, receivers, and feedback, all operating in a signaling environment.

Applied to the present example of social media as a signaling environment, this means that the customer as signaler sends information via social media to a known or unknown receiver—potentially the focal firm or future consumers—which then processes the signal to receive information. The receiver's reaction can be considered as feedback that is sent to the signaler. The process is visualized in Fig. 1. Signaling theory proposes that to reduce the uncertainty of social media information, receivers will screen signalers with a focus on the observability, usefulness, and trustworthiness of their signals (Banerjee et al., 2020). Despite social media communication being clearly observable and proven to be useful for organizations, the trustworthiness of the signals and their senders remains uncertain, as receivers (organizations) do not exercise control over crowds (Lukyanenko et al., 2019). In addition, the evaluation of the signals is subject to an often individualized process of interpretation (Branzei et al., 2004). The trustworthiness of these signals, and thus of the data from which information is generated for OSCM, is accordingly assessed on the basis of the data context and the expertise of the interpreter (Banerjee et al., 2020). Both understanding the cultural context in social media and domain expertise are therefore crucial to overcoming the veracity problem associated with social media data uncertainty for OSCM, which is discussed in greater detail below

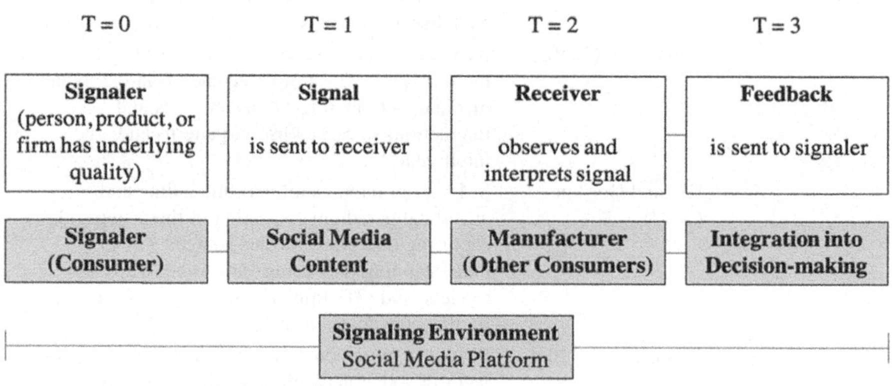

Fig. 1 The consumer–manufacturer signaling process in the social media environment (based on Connelly et al., 2011)

in the context of SMA challenges. First, we highlight the main opportunities and applications of SMA in OSCM in the next section.

4 SMA in OSCM: The Main Data Sources, Opportunities, and Applications

In this section, we make use of the supply chain operations reference (SCOR) model (APICS Supply Chain Council, 2017) to illustrate (1) how social media data can be used in OSCM for the main operational activities of planning, sourcing, making, delivery, and return; (2) the specific data sources that have been documented in the literature; and (3) how these can be used to enhance operational performance along the main performance dimensions of costs, time, quality, flexibility, and innovativeness (Kamble & Gunasekaran, 2020).

4.1 Big Data Sources and Social Media

Social media encompasses various Internet-based applications that allow content generation, sharing, and continuous modification by users in a collaborative fashion. In line with the broader definition applied earlier in this chapter, the content may include written messages, as well as pictures, videos, animation, audio materials, and web links to external sites, each constituting the interface between customers and the organization (Tóth et al., 2019).

As indicated above, social media is only one of many types of big data. The different data sources that are used by organizations to capture value from big data can be mapped by differentiating internal and external data sources. Internal data feeds from either existing data or self-generated data that may be crowdsourced or tracked, generated, or collected in a similar fashion. External data sources are populated by acquired data, customer-provided data, or freely available data. Freely available data might be open data, web-crawled data, or social media data, and the influential potential of this data for decision-making is shown by Hartmann and colleagues (2016), who state that nine out of ten organizations rely on external data sources. Figure 2 presents a taxonomy of SMA data sources for OSCM, categorizing social media as an external and freely available big data source and thus differentiating it from internal data sources and acquired or customer-provided data.

At present, unstructured data analysis methods are typically applied to the use of textual data (Adnan & Akbar, 2019a). This chapter thus forgoes analysis of image and video data, and instead focuses on the examination of text data, whose availability is a precondition of SMA. Social media data and web-crawled data are hereafter discussed from this point of view.

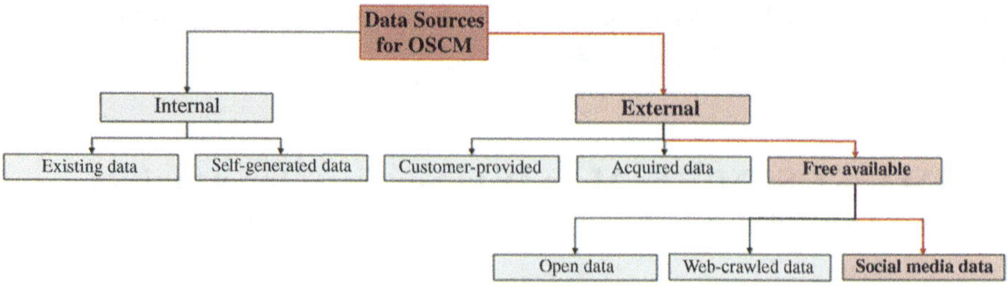

Fig. 2 Taxonomy of data sources for OSCM (based on Hartmann et al., 2014)

4.2 *Different Sources for SMA and how these Have Been Covered by the OSCM Literature*

Kinra et al. (2019) differentiate between traditional textual data sources and social media-based sources of textual data. While traditional textual data sources such as research articles, newspapers, and magazines, as well as company, consulting, and government reports, provide information to the group of readers, they lack an interactive "social" element present in contemporary social media. Social media can be classified into traditional social networking sites (e.g., Facebook, Instagram), web-based communities (e.g., brand communities), collaborative projects (e.g., Wikipedia), user-generated content communities (e.g., blogs), multimedia sharing sites (e.g., YouTube or TikTok), and virtual worlds (e.g., Second Life or the proposed Metaverse). Mobile social media include microblogs such as Twitter, and internal networks (Cheng & Krumwiede, 2018) such as WhatsApp and Telegram that allow for continuous mobile communication.

Applying a broader perspective, Abrahams et al. (2012) define social media as online services that provide for decentralized, user-level content creation, social interaction, and open membership, including discussion forums, public wikis, open online communities (social networks), and public groups, as well as customer product reviews, public visitor comments, and user-contributed news articles. We adopt this definition in order to provide an overview of SMA usage in the current OSCM literature. Our broad analysis of the literature shows that tweets and product reviews are the most frequently used SMA data sources. Tweets, for example, are often used as a source of transportation information, as they are produced at high speed and thus make it possible to obtain information in near real time (Chen et al., 2016; Gu, et al., 2016; Zavala & Ramirez-Marquez, 2019). With the exception of delivery, product reviews are used in all SCOR activities. OSCM makes use of the highly relevant data directly related to the product (Mudambi & Schuff, 2010), which enables a detailed understanding of the customer's perspective on the product or service (Min et al., 2018). It is striking that analysis of data not only focuses on the data itself, but also frequently considers the associated structured metadata. Examples are given by Gu et al. (2016), who use location data to map traffic incidents, and Mudambi and Schuff (2010), who incorporate the star ratings into the understanding of reviews of search and experience goods. A similar picture emerges when looking at the use of blogs and forum posts. Beheshti-Kashi et al. (2019) and Zavala and Ramirez-Marquez (2019) show how the combination of text and its metadata can be used for generating value-added information both for real-time decision-making and for longer time frames.

4.3 SMA Applications According to the SCOR Model

SMA is utilized by organizations in connection building with both the upstream and downstream supply chain, covering both the business-to-customer and business-to business markets. It supports the sharing of information, assisting the flow of information between customers, departments, and persons, and creating inter-organizational networks (Devi & Ganguly, 2021). On the basis of the resulting information flows, the functions of social media for OSCM can be categorized as company–public information exchange, inter-organizational information exchange, and intra-organizational information exchange. These flows enable efficient communication and effectiveness, but also increased environmental awareness (Huang et al., 2019). Operational efficiency benefits from enhanced communication, where social media data is used as information technology for profit maximization or cost reduction, helping firms to survive in competitive environments (Moyano-Fuentes et al., 2021). As an interface to the organization's environment, social media also serves as a sensing opportunity that enables higher situational awareness of companies. The improved coordination enabled by such access to additional data is shown to increase operational performance (Devi & Ganguly, 2021). These two basic functions—as connecting tool and data source—are exemplified in the SCOR activities detailed below.

4.3.1 Planning: Demand Forecasting and Inventory Management

Demand forecasting is the predominant application within SCOR activity planning, and benefits from using operations information, accounting variables, and market data for prediction (Devi & Ganguly, 2021). Sodero and Rabinovich (2017) develop a demand-forecasting model integrating the sentiments of discussion forum contributors into decision-making. Wood et al. (2016) aim to integrate sentiment analysis of product reviews into upstream firms' demand-sensing activities. Hou et al. (2017) and Chong et al. (2016) showcase the predicting power of sentiment in combination with quantitative review characteristics, while Lee et al. (2017) shed light on the issue of sentiment manipulation on Twitter. Papanagnou and Matthews-Amune (2018) combine sales data with unstructured multiple social media sources to improve inventory management. Yuan et al. (2018) investigate daily sentiments in online reviews through a joint sentiment–topic model approach.

In the fashion industry context, Beheshti-Kashi et al. (2019) demonstrate how to forecast fashion trends based on blog posts, and Choi (2018) develops a model to illustrate demand confidence of managers in the presence of social media. Irani et al. (2017) study the capabilities needed for collaborative co-design and collaborative design to order at the interface of joint product development with potentially disruptive effects on strategic inventory control. On the basis of the examples listed, it can be concluded that SMA can inform the planning process and reduce uncertainty in decision-making for operations planning.

4.3.2 Sourcing: Supplier Evaluation, Information Sharing, and Idea Capturing

Sourcing is a SCOR activity that has received comparatively little research attention (Huang et al., 2019). Mishra and Singh (2018) use twitter to identify and trace back product quality issues along the supply chain. Lin and colleagues (2017) demonstrate a supplier evaluation model integrating customer preferences in Google search and on Twitter. Grant and Preston (2019) illustrate that social influence plays a powerful role in supporting knowledge sharing with suppliers. Jiang et al. (2017) propose a method to locate quality-related reviews corresponding to different aspects of product quality and production systems at the interface of the making activity of the SCOR model. These examples show that SMA can be used to track the supply chain and evaluate how consumer requirements are being integrated even in the upstream supply chain.

4.3.3 Making: Product Development and Risk Management

The making activities of product development and business risk management are further OSCM areas that benefit from both supplier and customer involvement in new product design (Devi & Ganguly, 2021). Ramanathan et al. (2017) present a model for integrating review data to understand customer satisfaction. Cheng and Krumwiede (2018) use social media data from internal social networks to enhance supplier involvement in new product development. Sigala (2014) suggests considering customer input in the tourism sector, and Guo et al. (2015) identify critical factors in attraction management based on online reviews. These use cases suggest that decision-making in product and service development can benefit from SMA results through a better understanding of market needs.

4.3.4 Delivery: Transportation Information and Customer Service

Gu et al. (2016) and Liu and Qu (2016) present a methodology to crawl, process, and filter tweets in real time to detect traffic incidents, and Albuquerque et al. (2016) use tweets from authorities in charge of road networks or by news agencies to identify traffic-related events. Han et al. (2019) combine social media and RFDI data to harness the power of crowdsourcing and the Internet of Things in disaster response, and Chen et al. (2016) examine the discovery and utilization of relevant tweets for real-time disaster management. Bhattacharjya et al. (2016) analyze tweets related to logistics services for purposes of identifying effective and ineffective social media customer service strategies. Gkiotsalitis and Stathopoulos (2016) investigate social media users' willingness to travel in relation to varying daytimes, and Cottrill et al. (2017) investigate information management strategies during major events. Such decision-making benefits from coverage of the transport network by the crowd and from the metadata enabling localization to ensure optimal transportation and customer service.

4.3.5 Return: Returns Forecasting

Minnema et al. (2016) examine the impact of intrinsic review characteristics such as valence, volume, and variance on return decisions, finding that overly positive reviews induce more purchases, but also more returns. Sahoo et al. (2018) investigate how product reviews reduce uncertainty and the corresponding probability of returns among risk-averse, rational consumers. Zavala and Ramirez-Marquez (2019) propose a visualization framework to detect product disruptions based on customer sentiment from Twitter and Facebook to reduce response time. These examples show how operations management can use consumer input to obtain detailed information about product shortcomings and return behavior and thus decide on possible countermeasures at an early stage.

Table 2 presents examples where SMA is found in the OSCM literature (organized according to the SCOR activities of planning, sourcing, making, delivery, and return) and shows which data sources are used for different application fields. Our review reveals that planning and delivery are the SCOR activities in which SMA is used more frequently, with reviews being used strikingly more often for the former and Twitter data for the latter.

The next section delves into the various problems and challenges presented by the use of SMA in OSCM. The main challenges for the utilization of SMA can be associated with the various SMA techniques, big data characteristics, and the paradoxes that the use of big data poses for the effective deployment of SMA for OSCM.

Table 2 A selection of applications for SMA in OSCM

Contribution	Data source	SCOR activity	Application
Sodero and Rabinovich (2017)	Forum posts	Planning	Demand forecasting
Wood et al. (2016)	Reviews	Demand forecasting	
Hou et al. (2017)	Reviews	Demand forecasting	
Chong et al. (2016)	Reviews	Demand forecasting	
Papanagou and Matthews-Amune (2018)	Multiple	Demand forecasting	
Yuan et al. (2018)	Reviews	Demand forecasting	
Swain and Cao (2019)	Multiple	Demand forecasting	
Beheshti-Kashi et al. (2019)	Blogs	Demand forecasting	
Lee et al. (2017)	Reviews	Demand shaping	
Choi (2018)	General	Inventory management	
Irani et al. (2017)	Multiple	Inventory management	
Mishra and Singh (2018)	Tweets	Sourcing	Waste management
Grant and Preston (2019)	General	Knowledge sharing	
Lin et al. (2017)	Tweets, Google	Supplier evaluation	
Markova and Petkovska (2013)	General	Supplier evaluation	
Jiang et al. (2017)	Reviews	Supplier evaluation	
Ramanathan et al. (2017)	Reviews	Making	Product development
Cheng and Krumwiede (2018)	Internal networks	Product development	
Sigala (2014)	Reviews, general	Customer involvement	
Guo et al. (2015)	Reviews	Business risk management	
Singh et al. (2017)	Tweets	Delivery	Traffic monitoring
Albuquerque et al. (2016)	Tweets	Traffic monitoring	
Chen et al. (2016)	Tweets	Traffic monitoring	
Gkiotsalitis and Stathopoulos (2016)	Tweets	Traffic monitoring	
Liu and Qu (2016)	Internal networks	Traffic monitoring	
Han et al. (2019)	General, RFID	Traffic monitoring	
Cottrill et al. (2017)	Tweets	Traffic monitoring	
Gu et al. (2016)	Tweets	Traffic monitoring	
Bhattachajya et al. (2016)	Tweets	Customer service	
Minnema et al. (2016)	Reviews	Return	Returns forecasting
Sahoo et al. (2018)	Reviews	Returns forecasting	
Zavala and Ramirez-Marquez (2019)	Forum posts	Returns forecasting	

5 SMA in OSCM: Challenges and Characteristics

5.1 *Signal Processing: Some Current Challenges within the Dominant SMA Techniques in OSCM*

Recent advances in computer-aided natural language processing have led to a wide range of techniques for analyzing social media text. Topic modeling and sentiment analysis are two dominant techniques which are applied frequently in OSCM. Although these are not the only techniques and numerous other concepts for text processing have found their way into the OSCM literature, topic modeling and sentiment analysis are particularly illustrative of some of the difficulties that may arise in algorithm-driven language processing.

Topic modeling can be described as a statistical model that identifies topics as latent constructs that span a particular text corpus. The technique is typically used for finding clusters of words to identify major concepts or trends within and across corpuses or to reduce their dimensionality (Kinra et al., 2019). With regard to the OSCM domain, topic modeling has been applied to theorize the field and to reveal insights that might otherwise be lost in the abundance of data (Chae, 2015; Bansal et al., 2020). More practically, Yuan et al. (2018) extract latent information on product features to predict sales performance, benefiting from simplified corpus preparation compared to supervised models. Kinra et al. (2019) apply topic modeling to newspaper articles to gain insights on the adoption of driverless cars without the need of potentially biased data. Focusing on comparably long and targeted newspaper documents as data inputs, the authors avoid the common limitations associated with document length and topic quality (Albalawi et al., 2020).

Sentiment analysis is a similarly popular classification technique that assigns documents to sentiment categories, which are typically labeled as positive, neutral, or negative. Sentiment analysis relies on the input of keywords, topics, and character sequences for categorization. To reduce the amount of work required to generate this input data, standard corpora are frequently applied in OSCM for sentiment analysis (Kinra et al., 2019). Swain and Cao (2019) show how sentiment analysis in a supply chain context can be applied to unstructured social media documents to extract sentiments and opinions of customers, suppliers, and employees, drawing conclusions on supply chain performance. However, the limitations of the method go beyond the technical, as the true polarity of a document is influenced by contextual features such as negotiation, syntax, and modality (Abrahams et al., 2012). This becomes clear if we look at the word "good" in the comment "this design is not good." Although the supposedly positive word "good" is included in this sentence, an inference about its real sentiment depends upon the context of its use, which in this case is negative.

Even if advances in language processing have navigated simple pitfalls such as the example given, it is assumed that the understanding of complex context-depending language patterns, such as humor and irony, will remain a weak point in these techniques for the time being. To complicate matters, sentiment-indicative words may differ across domains, limiting the use of standard text corpora for sentiment analysis (Loughran & McDonald, 2011).

5.2 Dealing with Big Data Characteristics in SMA for Effective Signal Capture

The characteristics of big data—the four Vs outlined by Gartner (2017)—have implications for the use of SMA for OSCM. At first glance, the high volume of data and the velocity with which it is produced, as well as its variety and potentially unsettled veracity, represent enormous potential for comprehensively improving customer understanding and reducing uncertainty (Fosso Wamba et al., 2015; Hazen et al., 2018). The four Vs nevertheless pose distinct challenges for OSCM compared to handling of traditional structured data.

5.2.1 Volume

Built into the very notion of big data, volume poses a problem and is influenced by numerous factors. For example, advances in storage technology imply that data volumes that are now considered big data may not cease to expand in the future. The measurement of data volumes can also be misleading because, for example, two datasets of the same size may require different processing, and volume is therefore contextual. As a result, it is practically impossible to determine boundaries for what constitutes big data (Gandomi & Haider, 2015).

The practical handling of the volume in social media data also poses information technology challenges for OSCM. Parssian et al. (2004) highlight that data quality issues increase with the amounts of data collected, as implementing corresponding processes is costly in terms of software and associated human resources. Lukyanenko et al. (2019) state that little is known about data capture in the context of unanticipated phenomena or how to foster discoveries from user-generated content in the abundance of available data. Gu et al. (2016) point out that, in the context of real-time traffic incident detection, the volume of information that can be generated from tweets depends on the number of users and their spatial distribution.

The handling of high social media data volumes also poses a variety of cognitive challenges for OSCM. For example, excessive social media connectivity is argued to lead to emotional exhaustion, impairing turnover intentions of supply chain professionals (Tang et al., 2019). Exploring the question of how the volume of review data affects consumer behavior, Minnema et al. (2016) find that volume affects the purchase decision, but has little or no effect on product returns.

5.2.2 Velocity

The proliferation of mobile devices has led to an increase in the amount of data generated, particularly on social media, which requires real-time analysis to obtain the most current information possible. Given the limitations of traditional data management systems, big data technologies are needed to instantaneously process this continuously produced data (Gandomi & Haider, 2015). Even given the technical challenges of processing the data flows in real time, such processing requires compromises and hence may not be very precise. The respective tools are often designed without any hypotheses, favoring correlations over causation, resulting in susceptibility to errors (Scholz, 2017).

The OSCM literature provides various examples of how to manage the velocity at which social media data is generated. Kirac and Milburn (2018) illustrate the trade-off between accuracy and timeliness of social media analysis and show the strong potential for social data integration to improve disaster response operations. Liu and Qu (2016) utilize crowdsourced textual data from social media platforms to characterize the dynamics and uncertainty of road conditions and minimize collective travel time of vehicles. Gu et al. (2016) crawl, process, and filter tweets from Twitter in real time to detect traffic incidents. However, the trade-offs necessary for real-time data processing along supply chains result in a new type of uncertainty related to the data itself, as the velocity comes at the cost of accuracy. At a certain point, the efficiency of the tool ceases to compensate for the unreliability of its results, resulting in what Lechler et al. (2019) refer to as an "uncertainty dilemma."

5.2.3 Variety

The variety of big data is believed to benefit the granularity and accuracy of decision-making due to the variety of sources that can be explored (McAfee & Brynjolfsson, 2012). Unstructured data present on social media nevertheless bring enormous challenges as they lack schema or standardization and come in multiple formats (Adnan & Akbar, 2019b). Recent technological advances allow companies to use the various types of unstructured big data (Kinra et al., 2020). However, the range of types and sources is broad, as data in social media may take the form of text, images, audio, or video (Adnan & Akbar, 2019a), and methods such as image-based analytics are still in their infancy (Gandomi & Haider, 2015).

While numerous examples exist for textual SMA, the analysis of natural language is far from trivial. Papanagnou & Matthews-Amune (2018) use a combination of Google search, YouTube, and newspaper articles as data sources for predicting demand for medicines, highlighting the advantages of inclusion of different data structures. Challenges arising from different textual data sources are also illustrated by Zavala and Ramirez-Marquez (2019), who collect Facebook data when identifying product recalls, but base their analysis on supposedly unbiased Twitter data.

Kinra et al. (2019) state the need to examine data sources individually with an eye to their limitations and barriers.

5.2.4 Veracity

Due to the variety of big data sources and the accessibility that characterizes social media, the assurance of trustworthiness of data is a major challenge for OSCM (Wilkin et al., 2020), particularly in ensuring valid and relevant insights (Gandomi & Haider, 2015). Although larger text corpora are believed to reduce factors restricting data veracity, decision-makers need to have confidence in the generated results (Kinra et al., 2020).

In addressing data veracity issues, Zavala and Ramirez-Marquez (2019) use Twitter instead of Facebook data, referring to possible biases and errors caused by bots. Research also shows that the data generated via social media is prone to manipulation. For example, Lee et al. (2017) find evidence of sentiment manipulation on Twitter through organizations. Wu et al. (2020) state that studies focus on organizations as contributors of fake reviews while neglecting the role of users and the platforms themselves. Decision-makers are therefore challenged to validate the results derived from SMA to reduce stakeholder-related veracity issues (Bansal et al., 2020).

6 Coping with Big Data Paradoxes in Order to Overcome Signal Distortion in OSCM

The access among organizations and practitioners of OSCM to the socio-technical ecosystem of social media presents decision-makers with enormous challenges associated with the use of consumer data. The visibility of the signalers and the receiver's analytic capabilities require balanced decision-making to avoid generating long-term competitive disadvantages through opportunities that are beneficial to the operations function in the short term.

6.1 Connectivity Paradox

The connectivity paradox is described as a situation when one party fears being disconnected from the other party and starts to use technologies that establish a connection that is so close, the actor in fear of being disconnected also needs to take heed of practices to disconnect. Efforts to strengthen customer loyalty may result in information being provided to the operations function, but the company's long-term goals may be jeopardized by a dysfunctional relationship (Leonardi &

Treem, 2020). The connectivity paradox concerns the point in the signaling process where the signaler decides to send the signal but cannot control the recipients of the signals due to the public nature of the social media platform as a signaling environment. Considering the number of ways in which social media data is already being analyzed, it is easy to forget that customers are already deliberately avoiding the production of usable data.

Consequently, OSCM is faced with the challenge of balancing the extent to which the skimming of data produces added value or facilitates countermeasures and whether more connectivity ultimately leads to better outcomes. An example of such negative implications of social media usage is given by Tang et al. (2019), who demonstrate a negative effect of social media connectivity on turnover intentions of supply chain professionals. As a consequence, social media users may reduce the observability of their behavior, thus consciously limiting a necessary characteristic of signals to be examined.

6.2 Performance Paradox

As described above, SMA requires a great deal of effort to identify relevant data, clean it, and prepare the results. Therefore, much of the effort is invisible and the information generated is neither standardized nor explicit. This is one basis for the performance paradox, wherein actors expend so many resources to make task performance visible that this communication effort diminishes actual performance (Leonardi & Treem, 2020).

From the signaling perspective, the performance paradox is located between $T = 1$ and $T = 2$, when the receiver (i.e., the organization) observes and interprets the transmitted signals. Due to the lack of standard practices in BDA and their domain knowledge dependability (Waller & Fawcett, 2013), disturbances may occur in the dissemination of information generated from SMA. The performance paradox thus confronts OSCM with the task of not only considering the work itself and its underlying technology in order to measure performance, but also keeping track of the extent to which the results are tangible for others than the analysts.

With regard to the use of SMA in companies, this means that a certain understanding of the technology's results should be established in order to create a target-oriented balance between the workload and the communication effort. A key task is therefore to integrate the technology into established corporate processes (Spearman & Hopp, 2020). Hazen et al. (2014) detail approaches for combining the measurement of data quality with established methods in the OM field, such as control charts. Zavala and Ramirez-Marquez (2019) show how visualization frameworks can be used to prepare insights from Twitter data in an intelligible way.

6.3 Transparency Paradox

The transparency paradox describes the situation where organizations put effort into increasing transparency, but in doing so produce a volume and variety of communication and information that obstruct a clear view of their analysis processes. A high degree of transparency does not reduce secrecy, but counterintuitively increases it, since a flood of information that is difficult to process reduces visibility (Hald & Kinra, 2019). While a high degree of transparency in business processes is socially considered desirable, it allows companies to conceal aspects of their operations (Leonardi & Treem, 2020).

The transparency paradox relates to $T = 3$ of the signaling process, when the receiver sends feedback to the signaler. Connelly et al. (2011) emphasize the importance of this feedback in providing information to the signalers about the effectiveness of their signals in order to reduce information asymmetry. However, in the case of social media communication, the organization is not necessarily the primary addressee of the signal; hence, it faces the difficult task of creating transparency without being able to address the entirety of the signalers in response to the respective signals. Due to the variety of touchpoints between OSCM practitioners and consumers via social media, the challenge lies in providing an appropriate degree of visibility of relevant and critical analysis processes. Accordingly, the need for communication relates not only to internal stakeholders, but also to the signal providers themselves. Zavala and Ramirez-Marquez (2019) take steps toward resolving such issues by applying a visual analytics framework based on established control charts to support real-time decision-making with low-threshold, complementary, relevant information.

6.4 Power Paradox

Information processing along the phases identified by signaling theory shows that the entire process of SMA is accompanied by paradoxes, which are formed from the SMA-related integration of the customer's social context into operations management. The paradoxes occur when the SMA-enabled opportunity for a supposedly better customer understanding leads to actual deterioration. The connectivity paradox is particularly relevant in the interaction between signaler (e.g., customer) and receiver (i.e., observing organization). The performance paradox affects the interface between receiver and feedback (i.e., the integration of knowledge into business processes), while the transparency paradox affects the entire process from signal transmission to information integration. As these paradoxes reveal, the analysis of social media data creates winners and losers. Without a properly defined framework, both operations management and customers, with their respective needs, find themselves in an uncertain state that is not beneficial to either party—what is known as the power paradox (Richards & King, 2013).

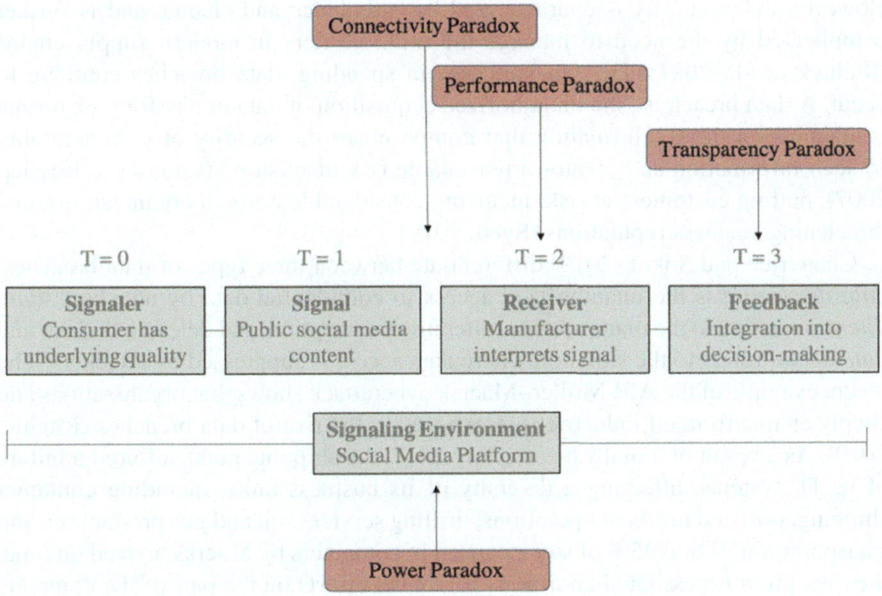

Fig. 3 SMA paradoxes in the signaling process

Although the subject needs further research, the different paradoxes are understood as emerging from and impacting the signaling process as visualized in Fig. 3. If a consensus cannot be reached on which analysis methods are appropriate, then the full potential of SMA will not be realized. The challenge is to strike a balance that allows operations management to add value without compromising the self-determination of the customer. Consequently, it is necessary to consider holistically what level of visibility is desired, and where restrictions may be needed to meet the needs of stakeholders.

The next section covers examples of real-life breakdowns that may occur in OSCM as a result of the challenges and paradoxes in the use of social media and SMA that have been discussed above.

7 Current Issues in the Practice of SMA in OSCM

7.1 Security and Data Breaches

OSCM decisions are increasingly becoming data driven. The sections above show why data is considered a key resource for the company and why companies invest in protecting it. This is reflected in corporate spending. Gartner expects annual expenditure in the area of IT security to increase by around 10% (Pettey, 2017).

However, cybersecurity is characterized by turbulence and change and is further complicated by the need to manage the multiple tiers in modern supply chains (Melnyk et al., 2021). Despite increases in spending, data breaches continue to occur. A data breach is "the unauthorized acquisition of data in any form or format containing sensitive information that compromises the security or confidentiality of such information and creates a reasonable risk of misuse" (Cannon & Kessler, 2007), putting customers at risk, incurring considerable costs to organizations, and threatening business reputations (Syed, 2019).

Chatterjee and Sokol (2019) differentiate between three types of data breaches: *data disclosure* is the unauthorized access to confidential data by attackers; *data alteration* refers to the manipulation, alteration, corruption, and deletion of data; and *data denial* refers to the situation where data access is suppressed by attackers. The recent example of the A.P. Moller–Maersk cyberattack shows that organizations and supply chains from all industries are exposed to the risk of data breaches (Ritchie, 2019). As a result of a malware attack in 2017, the shipping giant suffered a failure of its IT systems, affecting a diversity of its business units, including container shipping, port and tug-boat operations, drilling services, oil and gas production, and transportation. While 95% of stock carried in containers by Maersk arrived on time, the disruption necessitated enormous personnel efforts on the part of the company to deal with the consequences of the incident. Further illustration of potential data security problems can be seen with UPS and FedEx (whose data breaches leaked the information of thousands of customers; FedEx, 2017; Bisson, 2020), Total Quality Logistics (where carrier information was exposed due to a cyberattack; Forde, 2020), and Forward Air (which warned of revenue losses following a ransomware attack; Tabak, 2020).

The gateways for such risks are many and various and are based on technological as well as procedural and behavioral weaknesses, making them difficult to protect against. To deal with increasingly frequent malware and ransomware attacks (e.g., WannaCry, which infected 230,000 computers worldwide in 2017), organizations need to realize that such attacks represent a fundamental business problem, potentially affecting operations along the whole supply chain. Consumers are also becoming increasingly deliberate in what types of data they share, with media coverage of data breaches increasingly raising awareness of the risks involved. Such wide awareness nevertheless allowed Maersk to enhance its reputation as a trustworthy brand by openly communicating about the incident and its effects on its own systems. This example illustrates how, despite the business challenge, secure data handling and privacy can become a differentiator and even a source of competitive advantage (Kaplan et al., 2020).

7.2 Moral and Ethical Challenges

SMA is the automation of human decision-making by social media-based algorithms that produce probability-aided information. However, the information generated from this must inevitably be regarded as uncertain and is thus often unsuitable for triggering action. This is particularly true for unstructured data and user-generated content from social media. It is important to include this limitation when basing decisions on SMA-generated insights. Given the lack of transparency of algorithms, especially in the area of deep learning, the link between data and the information generated by the algorithm is often not traceable. In practice, this leads to problems when it comes to accountability for decisions, limiting the action-initiation ability of SMA insights (Mittelstadt et al., 2016). Opening this black box is critical in all analytics systems where supervised or unsupervised machine learning is used (Goebel et al., 2018; Kinra et al., 2019; Fieberg et al., 2022). As a remedy, explainable artificial intelligence approaches have been developed to increase interpretability of such decision support systems (Guidotti et al., 2018) and have begun to find their way into the OSCM literature (e.g., Senoner et al., 2021).

SMA algorithms are prone to the "garbage in, garbage out" principle. SMA-based insights can therefore only be as reliable as the input they process, and the open character of social media platforms can have serious ramifications for this reliability. As an example, Lee et al. (2017) find instances of sentiment manipulation in movie reviews and thus illustrate that the processing of social media data should not be considered infallible. It is also necessary to question the extent to which the recommendations for action derived from the insights can be reconciled with the company's long-term objectives (Mittelstadt et al., 2016). For example, while it may make sense to adjust prices according to the situation or customer group from an operational point of view, this may run counter to the organization's marketing strategy and thus reduce the long-term performance of the company and the entire supply chain. A practical example of this is provided by Ketzenberg et al. (2020), who clarify that identifying abusive potential customer returns is not sufficient, as this may jeopardize relationships with profitable customers.

These are only some of the examples that constitute the debate on the moral and ethical challenges of SMA in OSCM. The analysis of Mittelstadt et al. (2016) is recommended for further discussion of such issues.

8 Conclusion

This chapter provides a summary of current and future perspectives on the use of textual social media analytics in OSCM, with the aim of presenting the current state of the art, and identifying its opportunities and challenges. The detailed literature analysis demonstrates that the use of SMA is still in its infancy. This chapter also details the use of product reviews and Twitter content as the dominant SMA data sources. Activities in planning and delivery operations in particular benefit from the analysis of this type of data, while sourcing, making, and return operations activities have received comparatively little attention in the research literature to date.

To shed light on the problems that can arise in the use of SMA for decision-making in OSCM, the existing research reveals the characteristics of big data that hinder effective social media data processing. A set of paradoxes, the connectivity–performance–transparency–power paradoxes, are identified alongside the challenges they pose to OSCM, as well as how SMA activities may run counterproductive to their promised information gains. The impact of cybercrime as part of responsible management for the use of potentially sensitive consumer data is also discussed, as well as the moral and ethical challenges that organizations and managers face in advancing their applications of SMA.

The chapter is also one of the first studies to apply signaling theory as a lens to examine the use of social media data processing in OSCM. By identifying the inherent paradoxes it uniquely illustrates the behavioral visibility challenges for the signaling process in operations, and postulates why SMA may not have unfolded in OSCM as speculated by Waller and Fawcett (2013). The main implications of the study are that practitioners should note the shortcomings of analyzing textual social media data and act accordingly. Knowledge of these difficulties can serve as a guideline in the integration of SMA into business practices. Ideally, managers should try to bundle competencies along the interface between data science and OSCM. For future research directions, the study reveals the need to explore both the possible applications of the technology across the range of OSCM activities, as well as the reasonable depth of the insights gained from SMA.

To holistically reflect the state of research, the period and scope for articles included in future studies should be regularly adjusted to match the changing dynamics of the research field. Based on the research presented here, it is clear that the potential of SMA analytics is distributed across the entire breadth of the research field and that the challenges are as diverse as the data itself. The current state of research suggests that scholars should also seek to develop a deeper understanding of the data being analyzed, the patterns of behavior on social media, and the underlying analytics methods in order to fully realize the potential of SMA. From this perspective, more in-depth research is warranted into the identified paradoxes within OSCM. If research succeeds in making this interdisciplinary leap, this promising field can be expected to bear exciting and actionable results in both research and practice.

References

Abbott, D. (2014). *Applied predictive analytics: Principles and techniques for the professional data analyst*. John Wiley & Sons, Inc.

Abrahams, A. S., Jiao, J., Wang, G. A., & Fan, W. (2012). Vehicle defect discovery from social media. *Decision Support Systems, 54*(1), 87–97. https://doi.org/10.1016/j.dss.2012.04.005

Adnan, K., & Akbar, R. (2019a). An analytical study of information extraction from unstructured and multidimensional big data. *Journal of Big Data, 6*, 91. https://doi.org/10.1186/s40537-019-0254-8. Springer International Publishing.

Adnan, K., & Akbar, R. (2019b). Limitations of information extraction methods and techniques for heterogeneous unstructured big data. *International Journal of Engineering Business Management, 11*, 1–23. https://doi.org/10.1177/1847979019890771

Albalawi, R., Yeap, T. H., & Benyoucef, M. (2020). Using topic modeling methods for short-text data: A comparative analysis. *Frontiers in Artificial Intelligence, 3*(July), 1–14. https://doi.org/10.3389/frai.2020.00042

Albuquerque, F. C., Casanova, M. A., Lopes, H., Redlich, L. R., De Macedo, J. A. F., Lemos, M., De Carvalho, M. T. M., & Renso, C. (2016). A methodology for traffic-related twitter messages interpretation. *Computers in Industry, 78*, 57–69. https://doi.org/10.1016/j.compind.2015.10.005

APICS Supply Chain Council. (2017). *The supply chain operations reference model (SCOR)*. Available at: http://www.apics.org/docs/default-source/scor-p-toolkits/apics-scc-scor-quick-reference-guide.pdf.

Banerjee, A., Ries, J. M., & Wiertz, C. (2020). The impact of social media signals on supplier selection: Insights from two experiments. *International Journal of Operations and Production Management, 40*(5), 531–552. https://doi.org/10.1108/IJOPM-05-2019-0413

Bansal, P., Gualandris, J., & Kim, N. (2020). Theorizing supply chains with qualitative big data and topic modeling. *Journal of Supply Chain Management, 56*(2), 7–18. https://doi.org/10.1111/jscm.12224

Beheshti-Kashi, S., Pannek, J., & Kinra, A. (2019). Complementing decision support and forecasting risk in supply chain with unstructured data. *IFAC-PapersOnLine, 52*(13), 1721–1726. https://doi.org/10.1016/j.ifacol.2019.11.449

Bernardes, E. S., & Hanna, M. D. (2009). A theoretical review of flexibility, agility and responsiveness in the operations management literature: Toward a conceptual definition of customer responsiveness. *International Journal of Operations and Production Management, 29*(1), 30–53. https://doi.org/10.1108/01443570910925352

Bhattacharjya, J., Ellison, A., & Tripathi, S. (2016). An exploration of logistics related customer service provision on twitter: The case of e-retailers. *International Journal of Physical Distribution & Logistics Management, 46*(6), 659–680. 10.1108/IJPDLM-01-2015-0007

Bisson, D. (2020). *UPS says phishing incident might have exposed some customers' data*. Available at: https://securityboulevard.com/2020/01/ups-says-phishing-incident-might-have-exposed-some-customers-data/.

Branzei, O., Ursacki-Bryant, T. J., Vertinsky, I., & Zhang, W. (2004). The formation of green strategies in chinese firms: Matching corporate environmental responses and individual principles. *Strategic Management Journal, 25*(11), 1075–1095. https://doi.org/10.1002/smj.409

Cannon, D. M., & Kessler, L. (2007). Danger: Corporate data breach! *The Journal of Corporate Accounting & Finance, 18*(5), 41–49. https://doi.org/10.1002/jcaf

Chae, B. (2015). Insights from hashtag #supplychain and twitter analytics: Considering twitter and twitter data for supply chain practice and research. *International Journal of Production Economics, 165*, 247–259. https://doi.org/10.1016/j.ijpe.2014.12.037

Chatterjee, C., & Sokol, D. D. (2019). Data security, data breaches, and compliance. In C. Chatterjee & D. D. Sokol (Eds.), *Cambridge handbook of compliance* (pp. 936–948). Cambridge University Press.

Chen, H., Chiang, R. H. L. & Storey, V. C. (2012). Business Intelligence and Analytics: From Big Data to Big Impact, *Management Information Systems Quarterly, 36*(4), pp. 1165–1188.

Chen, X., Elmes, G., Ye, X., & Chang, J. (2016). Implementing a real-time twitter-based system for resource dispatch in disaster management. *GeoJournal, 81*(6), 863–873. https://doi.org/10.1007/s10708-016-9745-8

Cheng, C. C. J., & Krumwiede, D. (2018). Enhancing the performance of supplier involvement in new product development: The enabling roles of social media and firm capabilities. *Supply Chain Management, 23*(3), 171–187. https://doi.org/10.1108/SCM-07-2017-0230

Choi, T. M. (2018). Incorporating social media observations and bounded rationality into fashion quick response supply chains in the big data era. *Transportation Research Part E: Logistics and Transportation Review, 114*, 386–397. https://doi.org/10.1016/j.tre.2016.11.006

Chong, A. Y. L., Li, B., Ngai, E. W., Ch'ng, E., & Lee, F. (2016). Predicting online product sales via online reviews, sentiments, and promotion strategies: A big data architecture and neural network approach. *International Journal of Operations & Production Management., 36*(4), 358–383. https://doi.org/10.1108/IJOPM-03-2015-0151

Connelly, B. L., Certo, S. T., Ireland, R. D., & Reutzel, C. R. (2011). Signaling theory: A review and assessment. *Journal of Management, 37*(1), 39–67. https://doi.org/10.1177/0149206310388419

Cottrill, C., Gault, P., Yeboah, G., Nelson, J. D., Anable, J., & Budd, T. (2017). Tweeting transit: An examination of social media strategies for transport information management during a large event. *Transportation Research Part C: Emerging Technologies, 77*, 421–432. https://doi.org/10.1016/j.trc.2017.02.008

Devi, Y., & Ganguly, K. (2021). Social media in operations and supply chain management: A systematic literature review to explore the future. *Operations and Supply Chain Management: An International Journal, 14*(2), 232–248. https://doi.org/10.31387/oscm0450299

Dubey, R., Gunasekaran, A., Childe, S. J., Blome, C., & Papadopoulos, T. (2019). Big data and predictive analytics and manufacturing performance: Integrating institutional theory, resource-based view and big data culture. *British Journal of Management, 30*(2), 341–361. https://doi.org/10.1111/1467-8551.12355

Fan, W. & Gordon, M. D. (2014). The power of social media analytics, *Communications of the ACM, 57*(6), pp. 74–81. 10.1145/2602574.

FedEx. (2017). *FedEx files 10-K with additional disclosure on cyber-attack affecting TNT Express Systems*. Available at: https://investors.fedex.com/news-and-events/investor-news/investor-news-details/2017/FedEx-Files-10-K-with-Additional-Disclosure-on-Cyber-Attack-Affecting-TNT-Express-Systems/default.aspx.

Fieberg, C., Hesse, M., Loy, T., & Metko, D. (2022). Machine learning in accounting research. In L. Hornuf (Ed.), *Diginomics research perspectives: The role of digitalization in business and society*. Springer International Publishing.

Forde, M. (2020). *TQL cyber breach is latest example of the industry's vulnerability to hacking*. Available at: www.supplychaindive.com/news/tql-cyber-breach-industry-vulnerability-hacking/573174/.

Fosso Wamba, S., Akter, S., Edwards, A., Chopin, G., & Gnanzou, D. (2015). How "big data" can make big impact: Findings from a systematic review and a longitudinal case study. *International Journal of Production Economics, 165*, 234–246. https://doi.org/10.1016/j.ijpe.2014.12.031

Gandomi, A., & Haider, M. (2015). Beyond the hype: Big data concepts, methods, and analytics. *International Journal of Information Management, 35*(2), 137–144. https://doi.org/10.1016/j.ijinfomgt.2014.10.007

Gartner, (2022). *Big Data, Gartner Information Technology Glossary*. Available at: https://www.gartner.com/en/information-technology/glossary/big-data

George, G., Haas, M. R., & Pentland, A. (2014). Big data and management. *Academy of Management Journal, 57*(2), 321–326. https://doi.org/10.18352/bmgn-lchr.9536

Gkiotsalitis, K., & Stathopoulos, A. (2016). Joint leisure travel optimization with user-generated data via perceived utility maximization. *Transportation Research Part C: Emerging Technologies, 68*, 532–548. https://doi.org/10.1016/j.trc.2016.05.009

Goebel, R., Chander, A., Holzinger, K., Lecue, F., Stumpf, S., Kieseberg, P., Holzinger, A., Goebel, R., Chander, A., Holzinger, K., Lecue, F., Akata, Z., Goebel, R., Chander, A., Holzinger, K., & Lecue, F. (2018). Explainable AI: The new 42? To cite this version: HAL Id: hal-01934928', 2nd International Cross-Domain Conference for Machine Learning and Knowledge Extraction (CD-MAKE), Hamburg, Germany.

Grant, S. B., & Preston, T. A. (2019). Using social power and influence to mobilise the supply chain into knowledge sharing: A case in insurance. *Information and Management, 56*(5), 625–639. https://doi.org/10.1016/j.im.2018.10.004

Gu, Y., Qian, Z., & Chen, F. (2016). From twitter to detector: Real-time traffic incident detection using social media data. *Transportation Research Part C: Emerging Technologies, 67*, 321–342. https://doi.org/10.1016/j.trc.2016.02.011

Guidotti, R., Monreale, A., Ruggieri, S., Turini, F., Giannotti, F., & Pedreschi, D. (2018). A survey of methods for explaining black box models. *ACM Computing Surveys, 51*(5), 1–42. https://doi.org/10.1145/3236009

Guo, Y., Sun, S., Schuckert, M., & Law, R. (2015). Online feedback and attraction management: An exploration of the critical factors in effective operations. *Asia Pacific Journal of Tourism Research, 21*(8), 883–904. https://doi.org/10.1080/10941665.2015.1080740

Gupta, M., & George, J. F. (2016). Toward the development of a big data analytics capability, Information and Management. *Elsevier B.V., 53*(8), pp. 1049–1064. 10.1016/j.im.2016.07.004.

Hald, K. S., & Kinra, A. (2019). How the blockchain enables and constrains supply chain performance. *International Journal of Physical Distribution and Logistics Management, 49*(4), 376–397. https://doi.org/10.1108/IJPDLM-02-2019-0063

Han, S., Huang, H., Luo, Z., & Foropon, C. (2019). Harnessing the power of crowdsourcing and internet of things in disaster response. *Annals of Operations Research, 283*(1–2), 1175–1190. https://doi.org/10.1007/s10479-018-2884-1

Hartmann, P. M., Zaki, M., Feldmann, N., & Neely, A. (2014). Capturing value from big data: A taxonomy of data-driven business models used by start-up firms. *International Journal of Operations and Production Management, 36*(10), 1382–1406. https://doi.org/10.1108/IJOPM-02-2014-0098

Hazen, B. T., Boone, C. A., Ezell, J. D., & Jones-Farmer, L. A. (2014). Data quality for data science, predictive analytics, and big data in supply chain management: An introduction to the problem and suggestions for research and applications. *International Journal of Production Economics, 154*, 72–80. https://doi.org/10.1016/j.ijpe.2014.04.018

Hazen, B. T., Skipper, J. B., Boone, C. A., & Hill, R. R. (2018). Back in business: Operations research in support of big data analytics for operations and supply chain management. *Annals of Operations Research, 270*(1–2), 201–211. https://doi.org/10.1007/s10479-016-2226-0

Hou, F., Li, B., Chong, A. Y. L., Yannopoulou, N., & Liu, M. J. (2017). Understanding and predicting what influence online product sales? A neural network approach. *Production Planning and Control, 28*(11–12), 964–975. https://doi.org/10.1080/09537287.2017. 1336791

Hsuan, J., Skjott-Larsen, T., Kinra, A., & Kotzab, H. (2015). *Managing the global supply chain* (4th ed.). CBS Press.

Huang, S., Potter, A., & Eyers, D. (2019). Social media in operations and supply chain management: State-of-the-art and research directions. *International Journal of Production Research, 58*(6), 1893–1925. https://doi.org/10.1080/00207543.2019.1702228

Irani, Z., Sharif, A. M., Papadopoulos, T., & Love, P. E. D. (2017). Social media and web 2.0 for knowledge sharing in product design. *Production Planning and Control, 28*(13), 1047–1065. https://doi.org/10.1080/09537287.2017.1329955

Jeble, S., Dubey, R., Childe, S. J., Papadopoulos, T., Rouband, D. & Anand, P. (2018). Impact of big data & predictive analytics capability on supply chain sustainability, *International Journal of Logistics Management, 29*(2), pp. 513–538. 10.1108/IJLM-05-2017-0134.

Jiang, C., Liu, Y., Ding, Y., Liang, K., & Duan, R. (2017). Capturing helpful reviews from social media for product quality improvement: A multi-class classification approach. *International Journal of Production Research, 55*(12), 3528–3541. https://doi.org/10.1080/00207543.2017.1304664

Kamble, S. S., & Gunasekaran, A. (2020). Big data-driven supply chain performance measurement system: A review and framework for implementation. *International Journal of Production Research, 58*(1), 65–86. https://doi.org/10.1080/00207543.2019.1630770

Kaplan, J., Soller, H., Anant, V., & Donchak, L. (2020). *The consumer-data opportunity and the privacy imperative*. McKinsey & Company.

Ketzenberg, M. E., Abbey, J. D., Heim, G. R., & Kumar, S. (2020). Assessing customer return behaviors through data analytics. *Journal of Operations Management, 66*(6), 622–645. https://doi.org/10.1002/joom.1086

Kinra, A., Hald, K. S., Mukkamala, R. R., & Vatrapu, R. (2020). An unstructured big data approach for country logistics performance assessment in global supply chains. *International Journal of*

Operations and Production Management, 40(4), 439–458. https://doi.org/10.1108/IJOPM-07-2019-0544

Kinra, A., Kashi, S. B., Pereira, F. C., Combes, F., & Rothengatter, W. (2019). Textual data in transportation research: Techniques and opportunities. In *Mobility patterns, big data and transport analytics* (pp. 173–197). Elsevier. https://doi.org/10.1016/b978-0-12-812970-8.00008-7

Kirac, E., & Milburn, A. B. (2018). A general framework for assessing the value of social data for disaster response logistics planning. *European Journal of Operational Research, 269*(2), 486–500. https://doi.org/10.1016/j.ejor.2018.02.011

Krippendorff, K. (2004). *Content analysis: An introduction to its methodology* (2nd ed.). Sage Publications Limited. https://doi.org/10.2307/2288384

Lechler, S., Canzaniello, A., Roßmann, B., von der Gracht, H. A., & Hartmann, E. (2019). Real-time data processing in supply chain management: Revealing the uncertainty dilemma. *International Journal of Physical Distribution and Logistics Management, 49*(10), 1003–1019. https://doi.org/10.1108/IJPDLM-12-2017-0398

Lee, S.-Y., Qiu, L., & Whinston, A. (2017). Sentiment manipulation in online platforms: An analysis of movie tweets. *Production and Operations Management, 27*(3), 393–416. https://doi.org/10.1111/ijlh.12426

Leonardi, P. M., & Treem, J. W. (2020). Behavioral visibility: A new paradigm for organization studies in the age of digitization, digitalization, and datafication. *Organization Studies, 41*(12), 1601–1625. https://doi.org/10.1177/0170840620970728

Lin, K. P., Hung, K. C., Lin, Y. T., & Hsieh, Y. H. (2017). Green suppliers performance evaluation in belt and road using fuzzy weighted average with social media information. *Sustainability (Switzerland), 10*(1), 5. https://doi.org/10.3390/su10010005

Liu, S., & Qu, Q. (2016). Dynamic collective routing using crowdsourcing data. *Transportation Research Part B: Methodological, 93*, 450–469. https://doi.org/10.1016/j.trb.2016.08.005

Loughran, T., & McDonald, B. (2011). When is a liability not a liability? Textual analysis, dictionaries, and 10-Ks. *Journal of Finance, 66*(1), 35–65. https://doi.org/10.2469/dig.v41.n2.20

Lukyanenko, R., Parsons, J., Wiersma, Y. F., & Maddah, M. (2019). Expecting the unexpected: Effects of data collection design choices on the quality of crowdsourced user-generated content. *MIS Quarterly: Management Information Systems, 43*(2), 634–647. https://doi.org/10.25300/MISQ/2019/14439

Markova, S., & Petkovska-Mirčevska, T. (2013). Social Media and Supply Chain, *Supply Chain Management, 15*(33), pp. 89–102.

McAfee, A., & Brynjolfsson, E. (2012). Big data: The management revolution. *Harvard Business Review, 90*(10), 60–66.

Melnyk, S. A., Schoenherr, T., Speier-pero, C., Peters, C., Jeff, F., Friday, D., Melnyk, S. A., Schoenherr, T., & Speier-pero, C. (2021). New challenges in supply chain management: Cybersecurity across the supply chain. *International Journal of Production Research, 60*, 162–183. https://doi.org/10.1080/00207543.2021.1984606

Mentzer, J. T., Stank, T. P., & Esper, T. L. (2008). Supply chain management and its relationship to logistics, marketing, production, and operations management. *Journal of Business Logistics, 29*(1), 31–46. https://doi.org/10.1002/j.2158-1592.2008.tb00067.x

Min, H., Yun, J., & Geum, Y. (2018). Analyzing dynamic change in customer requirements: An approach using review-based Kano analysis. *Sustainability (Switzerland), 10*(3), 746. https://doi.org/10.3390/su10030746

Minnema, A., Bijmolt, T. H. A., Gensler, S., & Wiesel, T. (2016). To keep or not to keep: Effects of online customer reviews on product returns. *Journal of Retailing, 92*(3), 253–267. https://doi.org/10.1016/j.jretai.2016.03.001

Mishra, N., & Singh, A. (2018). Use of twitter data for waste minimisation in beef supply chain. *Annals of Operations Research, 270*(1–2), 337–359. https://doi.org/10.1007/s10479-016-2303-4

Mittelstadt, B. D., Allo, P., Taddeo, M., Wachter, S., & Floridi, L. (2016). The ethics of algorithms: Mapping the debate. *Big Data and Society, 3*(2), 1–21. https://doi.org/10.1177/2053951716679679

Moyano-Fuentes, J., Maqueira-Marín, J. M., Martínez-Jurado, P. J., & Sacristán-Díaz, M. (2021). Extending lean management along the supply chain: Impact on efficiency. *Journal of Manufacturing Technology Management, 32*(1), 63–84. https://doi.org/10.1108/JMTM-10-2019-0388

Mudambi, S. M., & Schuff, D. (2010). What makes a helpful online review? A study of customer reviews on Amazon.com. MIS quarterly: *Management Information Systems, 34*(1), 185–200.

Papanagnou, C. I., & Matthews-Amune, O. (2018). Coping with demand volatility in retail pharmacies with the aid of big data exploration. *Computers and Operations Research, 98*, 343–354. https://doi.org/10.1016/j.cor.2017.08.009

Parssian, A., Sarkar, S., & Jacob, V. S. (2004). Assessing data quality for information products: Impact of selection, projection, and cartesian product. *Management Science, 50*(7), 967–982. https://doi.org/10.1287/mnsc.1040.0237

Pettey, C. (2017). *5 reasons you're failing with social analytics: Drive stronger performance on your most critical priorities*. Available at: https://www.gartner.com/smarterwithgartner/5-reasons-youre-failing-with-social-analytics.

Rahimi, I., Gandomi, A. H., Fong, S. J., & Ülkü, M. A. (2020). *Big data analytics in supply chain management: Theory and applications*. CRC Press.

Ramanathan, U., Subramanian, N., & Parrott, G. (2017). Role of social media in retail network operations and marketing to enhance customer satisfaction. *International Journal of Operations and Production Management, 37*(1), 105–123. https://doi.org/10.1108/IJOPM-03-2015-0153

Richards, N. M., & King, J. H. (2013). Three paradoxes of big data. *Standford Law Review, 66*, 41–46.

Ritchie, R. (2019). *Maersk: Springing back from a catastrophic cyber-attack, I-Cio*. Available at: hhttps://www.i-cio.com/management/insight/item/maersk-springing-back-from-a-catastrophic-cyber-attack.

Sahoo, N., Dellarocas, C., & Srinivasan, S. (2018). The impact of online product reviews on product returns. *Information Systems Research, 29*(3), 723–738. https://doi.org/10.1287/isre.2017.0736

Scholz, T. M. (2017). *Big data in organizations and the role of human resource management, big data in organizations and the role of human resource management*. Peter Lang International Academic Publishers. https://doi.org/10.3726/b10907

Senoner, J., Netland, T., & Feuerriegel, S. (2021). Using explainable artificial intelligence to improve process quality: Evidence from semiconductor fabrication. *Management Science*, forthcoming.

Seyedghorban, Z., Samson, D., & Swink, M. (2021). Quo vadis OSCM? An analysis of past and future trends in operations and supply chain management research. *Decision Sciences, (April 2020)*, 1–23. https://doi.org/10.1111/deci.12519

Sigala, M. (2014). Customer involvement in sustainable supply chain management: A research framework and implications in tourism. *Cornell Hospitality Quarterly, 55*(1), 76–88. https://doi.org/10.1177/1938965513504030

Singh, A., Shukla, N., & Mishra, N. (2017). Social media data analytics to improve supply chain management in food industries. *Transportation Research Part E: Logistics and Transportation Review, 114*, 398–415. https://doi.org/10.1016/j.tre.2017.05.008

Slack, N., Chambers, S., & Johnston, R. (2010). *Operations management* (6th ed.). Pearson Education.

Sodero, A. C., & Rabinovich, E. (2017). Demand and revenue management of deteriorating inventory on the internet: An empirical study of flash sales markets. *Journal of Business Logistics, 38*(3), 170–183. https://doi.org/10.1111/jbl.12157

Spearman, M. L., & Hopp, W. J. (2020). The case for a unified science of operations. *Production and Operations Management, 30*(3), 802–814. https://doi.org/10.1111/poms.13318

Spence, M. (1974). *Market signaling, information transfer in hiring and related processes*. Harvard University Press.

Spence, M. (2002). Signaling in retrospect and the informational structure of markets. *American Economic Review, 92*(3), 434–459. https://doi.org/10.1257/00028280260136200

Swain, A. K., & Cao, R. Q. (2019). Using sentiment analysis to improve supply chain intelligence. *Information Systems Frontiers, 21*(2), 469–484. https://doi.org/10.1007/s10796-017-9762-2

Syed, R. (2019). Enterprise reputation threats on social media: A case of data breach framing. *Journal of Strategic Information Systems, 28*(3), 257–274. https://doi.org/10.1016/j.jsis.2018.12.001

Tabak, N. (2020). *Forward Air reveals ransomware attack, warns of revenue hit.* Available at: https://www.freightwaves.com/news/news-alert-forward-air-reveals-ransomware-attack-warns-of-revenue-hit.

Tang, G., Ren, S., Chadee, D., & Yuan, S. (2019). The dark side of social media connectivity: Influence on turnover intentions of supply chain professionals. *International Journal of Operations and Production Management, 40*(5), 603–623. https://doi.org/10.1108/IJOPM-05-2019-0391

Tóth, Z., Liu, M., Luo, J., & Braziotis, C. (2019). The role of social media in managing supplier attractiveness: An investigation of business-to-business markets. *International Journal of Operations and Production Management, 40*(5), 625–646. https://doi.org/10.1108/IJOPM-04-2019-0321

Wallenburg, C. M., Einmahl, L., Lee, K. B., & Rao, S. (2017). On packaging and product returns in online retail: Mailing boxes or sending signals? *Journal of Business Logistics, 42*(1), 291–308. https://doi.org/10.1111/jbl.12273

Waller, M. A., & Fawcett, S. E. (2013). Data science, predictive analytics, and big data: A revolution that will transform supply chain design and management. *Journal of Business Logistics, 34*(2), 77–84. https://doi.org/10.1111/jbl.12010

Wamba, S. F., Akter, S., Kang, H., Bhattacharya, M., & Upal, M. (2016). The primer of social media analytics. *Journal of Organizational and End User Computing, 28*(2), 1–12. https://doi.org/10.4018/JOEUC.2016040101

Wang, Y., Zhang, M., Tse, Y. K., & Chan, H. K. (2020). Unpacking the impact of social media analytics on customer satisfaction: Do external stakeholder characteristics matter? *International Journal of Operations and Production Management, 40*(5), 647–669. https://doi.org/10.1108/IJOPM-04-2019-0331

Wenzel, R., & Van Quaquebeke, N. (2018). The double-edged sword of big data in organizational and management research: A review of opportunities and risks. *Organizational Research Methods, 21*(3), 1–44. https://doi.org/10.1177/1094428117718627

Wilkin, C., Ferreira, A., Rotaru, K., & Gaerlan, L. R. (2020). Big data prioritization in SCM decision-making: Its role and performance implications. *International Journal of Accounting Information Systems, 38*, 100470. https://doi.org/10.1016/j.accinf.2020.100470

Wood, L. C., Reiners, T., & Srivastava, H. S. (2016). Think exogenous to excel: Alternative supply chain data to improve transparency and decisions. *International Journal of Logistics Research and Applications, 20*(5), 426–443. https://doi.org/10.1080/13675567.2016.1267126

Wu, Y., Ngai, E. W. T., Wu, P., & Wu, C. (2020). Fake online reviews: Literature review, synthesis, and directions for future research. *Decision Support Systems, 132*(February), 113280. https://doi.org/10.1016/j.dss.2020.113280

Yuan, H., Xu, W., Li, Q., & Lau, R. (2018). Topic sentiment mining for sales performance prediction in e-commerce. *Annals of Operations Research, 270*(1–2), 553–576. https://doi.org/10.1007/s10479-017-2421-7

Zavala, A., & Ramirez-Marquez, J. E. (2019). Visual analytics for identifying product disruptions and effects via social media. *International Journal of Production Economics, 208*(December), 544–559. https://doi.org/10.1016/j.ijpe.2018.12.020

Zeng, D., Chen, H., Lusch, R., & Li, S. (2010). Social Media Analytics and Intelligence, *IEEE Intelligent Systems, 25*(6), pp. 13–16. 10.1109/MIS.2010.151.

The manufacturer's authorised representative in the EU is Springer Nature Customer Service Centre GmbH, Europaplatz 3, 69115 Heidelberg, Germany. If you have any concerns regarding our products, please contact ProductSafety@springernature.com

Printed and bound by CPI Group (UK) Ltd, Croydon, CR0 4YY
28/09/2026
02224091-0004